SOMEDAY ALL THE ADULTS WILL DIE!

The Birth of Texas Punk

Pat Blashill

University of Texas Press *Austin*

Printed in the United States of America
First edition, 2025

An early draft of portions of Chapter 5. White Rage? was published in Volume 105 of the *Southwest Review*, whose support is gratefully acknowledged.

♾ The paper used in this book meets the minimum requirements of ANSI/NISO Z39.48–1992 (R1997) (Permanence of Paper).

Library of Congress Cataloging-in-Publication Data

Names: Blashill, Pat, author.
Title: Someday all the adults will die! : the birth of Texas punk / Pat Blashill.
Description: First edition. | Austin : University of Texas Press, 2025. | Includes index.
Identifiers: LCCN 2024049493 (print) | LCCN 2024049494 (ebook)
ISBN 978-1-4773-3247-4 (paperback)
ISBN 978-1-4773-3248-1 (pdf)
ISBN 978-1-4773-3249-8 (epub)
Subjects: LCSH: Punk rock music—Texas—Austin—Anecdotes. | Punk rock music—Texas—Austin—History and criticism. | Punk rock music—Social aspects—Texas—Austin—History. | Punk rock music—Political aspects—Texas—Austin—History. | Nightclubs—Texas—Austin—History. | Punk rock musicians—Texas—Austin. | Austin (Tex.)—Social life and customs.
Classification: LCC ML3534.3 .B535 2025 (print) | LCC ML3534.3 (ebook) | DDC 781.6609764/31—dc23/eng/20241211
LC record available at https://lccn.loc.gov/2024049493
LC ebook record available at https://lccn.loc.gov/2024049494

doi:10.7560/332474

SOMEDAY ALL THE ADULTS WILL DIE!

American Music Series
Hanif Abdurraqib, Jessica Hopper, and Charles L. Hughes, Editors

RECENT TITLES

Seth Neblett, *Mothership Connected: The Women of Parliament-Funkadelic*
Niko Stratis, *The Dad Rock That Made Me a Woman*
Franz Nicolay, *Band People: Life and Work in Popular Music*
Tara López, *Chuco Punk: Sonic Insurgency in El Paso*
Alex Pappademas and Joan LeMay, *Quantum Criminals: Ramblers, Wild Gamblers, and Other Sole Survivors from the Songs of Steely Dan*
Bruce Adams, *You're with Stupid: kranky, Chicago, and the Reinvention of Indie Music*
Margo Price, *Maybe We'll Make It: A Memoir*
Francesca T. Royster, *Black Country Music: Listening for Revolutions*
Lynn Melnick, *I've Had to Think Up a Way to Survive: On Trauma, Persistence, and Dolly Parton*
Lance Scott Walker, *DJ Screw: A Life in Slow Revolution*
Eddie Huffman, *John Prine: In Spite of Himself*
David Cantwell, *The Running Kind: Listening to Merle Haggard*
Stephen Deusner, *Where the Devil Don't Stay: Traveling the South with the Drive-By Truckers*
Eric Harvey, *Who Got the Camera? A History of Rap and Reality*
Kristin Hersh, *Seeing Sideways: A Memoir of Music and Motherhood*
Hannah Ewens, *Fangirls: Scenes from Modern Music Culture*
Sasha Geffen, *Glitter Up the Dark: How Pop Music Broke the Binary*
Hanif Abdurraqib, *Go Ahead in the Rain: Notes to A Tribe Called Quest*

Peter Blackstock and David Menconi, Founding Editors

This is dedicated to the musicians, artists, writers, designers, producers, loiterers, posers, style queens and kings, gadflies, runaways, and crazy motherfuckers who are making a scene RIGHT NOW somewhere in the world, closer than you think . . .

CONTENTS

SOMEDAY ALL THE ADULTS WILL DIE!

Dogpile at a Fang show, Liberty Lunch, Austin, July 1984. *From left:* Tales of Terror singer Rat's Ass, Fang singer Sam McBride, journalist Marc Savlov, Butthole Surfer Quinn Matthews, Tim Swingle of Doctors' Mob, Chris Gates of the Big Boys.

PROLOGUE
The Kids, the Huns, and Texas Drag

They weren't bad kids, but oh, they were a handful. "Texas" Terri Laird had a mouth like a sailor, and she was forever with the troublemakers down at that ditch with the sewer pipes. Ty Gavin was always in trouble, so he was always grounded. Chris Gates was a fast learner at school, but you got the feeling he could charm the pants off a snake. Teresa Taylor loved John F. Kennedy and his family—a little too much maybe—and we all know how that turned out. I was teacher's pet, a goody-goody, but I also knew an awful lot about horror movies.

Our real vice was music, and not just the Beatles or Glen Campbell, but the weird stuff too. David Yow was an army brat, and when he was living in England with his family, he heard a song called "Killer Queen" and immediately knew Queen was gonna be huge. Dayna Blackwell, on the other hand, was obsessed with the Bay City Rollers. By the time I was twelve, I was buying scratchy Roxy Music records at Pirate's Den, a run-down flea market just past the city limits.

Even then, Austin was a good place for wild music. Texas music in the twentieth century was just as rough and ready as everything else about the place. Journalist and *Deep Blues* author Robert Palmer has argued that blues music is just as likely to have been born in Texas as in Mississippi. Later Lone Star innovators such as Bob Wills and Buddy Holly were crucial to early country and rock and roll. In the 1960s, Texas garage bands like the Chessmen, from Denton, and the Outcasts, from San Antonio, formed all across the state. But the 13th Floor Elevators flew the highest. Their warped and gorgeous music transcended any of the labels—psychedelic, garage, or protopunk—that have been flung at them. The band members themselves ingested LSD and other hallucinogenics almost daily for years. Their singer, Austin native Roky Erickson, howled like a werewolf, then crooned like a wounded romantic. Their nominal leader, Tommy Hall, played a little brown jug.

"Texas" Terri discovered them accidentally. "When I was in seventh or eighth grade, the white trash girl from my junior high school threw a party at the Austin Country Club," she remembers. "When we got there, a band had set up in the corner, and there was this jug sitting there. We started playing with it—pretending we were drinking alcohol—and all this spit came out. Then the band showed up. It was Roky Erickson and the 13th Floor Elevators. I must have stood there through the whole set with my jaw on the floor. I was always drawn to the bad boys."

In the seventies, in Texas and elsewhere, rock and roll bloated into the virtuosic pretension of bands like Genesis and Wishbone Ash. On the other hand, glam artists like David Bowie and shock rockers like Alice Cooper took musical left turns that would later seem prophetic. In Upper Heyford, UK, David Yow was glued to the screen when T. Rex played *Top of the Pops*; whenever they heard "D.O.A." a gruesome hit about a plane crash by Fort Worth's own Bloodrock, David and his sister playacted their own most horrible deaths.

"I grew up in New York City, and then my family moved to San Antonio," says Ty Gavin. "When we were high school kids, the stuff we were listening to was the Doors and Iggy Pop. Then I saw Alice Cooper on TV. I was at the breakfast table, and he was on *The Dick Cavett Show*. At the end of the song, the motherfucking drummer jumps completely over his fucking drum set and lands on his feet. I was seeing magic in the circus, and I said, 'I wanna be in it.'"

In Austin, some freaks tried to vanquish their sixties hangovers by seeking refuge in older forms, particularly country and blues. Because of clubs like the Armadillo World Headquarters and record stores such as Inner Sanctum, our town was already an oasis for underground music fans, who could soak up everything from cosmic country to weirdo English electronic innovators like Brian Eno. I grew up in what was once far-north Austin, just down the street from a rickety old hangar called the Skyline Club. Elvis played the Skyline in 1955; Black Flag would play there in 1984. I went to Luckenbach, Texas, when I was a little kid, but by 1976, I was reading about punk rock in the pages of *Creem* magazine. It sounded like a good idea.

"When I first heard about punk," Teresa Taylor told me, "I went to Inner Sanctum, got a copy of the *NME*, and read all about English punk. I was converted overnight. I thought, 'Finally, I found some shit I could relate to.' I had a lot of hatred for my parents. Now I love my parents, but I was a *really* rebellious teenager."

Like Taylor, many of us heard *about* punk before we actually heard any of the music. When I first heard Cheap Trick, I thought, "This must be punk rock, right?" For her part, young Dayna Blackwell walked into a trap.

"In fourth grade, my best friend Karla and I were both outcasts—just weird, wonky, and strange," Dayna says. "We both loved the Bay City Rollers. Every weekend, my mother would take us to Zebra Records, and we'd ask, 'Do you have any new Bay City Rollers?' Then, one time, Neil Ruttenberg was working there. And he said, 'No Bay City Rollers. However, I do have this album you might find interesting. Go into the listening booth and I'll put it on for you.' It was *Never Mind the Bollocks*. My mom said she saw this glaze pass over our faces, and it was all over. Then he played us the Ramones. It was fast, loud, and powerful. It just set everything on fire. Within a week, Karla and I both had spiked hair."

We didn't know one another yet, but we were all converging on a small Tejano bar across from the University of Texas campus in Austin. The only thing we really shared was firsthand experience of the pleasures and terrors of Texas. The legend and the reality of the state would cast a long shadow over us.

"Nobody knew then that any of it was important," remembers Chris Gates. "This was just the crap we were doing as young people. I don't think a single band that was part of our generation of bands thought that what they were doing was for posterity. Not one of them thought anybody would remember them ten minutes later. It was all about right here, right now. We thought, 'All we have is a minute.'"

1978 was midnight in America, a time of self-doubt, confusion, and drift. You could feel it. A nice guy peanut farmer was president, but it seemed like no one took him seriously. Everyone had a hangover from Watergate, Vietnam, gas prices, and the terrorists at the Munich Olympics. Out in Austin, liberals like me were coming of voting age, but maybe it didn't matter. It felt like someone—Nixon? Kissinger? LBJ?—had fucked around, and now we were all gonna find out.

The Huns were ready. They were five comically unskilled musicians who were sick of it all: bored with nice guys, disgusted with bar bands, tired of Texas. The Huns made jokes about the JFK assassination. They proclaimed their homosexual love for Leif Garrett. They urinated on their enemies' doorsteps. And now, at last, they were set to make their debut at Raul's Club, the first punk venue in Austin.

"[Singer] Phil Tolstead told me the night before our first show that we were going to be overnight sensations," Huns drummer Tom Huckabee told me. "We'd barely learned ten songs and were quite aware of our ineptitude. So I said, 'Aw, Phil, let's get practical. We're gonna have to learn our instruments and learn our songs.' But he was totally right."

The Huns took the stage at Raul's just before midnight on September 19. Tolstead immediately told the audience, 'We're not here for your entertainment—you're here for ours.' Then they played the Sex Pistols' "Belsen Was a Gas."

The band finished three songs before the cops walked into Raul's. When the Huns launched into their fourth tune, "Eat Death Scum," Tolstead was glaring at [Austin Police Department] Patrolman Steve Bridgewater. The Huns singer suddenly popped like a pimple and began screaming at the cop, "I hate you! I hate you!"

Bridgewater and several undercover officers climbed onstage to confront Tolstead. The audience erupted. At the moment of truth, Tolstead switched up and did the one thing a Texas man should never, ever do: He kissed the policeman.

In the melee that followed, six people, including two Huns and the future publisher of *The Austin Chronicle*, were taken into custody. Texas music would never be the same.

The Huns were not the first Austin punk band, nor the best, but their debut performance tells us a great deal about the genre as a whole and almost everything about the Texas punk, hardcore, and postpunk music that would follow. It was all in play: theatricality, wild provocation, genderfuckery, and, most especially, a defiant challenge to the rules and norms of one of the most conservative places in the United States.

Punk has always had two voices: anger and abandon. In his book *Major Labels*, music critic Kelefa Sanneh has written that the Ramones song "I Wanna Be Sedated" perfectly represents punk's "twin preoccupations with fun and hopelessness." From Patti Smith to Amyl and the Sniffers, punk performers have made it clear that the kids are not alright. They address an older generation and the world they have inherited and howl, "We're part of the problem . . . but you killed us first." Then punk's second voice rings in and suggests that now, as Peggy Lee once sang, we "break out the booze and have a ball."

Punk music and art have been a way of understanding a world of pain and complicated joy, kitchen sink horror and imperfect solutions, unreliable narrators and broken fathers. They have confronted almost all the aesthetic and ethical dilemmas of the twentieth century—the police state, genocide, abstraction, corruption, randomness, addiction, pornography, even love—and, in so doing, helped us to process that shit.

"Punk was the gateway drug," says Bill Daniel, perhaps the most gifted photographer to document Texas punk. "I was an idiot. I was a cultural blank sheet of paper from Richardson, Texas. The situationist anthology was available at Inner Sanctum Records! But the point is that jazz, experimental music, John Cage . . . all of that came to me after the fucking blank white wall was broken by punk."

But if punk gave many of us a way to understand the world, it also became a way for us to explain Texas and Texans to the rest of the planet. Punk didn't flourish in the Lone Star State in spite of local conditions but because of them. From the jump, punks in Austin, Dallas, Houston, and San Antonio roared and railed against bad cops, racism, religious hypocrisy, sexism, homophobia, and everything else about Texas that's not funny because it's true.

"We were doing Texas drag, just playing up the hillbilly role," says Jeffrey "King" Coffey of the Butthole Surfers. "But we were also taking a lot of acid. It was like primal therapy. It was like we were saying, 'We're from Texas, it's fucked up, we're here. We'll wear trashy clothes onstage. We'll even pay tribute to our culture by playing all the tropes of Texas because it's our birthright. But as punks, it's also our right to want to destroy it.'"

Punk had been designed to fail, to reject, to self-destruct and destroy. Punks often thought of themselves as born to lose, as New York Doll Johnny Thunders put it. But as a Texan, I've never really identified with that nihilistic, nasty, low-down aspect of punk. In Texas, punk was angry but somehow positive. Sloppy, dirty, and broke but also self-parodic and side-splittingly funny. There was always a wink, a crooked smile from the corner of the room.

What if punk were to succeed? What if it created a space of triumph and affirmation, or if nothing else, a way to have good, clean fun without asking permission or paying admission? These questions were never asked out loud, at least not in Texas. But maybe someone dreamed them. Maybe these ideas were on the tips of our tongues, in the back of our heads. What if punk could show us a new way to say, "Yes, please!"

Stories about individual musicians tend to follow an arc: inspiration, revelry, a grand breakthrough, commercial success, then a long, slow decline into irrelevance or Percodan. I've always been more captivated by stories about bands, genres, salons, and scenes, which are much messier and more inexplicable. Because something very strange is happening when people get together to play and dance and then realize that it sounds . . . unique. That ought to be enough.

I nevertheless know some things to be true, and the story of Texas punk has a basic outline. In the middle 1970s, as rock music stagnated, a few musicians in New York and the UK went back to the future to strip the music down and adrenalize the best parts. In Texas, we got some half-ass intel about all of this, and it set our imaginations to work. Then the Ramones and Sex Pistols blitzed the Lone Star State in 1978. When their tour buses left town, we had to fend for ourselves.

What happened next involved two aspects of Texas life that many would regard as disadvantages: Texas was remote from the capitals of culture and had a violent history of defying anything from those locales. When punk bands, shows, and clubs began blaring across the state, some performers imitated music from the East Coast and England, but the better bands—true to a heritage of independence—crafted their own hairy kind of punk rock. It wasn't always a caveman sound, but it was usually wild.

For the next ten years, punk fans, bands, artists, writers, and clubs in Texas turned the precepts of the music every which way but loose. With some exceptions, punk had been a straight white male thing, but in Austin, it was more feminist and queer. In New York and Washington, DC, punk accelerated and standardized as it morphed into hardcore; in Dallas and Houston, bands slowed down and got weirder. In Cleveland and Leeds, punks thrived in industrial wastelands; in Texas, they played backyard barbecues and swimming holes. While death drugs like heroin and cocaine decimated punk scenes in LA, Detroit, and Minneapolis, they barely mattered in most of Texas, where people ate acid and psilocybin for breakfast. That figures: Psychedelics are less about obliterating yourself and more about deranging your senses. Texas punks were more interested in reimagining the world than incinerating it.

Unlike a typical showbiz story, this one doesn't peak with mega fame or end in tragedy. No one became a superstar, although several of the most unlikely characters became infamous for a few minutes. It wasn't about notoriety so much as derring-do. And even though some of our "stars" met unfortunate fates, more of them are now teachers, homeowners, and even accountants. Texas punk itself hasn't ended at all: A new generation of punk and postpunk performers, including Surfbort, Spoon, and St. Vincent, are defying punk norms while honoring 1980s Lone Star luminaries like the Butthole Surfers and Reversible Cords. Meanwhile, in 2023, Jeff Smith, cofounder of Hickoids—who released their classic cowpunk debut in 1985—led the latest version of the band onto the largest festival stage of their career at Luna Fest in Coimbra, Portugal, where they shared a bill with Buzzcocks and Gang of Four.

So this isn't about a rise and a fall. It's just a story about a moment in time.

For me, that moment began in November 1979. I was working in a multiplex movie theater with drummer Steve Collier, and he invited me to come see him play with his new band, the Big Boys, at Raul's. When I arrived, Steve and the rest of the group were in drag, and the singer, Randy "Biscuit" Turner, was introducing them as Kaye Mart and the Shoppers. It was overwhelming, a reset of everything: the Big Boys' sinewy, off-kilter grooves, the speed and the screaming, the mascara on my friend's face.

I got closer. I had my camera, and as I took one picture, Biscuit stuck his tongue out at me. He *saw* me. I flushed and retreated to the side of the stage. But I didn't leave the club. I couldn't. I was in.

1 | THE FIRST WAVE

I'm pretty sure I had seen Biscuit before that night. Before I knew about Raul's, I had begun to lurk around Discount Records in Highland Mall. That's where I bought my first rock fashion statement: a black silk Cheap Trick baseball jacket.

I saw my first punk rockers at the mall too. I was on the down escalator, and strolling across the atrium floor below me were two giant men dressed from head to toe in pink cowboy outfits. To this day, I am convinced they were Biscuit and Gary Floyd, who would later become the singer for the Dicks. But who knows?

I remember looking at these two pink cowboys and thinking, "Oh, that's too much!" or "Is this allowed?" I may have unconsciously looked around the atrium to see if a security team was on its way to stop this display of flaming Texanity.

In 1978, this was unusual, but initially punk always provokes one or both of those questions: "Isn't this too much?" and "Is this allowed?" The first encounter is always a shock. And it's different for everyone . . .

Neil Ruttenberg, a.k.a. the Reverend Neil X (Inner Sanctum Records, Radio Free Europe, F-Systems): It all started when Richard Dorsett, one of my coworkers at Inner Sanctum, came back from New York with the first Ramones album. He played it, and my brain exploded. It was like garage rock meets the Beach Boys.

Steve Collier (Big Boys, Doctors' Mob): Devo was my gateway. My friend Jody and I saw them on *Saturday Night Live* in the fall of 1978. We thought they were hilarious and silly. I bought their first album, and we listened to it like a comedy album. I was working at the skate park at the time. One night, we were driving home, and all of a sudden "Uncontrollable Urge" just sounded *great*. And not in a funny way. We played it over and over. . . .

That night, I phoned my high school girlfriend. She was a classical pianist. I told her I liked Devo, and she started bawling. She was in tears. She thought I was ruined—beyond redemption. I guess Devo was just so challenging.

Teresa Taylor (Butthole Surfers): I loved John F. Kennedy, and Jackie and John-John too. I always had a reverence for that family. I bought into Camelot. So when I heard the Huns song "Glad He's Dead" and they sang, "I'm glad he's dead / I helped Lee Oswald shoot him in the head!" it seemed sacrilegious! But I loved the fact that nothing was safe.

Maria Cotera (fan and friend): I dabbled in punk rock in high school. The most punk rock I had gotten was I went to see . . . the B-52s. I was pretty green. And we had this annual Spring Fling party that the protofraternity and -sorority people would put on at school, and they would accept bands. In my junior year, David Yow's first band, Toxic Shock, played at our Spring Fling. They got unplugged! The vice principal—the guy with the paddle—took them down. It was awesome! OMG! I loved seeing the Spring Fling ruined. That's what I mainly loved about punk rock—*just ruining shit*. I *loved* that! My favorite thing.

"Texas" Terri Laird (fan and singer): That's the great thing about all this punk rock shit: Even in the angriest songs of the Dicks, there was always love, love in [Dicks' singer] Gary's heart. The first time I heard punk, I was in love. And it made me feel like I was in love. All. The. Time. And who doesn't want to feel like that?

As it happened, Texans didn't have to go to punk rock—it came to us. Before we learned about CBGB and Pere Ubu, some of us thought the Sex Pistols invented punk. So we were psyched when Malcolm McLaren announced that the band was coming to San Antonio and Dallas in 1978 as part of a carefully contrived plan to incite some riots and maybe even play some songs. In fact, the Pistols were on their last legs: Back in the UK, punk was already passé. But after their Texas shows, Johnny Rotten and Sid Vicious left behind an idea. And like a cutting from some strange ivy, this premise wrapped itself around the people and surfaces of Texas and grew into something singular.

Diane "Muffy" McGee Hardin (fan): I remember seeing the Sex Pistols on TV and thinking, "I don't ever want to be one of those awful punk rockers." Within a few months, I was thinking, "I *do* want to be one of those awful punk rock rockers."

Ty Gavin (the Next): In 1978, we already had the Sex Pistols record and that thing was just smoking on the turntable. We never stopped listening to it.

Jeff Smith (Hickoids): I was a big Sex Pistols fan. The band name telegraphs fornication and violence simultaneously. They were on the covers of both San Antonio newspapers two or three times that week—before *and* after their show at Randy's Rodeo. That would be like Kanye West wearing a swastika armband today. That's the only time you're gonna see a musician on the front page of those papers.

Ty Gavin: When we got to their show at Randy's Rodeo, it was just incredible. It was . . . *magic*. I didn't anticipate the pandemonium. I just thought in San Antonio, people are rowdy, you know? If they're rowdy, shit man, it's gonna be a great party. The San Antonio rocker is an incredible breed of creature.

Kathy Valentine (Violators, Go-Go's): Our band, the Violators, was almost ready to play clubs. We were rehearsing. We played our first gig about ten days after we went to the Sex Pistols show at Randy's Rodeo. That show was crazy, and that was by design. But the meaning of anarchy in England under Thatcher was very different from the meaning of anarchy at Randy's Rodeo. I understood anarchy. I understood class oppression, but I didn't understand wanting people to hate you. Because it seemed to me like they really got off on the audience not liking them, you know? I didn't understand that antagonism. I *like* people to *like* me. I can't imagine subjecting myself to people booing and hissing and throwing shit. That was not what I became a musician for.

Jeff Smith: When the Sex Pistols announced they were gonna play in San Antonio, it was like someone had given me a gold mine—I was over the moon about it. My older brother and I would always go to the record store together on Saturday mornings, and we'd go back and forth about how to spend my money. We'd always pick up the *New Music Express* and *Melody Maker*, so I'd been reading about the Sex Pistols for a couple of years.

I bought both myself and my brother a $3.50 ticket for the Sex Pistols show—that was the price mandated by Malcolm McLaren for all the US tour dates. And my brother disappeared with my ticket the day of the show—he took some girl he had dated for about two weeks to Randy's Rodeo.

I was pretty heartbroken. And my brother broke up with that girl a few days later.

Jeffrey Liles (fan): The Sex Pistols wanted some kind of culture clash confrontation and that's what they got at the Longhorn Ballroom in Dallas.

The day after the show, January 10, 1978, I wore my black leather pants to high school, and before first period biology, our teacher, Coach Moore, heard me talking to some other kids. I was telling them about the show and what punk rock was. But Coach Moore was sitting so far away he couldn't really hear the conversation.

As soon as the bell rang, Coach Moore said, "Before we start class, I think I'm gonna let Jeff come up to the front of class and tell everyone about his sex pistol."

I thought, "Okay, fuck it." I went up there and I said, "Last night, me and three other guys jumped into a pickup truck and went down to this country and western bar on the other side of Dallas. These dudes from England were there, and they're called the Sex Pistols, and they were punching each other in the face and people were spitting on each other—"

Coach says, "Jeff, *stop*."

Then he says, "Are you high on drugs?"

"*Coach, no!*" I said. "It's 8:30 in the morning!"

When I got to second period class, which was world geography, the teacher said, "Jeff, come out in the hall with me." She was a young woman.

We go out to the hall, and she says, "Listen, those pants are great, but don't ever wear them to school again. You're being a distraction."

The Sex Pistols didn't play a show in Austin, but just a few weeks later, punk bands were performing at the dank little bar on the Drag called Raul's. The conditions were right: Central Austin was nervous with college students and bored teenagers, fast food joints and oddball emporiums, cheap rents and thinly veiled ambition.

The New York and especially the English bands had proclaimed that punk was a necessary corrective to the big fat blob that rock and roll had become. Johnny Rotten said as much when he wore a T-shirt that read, "I HATE PINK FLOYD." But we may have missed something else important about the music. Punk was about a reduction in scale—it zoomed in. We thought it was just cheap sunglasses and shocking lyrics, so we looked right over the obvious—it was also about the local, about seeing your bands at your club on your street.

The first Austin bands aped the Pistols, Talking Heads, or Blondie, but that was okay because it was thrilling to see hometown bands who were fast and snotty. I didn't get to Raul's until 1979, when I was seventeen. After years of stadium rock concerts, I was just excited to be able to walk up to Standing Waves and tell them I liked their music. By that time, Raul's was hosting punk shows almost every night of the week, and the place was alive with a Felliniesque cast of characters. Joe "King" Carrasco played a sort of Tex-Mex new wave and wore a crown during solos. Billy Pringle sang for Boy Problems and seemed to be made out of Flubber. Then there were those witches, Clair and Sarita.

"Texas" Terri had become *the* punk rock haircutter in Austin, but her true occupation was hell-raiser. Every time I saw her, she wanted to show me her latest tattoo, so she was always pulling off her shirt. She had a Sid Vicious punk rock sneer, but she was always a sweetheart to me. She was usually up by the band, where she would grab a partner and begin knocking people over with a slam dancing style that was equal parts two-step and kamikaze. None of us would have guessed that before punk, she had been a friend and confidante of blues wunderkind Stevie Ray Vaughan.

Clair LaVaye (fan): In 1978, Raul's owner, Roy "Raul" Gomez, and manager, Joseph Gonzalez, let punk bands take over their Tejano music bar. Until the punks showed up, Raul's had been a stinky, beer-soaked dive, a watering hole for day drinkers.

Lynn Keller (Reversible Cords): Those guys at Raul's—[bouncer] Bobby Morales and Joseph Gonzalez? They could have given a shit about everybody there. I mean, they liked me—I grew up in El Paso and I understood where they were coming from. But it's not like they were responsible for the punk scene. They weren't into the music or anything. They opened a bar. The punks came in and took over their bar. And those guys accepted it because it was bringing in money.

Kathy Valentine: I'm a Texan, [but in 1973] I saw punk rock in England, and I came back to Texas to start a punk band. I saw an opening. I just knew it would be the first, and being first is always good. The Violators were the first band to play Raul's.

Neil Ruttenberg: The Violators were protopunk—like Austin's Runaways.

Kathy Valentine: The Violators did a lot of covers at the beginning, but we realized quickly that we wouldn't get anywhere by playing covers.

Ty Gavin: When you start out as a cover band, you already have cancer of the influences.

Kathy Valentine: [Violators bassist] Jesse Sublett and I decided to try our hand at writing some punk songs. The only one I really recall was "Gross Encounters." We put the notes of the theme from *Close Encounters of the Third Kind* into the song. We thought it was very clever. But it wasn't exactly "Anarchy in the U.K."

Joe Nick Patoski (journalist and manager): All these bands at Raul's were looking to London, to New York, and, to a lesser extent, to LA for their music cues. I didn't hear much originality until Roky Erickson showed up at Raul's. He was the missing link for all these bands. Roky showed them that, "Hey, punk comes from somewhere."

That woke people up—it got people to think, "Don't be the Sex Pistols, don't be the Ramones." Make your own shit up.

"Texas" Terri Laird: I left Raul's once and got in a friend's car—he had this big white Cadillac. And this head pops up from the backseat and says, "Hey, Terri, you want to go to my mom's house and eat some acid?" It was Roky Erickson.

Larry Seaman (Standing Waves): Summer of '78, I was going to Southwest Texas University, working in a bookstore, and reading *Creem* magazine.

I had veered off the mainstream rock path and was listening to Eno and Roxy Music and the Velvet Underground. I was friends with Roland Swenson, and he told me, "You need to come to Austin and check out this club because it's on your wavelength."

I went down that weekend and saw the Skunks and the Next at Raul's. I really loved Skip Seven's guitar playing. But it was really hot, and I took off my T-shirt. And Bobby Morales, the bouncer, came over and said, "Put your shirt on."

I said, "It's *really* hot."

And Roland was like, [*whispers urgently*] "*Don't argue with him!*"

Beth Kerr (manager, Big Boys): At first, I thought Raul's was scary. Tim [Kerr] and I didn't really go to nightclubs. There was a Battle of the Bands going on and there were people you weren't used to seeing on the street. It was loud. I was in my work clothes, so I *looked* like a UT librarian. But after half an hour, I realized nobody was gonna hurt us. They were really friendly. Billy Pringle and Boy Problems were dressed all in shirts with red stripes. I think they won the Battle of the Bands.

David Wm. Sims (Scratch Acid, the Jesus Lizard): My first show at Raul's was Joe "King" Carrasco. So many cute girls with short hair.

Joe Nick Patoski: Joe "King" was a white guy with a Mexican name from the Panhandle, but he was a punk first. He played with Mexican bands in Austin—he was really drawn to the sound. And when Kris Cummings started playing a Vox organ with Joe "King," it was a whole new iteration of the way that Augie Meyers's Vox organ playing in the Sir Douglas Quintet defined the Texas punk sound of the sixties.

Even today, Joe "King" is all jacked up, all wound up. Someone once said that Joe "King" was the embodiment of cocaine. But the only time I ever saw Joe do coke was in Europe, and then he got really circumspect and quiet. He was like a Ritalin kid: you give 'em speed to slow 'em down. He's *that* guy.

Kathy Valentine: Punk made sense to me and welcomed me because I was just very, very *hurt*. I had some really awful experiences, and I was a misfit and an outcast, and I'd been betrayed and lied about all through my adolescence. When you don't have a dad in your life, all you feel like is that if you mattered enough, he *would* be there. That's likely what sent me running to punk rock—because that was a place where misfits were embraced. That's where I could see that there was nothing wrong with me. Punk was a realm where nonconforming, non-standard-issue people were not only accepted but revered. My ambition and drive was largely informed by wanting to feel like I *mattered*. A lot of successful musicians are like that.

"Texas" Terri Laird: The Violators were great. I knew Kathy in those punk rock days. We always got along. She was younger than everybody. But she was always excited about being around the music. I mean, she just has music running through her veins. She moved out to LA with Carla Olson to start the Textones. I used to call them the Sex Groans. They had two hot chicks in the band, so I'm sure a lot of the guys were having some sex groans over the Textones.

Kathy Valentine: [Jesse Sublett had started] the Skunks, and they were getting popular. One of the reasons the Violators wanted to get out of Austin was that the Skunks were taking over this mantle. We were ready to move on. My eyes were set on much bigger things.

Ty Gavin: The Violators were cool, and I liked the first lineup of the Skunks. That's when they had "Fast" Eddie Munoz. He was a real rock star.

Steve Collier: One of the eye-opening things about Raul's was you felt like it was this whole self-sustained environment. I thought, "We don't need arena shows—we have rock stars right *here*! We have Ty Gavin and Billy Pringle." It was all right there. Something was going on every night. And the audience was full of characters, larger-than-life personalities.

Marcy Buffington (fan): I don't know that punk *music* ever *really* captured my imagination, except for the fact that it was a fuck-you to the scene and music that felt suffocating to me in high school. My peers were in thrall to Farrah Fawcett, Bonne Bell lip gloss, Peter Frampton, Fleetwood Mac. It all seemed like music for the rich, the bombastic, the bored, the self-satisfied. It was the soundtrack for parties with Everclear punch, a backyard pool, and absent parents.

So I started going to clubs. Punk rock was a contact sport for kids who hated football. We were like puppies, knocking up against each other. For me, the music was secondary.

Standing Waves play in the parking lot of Inner Sanctum Records, Austin, fall 1979. *From left:* Shona Lay, Larry Seaman, David Cardwell, Randy Franklin.

"Texas" Terri Laird: I've always gone for sleazy boys. Back then, I was all about hard drugs and alcohol. But punk was just so raw. The Next? The Dicks? These bands were like *sex, sex, sex*! The Dicks were the sleaziest fuckin' most dangerous punk rockers! Dirty, dirty, dirty! But their music made me want to have sex.

Dayna Blackwell (fan): I was thirteen, so I don't know why Raul's would let me in. Joseph Gonzalez would just say, "Keep an eye on her. And if the police come, make sure you get her out the back door." They had an escape route for me. In case the po-po came: out of that door, under that fence, and go home.

"Texas" Terri Laird: Mike Runnels from the Reactors came over to my house once, and he said, "I want you to know that people at Raul's have been talking . . . and a lot of people don't like you. I mean, *nobody likes* you—they either love you or they hate you."

So I asked him, "Well, what's the ratio?"

And he said, "About fifty-fifty."

I couldn't believe it! I thought everybody loved me. Who wouldn't love me, the craziest girl in town, right?

But then, I thought, "I just have to hang out with the people that love me!"

Steve Collier: I'd heard these rumors about Clair and Sarita. "Oh, they're witches." "They dig up graves." I heard they slept in coffins and had a severed head in their house.

Clair LaVaye: Sarita and I did indeed sleep in coffins. The rumors that we had preserved human body parts (and not just a head) in our house were true. I dressed in lovely attire from the 1920s. After Sarita joined me in Austin, we started to paint our throats as cut open or make Frankenstein gashes on our arms. But we never met anyone else who dressed in costume. The word *Goth* was unknown. We were almost complete recluses until we entered Raul's for the first time.

Lynn Keller: I don't even know if Clair and Sarita were gay. I *think* they were a couple. I mean, they had their own trip, a whole other chaos.

Clair LaVaye: One night, Sarita and I went to Swensen's ice cream on the Drag to get chocolate malted sodas. A bona fide punk rocker named Elizabeth June Gall was behind the counter. She was not yet in a band called the Buffalo Gals, but she sported a wonderful shock of gauzy white hair that stood straight up. She smiled at us and said, "Why do you *look* like that?"

I decided to bluff. "We're punk rockers."

She replied loudly, "You are *not* punk rockers. I know because *I am a punk rocker*. I've never seen you in *Raw-oools*!"

We were thrilled with her forthright manner and admitted that we had never gone to Raul's. She invited us to meet her there.

So one night, we covered ourselves from skull to feet in dark mosquito netting and made our way to Raul's. Holding hands, we walked slowly from the front door through the club and glided—like Cousin Itt of the *Addams Family*—into the women's restroom.

"I want to go home—now!" Sarita said.

I wanted to stay, but she won.

We glided back to the front door. As we reached it, I heard a voice calling to us, "Come back! Come back. Be one of us!"

I returned alone an hour later and took off my giant net. The Next were on stage. Ty Gavin was leaping onto amplifiers and grabbing some pipes above the stage. He'd hang there, his arms covered with sweat. He was like an animal, alive and young and wanting to escape. I wanted to escape too. And I thought I'd found the door out of my cage.

Steve Collier: When I worked at [record store] Sound Warehouse, Clair would come in with the complete Goth look: pancake makeup, wearing a shroud. I was at the cash register, and she gave me a check—it was personalized with little tombstones and bats next to her name. I thought, "Wow, she's all in."

Clair LaVaye: Sarita painted the rat mural at Raul's for fun. Joseph agreed to the project and paid for paints and supplies. We arrived at closing time and worked overnight during spring break. Sarita chose to paint rats running along pipes as a personal whim. My contribution was to fill in colors for the pipes and read aloud to her, probably selections from Marquis de Sade, Oscar Wilde, or E. A. Poe.

Not many saw the *second rat mural* that Sarita painted under the Perry-Castañeda Library on the UT campus. It's on a side wall near the sump pumps, accessible via the tunnels and by lifting up grates in the HVAC room next to the PCL loading dock. Perhaps it is still there.

Dayna Blackwell: The girls who did the mural of the rats on the wall—Sarita and Clair—I always loved it when they would come in. Because they'd come in dressed to the nines. I was like, "Great outfits!" I wasn't scared of them; they were always real sweet to me. But you gotta remember, a lot of these people looked at me as their pet child. "There's the little baby punk—come here, sweetie!"

Clair LaVaye: But the best part of being at Raul's was to stand *outside* of Raul's. To lean against the wall and stare at passersby, dare the passengers in the cars to insult us. To be "weary" of it all: That was the game. I was outside more than I was inside. Standing with Roky Erickson, listening to him play word games with people.

Gary Floyd (Dicks): It was a time of discovering yourself. Raul's was like this huge chalkboard, and you could draw whatever you wanted to on it. It was so . . . opening. Usually at the end of every day, I was happy because

I was doing exactly what I wanted to, and I had no limits. I didn't think, "Oh, I better not do this, everybody will be freaked out." I thought, "I *better* do this—everybody will be freaked out!"

You couldn't just *glimmer* in Austin. If you wanted to shine, you had to be pretty bright.

The Next were the third Austin punk band—give or take—and the first to really understand that punk had roots that went deeper than the first Ramones album. The band summoned all the dark arts of the Stooges and other protopunks and fashioned something new, loose, and mean. They knew their guitars didn't need to sound polished and the beats could clatter together into a heap as long as the whole thing was raw and immediate. The Next led with expressionist force instead of virtuosity.

They also made the first really great Texas punk recordings, including the astonishing *Make It Quick* EP. Ty Gavin could go from bobcat shrieks to baritone sarcasm in two seconds flat, but his lyrics packed a punch as well. On "Real Love," the Next's contribution to the 1979 *Live at Raul's* record, guitarist Skip Seven uncoils a zombie walk of a riff and Gavin ponders the nature of desire. Then he sabotages himself, babbling that he's "spilling my little-bitty brains out." His pain is real, but it's a cliché, embarrassing. This discursive turn was a shade more complex than songs about a girlfriend named Sharona. It meant you could confess your feelings and ridicule them at the same time—the essence of human ambivalence. The people who would soon form the Dicks and Scratch Acid were listening.

I once discovered Ty at Inner Sanctum Records marveling over a Frank Sinatra record. "Look," he said, pointing to the cover photo. "He was a punk." Sure enough, in the picture, Sinatra was wearing a safety pin on his lapel.

Ty Gavin: My parents listened to Sinatra, Tony Bennett, stuff like that. When I was a kid, I was constantly in trouble. I was always stuck in the house. I had to be a sneaky person and smoke weed and drink and run around and everything else. But that's really not such an abnormal youth.

After we moved to Texas, my friend Will Sharp and I were both working in restaurants in San Antonio. We were still in high school. I said, "I'm gonna buy a tape recorder, and I'm going to sing into it for a year to figure out how to sing. And then we'll look for musicians." A year later, Will was working at Record Hole in North Star Mall, and he was in charge of the imports. That meant that we got to hear all the cool stuff before anybody else—we got all the magazines and papers from Europe and England. And I already had Arthur Hays in mind as a drummer.

At the Sex Pistols concert in San Antonio, Will introduced us to Skip Seven, who had just got back from England. He was a punk rock guitar player. From there, we just started. The first time we played, there was probably six people there. The second time—twelve people. And then fifteen, and then twenty.

Kathy Valentine: I met Skip Seven and Ty at the Sex Pistols show too. I brought them back to Austin with me, and I went out with Skip. I saw the Next. Ty was a star—he was a really great front man!

Ty Gavin: We looked the way we looked—like people you didn't want around. I remember going into 7-Eleven stores and they'd wait on me right away, just because they wanted to get me out of the place. If I was wearing mascara or eye shadow, some people would get freaked out and some would want to fight you.

E. A. Srere (editor, *Sluggo!* fanzine): I *love, loved* the Next. I loved Ty Gavin. He was so cute. So, so very *engaging*. All the girls loved him.

Ty Gavin: When we started the band, I moved to Austin. We just split. We just left San Antonio, and we didn't tell anybody. I got this nasty letter a week later from my oldest sister saying, "What do you think you're doing? How irresponsible, how selfish. You don't care about other people." That's where the lyrics for the Next song "Mr. Wonderful" came from. But when we recorded that *Make It Quick* EP, I had snot hanging out of my nose—I had the flu or something. I was all fucked up.

Carlos Lowry (artist): The Next was the bridge to hardcore punk in Austin.

Ty Gavin: The only time I ever got put in jail was for fighting with rednecks in the Raul's parking lot. We weren't playing that night, but we did some mushrooms. And then this redneck started going after the girls. I ended up getting into a fight with him. And, um, you know . . . it was a pretty good fight. I was gonna hit him one more time before I walked away. Then this cop taps me on the shoulder. Fighting in public is against the law.

We got down to jail, and I was waiting to get booked. That's when I started getting off on the mushrooms. I had to go into maximum meditation mode, like Bruce Lee, because it was freezing cold in there. And my legs start shaking a little bit.

Meanwhile, back at Raul's, people were saying, "Ty got taken downtown to jail." It was closing time, so everybody from Raul's comes down to the jail. The lobby of the jail was full of punk rockers. The cops said, "You want to call somebody?" And I told them, "Well, everyone I know is here."

But I called my dad. It was two o'clock in the morning. I said, "I got put in jail."

And he just said, "Well, get some sleep before you talk to the judge in the morning."

I said, "Okay, talk to you later."

David Yow (Toxic Shock, Scratch Acid, the Jesus Lizard): One night, I was watching the Next, and you know, the stage at Raul's was what, like eight or ten inches tall? And I flicked my cigarette at Ty Gavin. He didn't stop singing, but he slowly, nonchalantly, walked over to me and just went *boom!* with his fist. Hit me in my center of gravity, and I went flying! I just loved that—it was so cool. Before punk rock, there was never that kind of connection—a possibly dangerous connection—between the audience and the band.

Ty Gavin: I was responsible back then too. That's why I survived. Because I did everything that everyone else did. I didn't hold back from nothing. But I had some street sense, and that's what kept me from becoming a fucking basket case. I was seeing people fall all around me from drugs and crank, and I'm going, "Man, these dumbasses have never been away from home. They can't handle it!" And then you got all these fucking drug predators—you know, "Oh wow, let's do some speed." And before you know it, the new college kid is on the way back home because they're fucked up on speed and they can't go to school.

Neil Ruttenberg: I've always thought that the Next were the best band in town. They could have been *big*. But they failed to *change*; you know, they failed to develop further. They were really great at that moment in time, and then they kind of just got stuck there.

Ty Gavin: At that time, there was nothing downtown. It was just office buildings. A couple of hotels. So at 5:30, downtown Austin was a *ghost land*. Vacant. There were abandoned buildings. We rehearsed in this old building. These prostitutes would hang out in front of the building, and then in the wintertime, they'd come in and sit on the couch while we were practicing. That was at [Reversible Cords accordionist] Bert Crews's place—it was just a big warehouse on Seventh and Trinity.

That's when the night riders started because it was so hot that you couldn't even ride your bike in the daytime. I had this cruiser bike—it was like having wings. There was this group of night riders—you'd start riding around downtown by yourself, and you'd see another rider, and then another rider and before you knew it, you had, like, a half dozen riders. We'd ride all night drunk and everything else. We were free spirits. No one would touch us. Police didn't give a shit about us. We had this fantastic romantic moment—bike riding at midnight. The midnight riders.

Meanwhile, across the state, punk scenes were sputtering to life or foundering. Really Red and Legionaire's Disease were playing at Rock Island in Houston, while in Dallas, DJs was the place to see the Infants performing their ode to elementary school love, "Giant Girl in the Fifth Grade." In San Antonio, the Vamps, who had opened for the Pistols at Randy's Rodeo, now shared the stage with John Cale and Iron Butterfly at an outdoor venue called Sunken Gardens. But instead of opening for touring dinosaurs, lots of Texas punks just packed up and moved to Austin.

Pat Doyle (Offenders): The punk rock scene in Killeen only existed because of Renaissance Records. Before that, most of us there got our records from Woolworth's, Winn's, TG&Y, or by mail order. Dave Spriggs decided to fix that. He was a rabid record collector who had been stationed at Fort Hood during a stint in the US Army. When he finished his army tour, he opened a proper record store in 1977. It featured lots of album-oriented seventies rock, except he also carried a lot of limited editions and imports, which was unheard of in Killeen. He began stocking a lot of punk and new wave bands. The soldiers coming into Killeen from all over the world demanded to hear something different from what was on the radio.

By 1978, Dave began hosting a few punk bands at the Crazy Horse Saloon, this hesher's bar on the outskirts of town. I was underage at the time, but we'd already formed the Offenders and we opened a few of those shows. Dave brought in the Runaways, Pearl Harbor and the Explosions, and cool Austin bands like the Skunks and Terminal Mind. Dave also played drums for the Ideals, a band he started with another Fort Hood soldier, Davy Jones. The Ideals would open all these shows at the Crazy Horse. They would play sixties covers and [original] songs like "FTA [Fuck the Army]," which were intended to piss off the local GIs. It worked. One night, the crowd asked the Ideals to play "Free Bird," which prompted [Ideals member] Richard Hays to play the intro on his bass using a beer bottle for a slide. The soldiers got offended and began chanting, "You suck, you suck, you suck!" like they were in marching formation.

I had my eyes set on moving to Austin even before I joined the Offenders. I mean, you had to drive [about thirty-five minutes] from Killeen to Temple just to buy drumsticks. So we thought, "We've got to get out of Killeen and establish ourselves in Austin."

Laurie Greenwell (fan): I worked in a record store in Houston when I was in high school, Cactus Records and Tapes. Some of the people that used to come in also went to [punk shows at] the Island. My friend's brother was in Verbal Abuse. I hated all the stuff that was popular: REO Speedwagon, Journey, and Kansas, all those faceless bands. But I hadn't quite figured out punk yet. I just had this disdain of conformity. When I moved to Austin, I couldn't stand the fraternities and sororities. They were repulsive to me. And it just seemed like the punks were my people.

Jeffrey Liles: Right after I got out of high school, I threw everything into a station wagon and drove from Dallas down to Austin. I didn't know what I was gonna do. I went to one semester of classes at Austin Community College. My parents were just trying to get rid of me, so they put me up in a dorm called the Castillian.

Of course, I hung out at Inner Sanctum Records, which was right across the street from the Castillian. One day I walked in there, and the cover of the first Mötley Crüe record was nailed to the wall. The nail was in Vince Neil's crotch. And underneath that, someone had written, "THE NEXT BIG THING?"

Laurie Greenwell: My friend Melissa Merryman got me a job at Inner Sanctum. I was a shitty employee. I was one of the snooty employees who passed judgment on your musical taste. I just went there to play records and talk to my friends. Biscuit worked in the skate shop upstairs, and Roky Erickson would always meander into the store and ask me to play that one Peter Tosh song with Mick Jagger ["(You Got to Walk and) Don't Look Back"]. I also got in trouble for playing too much punk rock.

Pat Doyle: [After Killeen,] Austin was Shangri-la, and not just for schlubs like us from small-town hellholes. It was a town with pretty young people, trees, swimming holes, and a real-deal punk rock scene. A pristine environment for nurturing the creative tendencies of artists and weirdos.

Cindy Melbie (fan): A friend and I moved from New York to Texas when we were twenty-one. We were tired of the cold winters. When we got to Austin, we went to some clubs. Then we went to Eeyore's Birthday Party at Pease Park. We met Dayna Blackwell there, and she started talking to us. I guess because we looked punk. Then she took us to Raul's.

As soon as we got there, Joseph and Bobby were so welcoming. They played pool with us, and they were so nice. Years later, I asked them about that, and Joseph said, "Bars have to have girls. Guys won't come if there aren't any girls."

Joseph Gonzalez, Bobby Morales, and Rudy Hyde, everyone's favorite door man, ran Raul's like a family business and didn't take shit from any of the occasional troublemakers. Regulars remember seeing a biker pull a knife on Morales at the entrance one night. The bouncer did not blink; he just slowly backed the man out of the club. For all sorts of unusual characters, Raul's became a safe house.

John Slate, a.k.a. Control Rat X, was a Raul's regular and part of the underage McCallum Senior High crew, along with Dayna Blackwell and Chris Gates. Unlike other regulars, John never stopped extolling the virtues of other kinds of music, especially those from Black superstars like James Brown and Parliament/Funkadelic. He threw an annual disco party (costumes mandatory) and was not above jumping onstage between bands to do his Funky Rat magic show. He knew about every JFK conspiracy theory (and later displayed this knowledge in his role in the Richard Linklater film *Slacker*). John was always carrying a book or flyers, a rolled-up magazine, a record, or a copy of his own fanzine. If you blurted a statistic, John would fact-check you in real time.

But do-it-yourself creative communities don't flourish just because of a few oddballs or the atmosphere at one nightclub. They live and grow from what happens offstage, out on the sidewalk, and in the coffee conversations the day after the show. When musicians and fans can't stop talking about what they were doing Saturday night, and especially when they start connecting play with school or work—by using the office copier to make flyers for a band, for example—a sort of human algorithm begins to tick. This is what happened in Austin, and it was the ants in the pants of the scene.

Neil Ruttenberg, a.k.a. the Reverend Neil X, was the most extreme case in point. Originally a rocker from San Antonio, Ruttenberg was studying film at UT, working at the record store at the center of Austin punk, DJing a late-night punk show on the student radio station, and playing in both the experimental noise group Radio Free Europe and the post-punk band F-Systems. He made a no-budget horror film called *Mask of Sarnath* with Louis Black, another film student who was also working as a newspaper critic and a repertory film programmer. Like many other UT Radio, Television, and Film (RTF) majors, their passions bled into their professions.

Chris Gates (Big Boys, Poison 13): In the fall of 1978, I saw a flyer on the Drag for a radio show on KUT called *The Reverend Neil X Show*. I tuned in on Sunday night at 10:00 p.m., and the first five songs he played were by the Buzzcocks, the Clash, Stiff Little Fingers, Generation X, and the Stranglers. After that, I was hooked. At some point during the show, he mentioned Inner Sanctum, and I made a beeline down there . . . after school that Monday. I started asking about the Buzzcocks, and someone pointed me to Neil, who also worked at Inner Sanctum. For a long time, his radio show was the *only* place to hear punk in Austin, and Inner Sanctum was the only place to find the records. It had also been ground zero for the cosmic cowboy movement earlier in the seventies.

Neil Ruttenberg: I had Phil Tolstead and the Huns on my show, and they did an on-air sex show where they simulated having sex. I was close to being fired so many times at that radio station. Sometimes I would put on *Metal Machine Music* by Lou Reed so that I could go across the street to eat at Jack in the Box. People at the station thought there was something wrong with our transmitter.

I had Patti Smith on the show, and she did a poetry reading. She spit on the table a lot. I thought, "What the hell was that all about?"

The Big Boys, Raul's Club, Austin, fall 1979. *From left*: Chris Gates, Steve Collier, Randy "Biscuit" Turner (RIP), Tim Kerr. On this night, Turner introduced the band as Kaye Mart and the Shoppers.

Clair LaVaye: The location of Raul's Club was key to who it first influenced—and how that influence spread virally to the greater population. The club was across the street from the University of Texas at Austin's Radio, Television, and Film building, the home of the *Daily Texan* student newspaper, and the location for Austin's public radio station, KUT-FM. Journalism and photojournalism students would cross Guadalupe Street to Raul's to drink beer, hear music, take photos, and then return to the *Texan* to publish stories in the student newspaper. Bands crossed over to practice in Studio B on campus. Neil Ruttenberg played punk and underground music on his show, and he occasionally used Studio B to host a live punk performance.

Louis Black (cofounder, *The Austin Chronicle* and South by Southwest Festival): In those Raul's days, we were running [the UT repertory film program] Cinema Texas, and we were on the board for the Student Union. So we'd watch a film at Jester Auditorium, then go by the Union and pick up the film that they had just shown. Then we'd go to Raul's or Dukes, and when the clubs closed, we'd go home and watch the film we'd picked up from the Union. It was so exciting, and it just never stopped.

Ty Gavin: Raul's was two blocks from the RTF school. It was easy for people to be curious about each other—you can smell each other at that distance. At Raul's, it didn't matter what you did; it didn't matter who you were. But if you wanted to come to Raul's and you did something, then *do the motherfucker*. If you're an artist, make a fucking flyer. If you're a painter, paint a fucking wall. That was the main idea of it.

Louis Black: In Austin, people would call you up to be in their movie, and you'd say, "Where?" instead of "Why?" And at the beginning, punk was all about saying, "I'm more important than my instrument. I don't know how to play it. I just have the guts to get on stage to go inside myself."

Clair LaVaye: Most bands included at least one painter, writer, actor, or filmmaker. Their musical contribution was sometimes minimal, but their moral support and friendship was integral. When the Huns' singer, Phil Tolstead, was arrested for kissing a cop, the *Texan* and other student media were ready to use that to put Raul's on the map.

The great punk artist Raymond Pettibon once illustrated an album by the postpunk band Sonic Youth with a cartoon that included the words, "It was all whirlwind, heat, and flash. Within a week we killed my parents." The Huns were a little like that, even if they did shine a spotlight on Texas punk. Musical talent notwithstanding, they appeared suddenly, made international headlines, then disappeared in a puff of smoke. Maybe they had decided fifteen minutes of fame was self-indulgent, so they just took five. The only leftover was a seven-inch single called "Busy Kids"—two and a half minutes of quasi-Ramones bombast and Alvin and the Chipmunks vocals. It's a wonder it still sounds so good.

Clair LaVaye: My favorite band, unreservedly, was the Huns. But I was not there for the music. I was there for the theater. There was a phase where a feud broke out between fans of the Standing Waves and followers of the Huns. The Standing Waves could actually play music well and people loved them because their songs made them happy. I hated the Standing Waves because I knew that they were sincere. I preferred the Huns' total immersion in irony, cynicism, and wickedness.

Neil Ruttenberg: The Huns were a joke.

Teresa Taylor: Phil Tolstead was a very charismatic singer. He always wore makeup—he was a pretty boy. He just started calling himself a rock star. And then he was one.

Tom Huckabee (Huns, Reversible Cords): [Before our first show at Raul's] we'd put up posters—mine said, "Legalize Crime." [Keyboardist] Dan Puckett's said, "No Police." Our third song that night was "Something About You Bores Me." It was a satire of the Skunks song "Something About You Scares Me." Phil wanted to bait the Skunks, who were the reigning band.

Then we started our fourth song. I had a very good view of the entire club. I was protected by the drums and didn't have any fear. I saw the guy walk in—the policeman. I think the undercover cops came in behind him as backup. And they were just ready. He came in by himself to a club full of punk rockers, and they probably barely understood what that scene *was*. So [APD Patrolman] Steve Bridgewater—being the cowboy that he was . . .

Rock Club Raid Leads to 6 Arrests

> Six persons were arrested early Wednesday morning when police broke up the debut performance of Austin punk rock band The Huns at Raul's. . . . Phil Tolstead, the lead singer, was pointing at the uniformed officer, singing a song titled "Eat Death Scum," which included the lyrics, "I hate you, I hate you," and the officer approached the stage.
>
> Larry Osier, a University communication student, who was present, said that when the singer responded by trying to kiss the officer, the officer handcuffed Tolstead and the audience then rushed the stage.
>
> *DAILY TEXAN*, SEPTEMBER 20, 1978

Tom Huckabee: [After the story was picked up by] *Rolling Stone* and *New Musical Express*, it just fed Phil's massive ego. The band had been a democracy before the first show. But after that, Phil just totally took charge, and it made sense. All we had going for us at that point was Phil's cheekiness.

He had star quality. Totally unpredictable. It was like gigging with Jim Morrison. He was beautiful at that time of his life—a really snappy dresser and an *amazing* dancer. The stage patter was phenomenal. He just couldn't carry a tune.

Teresa Taylor: The Huns keyboard player would put a poster of [teen Top 40 star] Leif Garrett behind his keyboard when they played. He looked like a hillbilly, but he was gay as shit. He'd put up flyers of Leif Garrett and wear a Leif Garrett T-shirt. He'd wear a gimme cap and a Western shirt and talk about "Leif Garrett's little honey balls."

David Yow: I saw the Huns play at Raul's on Halloween night in 1979. Me and my buddy Rob Lapoint both wore sweatshirts and skinny ties. Phil Tolstead was just wearing a jockstrap and had painted his entire body silver. I had never heard or seen anything like it. I know people always say things like, "It changed my life." But . . . it changed my life. I blew off college and just thought, "Okay, this is the most important thing to me."

E. A. Srere: [*laughs*] There were people who would say, "We hate everything, we hate the world." But the only person I knew to be *willfully* malignant was Phil Tolstead. He always wanted to go pee on somebody's door. That was some kind of fetish with him. "I'm gonna go down to [radio station] KLBJ and pee on their door—they won't play our music." "Oh, there's David Cardwell; he's in Standing Waves. I'm gonna go pee on his door."

Clair LaVaye: Sarita and I won a KUT radio contest in which the winner could perform a song with the Huns. For the performance—at Raul's—we called ourselves Dykes with Dicks. We were both covered in fake blood and dressed as *Carrie* at the prom, carrying a feather pillow and a huge knife. As Sarita held the pillow to her chest and yelled, "But momma, it's just a dirty pillow!" I stabbed the pillow. She screamed like Yoko Ono on fire. An explosion of feathers obscured the view. It was a crowd-pleasing performance.

After that, we still occasionally went to Huns shows in costume, and we'd sing, "Dykes with Dicks" and "Huns Go Hey Hey Hey." They never socialized with us, but they never said, "You can't do this anymore." They had to live with the suspense of whether the Dykes with Dicks were going to appear and fuck up their set.

Teresa Taylor: Then Phil Tolstead moved to LA and became an evangelical Christian. He told everyone, "I started punk rock in Austin, Texas, and then I got saved by Jesus!" Very arrogant.

Louis Black: The night that Reagan got elected, after Gang of Four played at Club Foot, I went home, started watching TV, and saw Phil Tolstead on one of the Christian channels. Up until Reagan's election, I would watch *The PTL Club* all the time. After the election, I couldn't watch it anymore. I didn't realize the reactionaries were gonna come at us in full force.

By the spring of 1980, the Vulcan Gas Company—the same downtown concert hall that had once hosted shows by the 13th Floor Elevators and the Velvet Underground—had reopened as Duke's Royal Coach Inn and was booking nightly punk shows. New subspecies of punk were appearing every week at Raul's and Duke's: The Foams were an all-female art school clatter, the Reactors an itchy minimalist sneer. After most of the Violators left town, bassist Jesse Sublett made slick and nasty power pop with the Skunks, who soon became the most popular band in the scene. Only slightly less successful, Standing Waves played a wiry but melodic strain of New York–influenced new wave. Terminal Mind was much beloved as well: They spiked their chords with black humor and played anthems like "I Wanna Die Young" and "(I Wanna Be) Radioactive."

But a rift was forming among some of these bands, and it echoed developments far afield in New York and London. Many of the first punk bands in those cities had immediately signed to corporate record labels, which began to develop and market other bands as "new wave." In the music business and media clusterfuck that followed, genuinely weird and innovative groups such as Devo and the B-52s were usually described as new wave, while formulaic, rehabilitated pub rockers like the Vibrators were identified as punk. Nevertheless, some onlookers developed a kind of second sight and believed they were able to divine which groups were poseurs and which were the real deal. For some of us in Austin, this manifested as a sneaking suspicion rather than something articulated with words: I hated the Explosives, who wore skinny ties and sunglasses and were way too professional. I didn't know they were also Roky Erickson's backing band for a year or two.

Beth Kerr: We saw the Huns' last night. They showed up in a limo. But that kind of points up the difference between that wave of bands and the next.

"Oh, here comes the band, and they're in a big gold limo. Don't get up on the stage—the audience isn't part of the show."

Lynn Keller: I went to Raul's right after the arrest of the Huns because I actually didn't know about the club. I'd [read about the bust in the] paper, and then I was like, "Oh, there's a punk club here!"

Larry Seaman: [Bassist] David Cardwell got us a gig opening for the Huns at their postbust gig at the Texas Union Ballroom. We were billed as the Latent Homos. That was also the first gig for Terminal Mind, who were called Red at first. We didn't come up with the name Standing Waves until the day before the gig. I got the name from my physics textbook.

Steve Marsh (Terminal Mind): I was an angry young man. I was storming around campus, determined to establish myself as different from everything that I had been brought up with—the nine-to-five, straight-and-narrow, going-to-church kind of thing. My dad was a preacher and a professor at a seminary in Fort Worth. In high school, I was a dedicated Christian, and I was doing everything I could to figure out how to please my father, until I realized there *was* no way that I could gain my father's approval—I was obviously a weirdo. That's what it was about.

Kathy McCarty (Buffalo Gals, Glass Eye): I was a suburban white kid, and I didn't know where music *came from*. The first time I went to Raul's, I saw Steve Marsh's band, Terminal Mind, and I thought they were great and *hee-larious*. I thought the people who played in the bands at Raul's were famous and rich. Then one day, I went to Thundercloud Subs and Steve Marsh made my sub. And I said, "You have a *job*?!"

Beth Kerr: Terminal Mind was one of my favorite bands all along. Except Steve Marsh would get so pissed that people were dancing to this amazing dance music they were playing. He'd stop in the middle of the song and say, "Stop dancing!" It was funny. I think he thought they weren't paying attention to the lyrics.

Steve Marsh: [*sighs*] I was a little overly serious. I was definitely about the mind. So I was trying to get people to pay attention to the lyrics, to pay attention to us, to pay attention to *me*.

Paul Leary (Butthole Surfers): I liked Terminal Mind a lot. I remember thinking that was so cool that I got to hang out with Terminal Mind a couple of times. It made me feel like a big shit.

Louis Black: I loved the Standing Waves. I loved the Big Boys.

Dave Dictor (Stains, a.k.a. MDC, a.k.a. Millions of Dead Cops): I didn't have a band yet, but I went to Raul's, and I watched the Huns. I was into Devo. I had one of those plastic suits. I liked the Skunks a little, but they weren't friendly with me. There were a lot of RTF majors at Raul's. There were a lot of people in the new wave bands who were snooty toward the punk bands. They really wanted to create a "Rock Lobster" vibe and thought new wave was going to sweep them to popularity and success.

Ty Gavin: I felt like an outsider to the younger people. The younger people weren't interested in history. They had no interest in what we were doing because they were involved with their own little scene, which was just growing and being born. That's the way it should be.

Rob Buford (Crotch Rot): A lot of the "first wave" bands and people were very cool. The Inserts were cool. Billy Problem was very cool. Sharon Tate's Baby had one of the coolest band names ever. We really didn't know many of the others—they were older. They probably thought we were just a bunch of stupid little kids. We thought they were posers and dorks. But as they say in AA, "If you spot it, you got it." I guess we were posers too. We were just the new "cooler" posers.

Larry Seaman: I was in the back of Raul's one night, and I saw that there were two groups of people standing in these elongated circles. Everybody in our group was wearing jean jackets, sort of a nerdy student look. And everybody in the other circle had a leather jacket on. I thought, "Oh, okay, they're the professional rockers."

Lynn Keller: The people I had difficulty with were the "intellectual" types. They were older than I was, and maybe they knew something I didn't know. I just thought they were phonies. They also hated our band. They liked that 1950s sound, so they were into groups like the Skunks and Standing Waves. Standing Waves for me were trying to be Talking Heads.

Tim Kerr (Big Boys, Poison 13): The first time Black Flag rolled through Austin, I thought it was a bunch of racket. You didn't know what to say . . . you didn't *not* like it, but you didn't know if you liked it either. After Black Flag, Fear came to town, and all these bands' singles started showing up at Inner Sanctum. It was like free jazz—once you started hearing it a lot, you could distinguish the differences, and you acquired a taste for it.

Gary Floyd: I called an old friend of mine, a hippie guy, and I told him, "I don't want any of this hippie music anymore. I've got all these albums—I'll give them to you. 'Cause I don't want 'em. I only want the punk rock music." And he came over, and I gave him the music.

But I took all the Neil Young and Joni Mitchell's *Blue* and *Ladies of the Canyon*, and I hid those under my bed. I thought, "I want to be really punk rock, but I think I'll save these . . . just in case."

2 | PINK FLAMINGOS

Gretchen Phillips (Meat Joy): Our scene was dominated by these two big, fat fags, and that created a context . . . which felt like "anything goes," and that was amazingly exciting. I was enthralled by Biscuit and Gary because they were the first fag musical perspective I'd been exposed to, aside from the Village People. It was so *affirming* to be at their shows, packed full of sweaty young bodies—male and female, queer and not—who were being moved by their music to slam dance and touch each other and to try to physically get out all of our powerful, overwhelming emotions of youth.

Chris Gates: One night, I was standing at the door of Raul's with Tuck, the bouncer. These five drunken frat boys show up. They're trying to get in, and they're talking about beating up fags. And Tuck said, "You better get more guys—our fags are pretty dangerous."

At the heart of the Austin punk rock scene were two bands: the sun and the moon of Raul's. Eight people who were so tightly bound together that they sounded like two halves of the same dirty joke: the Big Boys and the Dicks. And at the center of this center was a deep friendship between two gay men who shared a good-natured competition and a deep mutual admiration: Randy and Gary. Or, as one of them would later write beneath a snapshot of them both in drag, "Les Bad Bitches."

Randy "Biscuit" Turner and Gary Floyd were both heavily influenced by the performer Divine and the films of John Waters, who once remarked,

"When punk came along, it was so great—because we felt that we had *always* been punks, there just wasn't a word for it" (as quoted in Liam Warfield, Walter Crasshole, and Yony Leyser's *Queercore: How to Punk a Revolution: An Oral History*). In the last fifty years, queerness—as a cultural practice that includes drag and performance art—has been much more rigorously discussed, but not defanged: It may still be confrontational enough to destroy the Republican Party. In *Queer Art: A Freak Theory*, the German filmmaker and artist Renate Lorenz wrote, "Everyone participating in artistic practices gets their own possibilities of agency, precisely because a space—a deferral and a gap—is opened up to experiment with what this wish for belonging might mean for *their* lives."

This is how a queer aesthetic became the key that opened the golden age of Texas punk rock: It signaled that nothing was forbidden, everything was permitted. Between May 1980 and August 1982, the Big Boys and the Dicks played thirty-four shows together. They took Black music forms—blues and funk—and adrenalized them in performances with cross-dressing, meat-throwing, and the occasional horn section. Witnesses took home a sort of manifesto: "Do your own thing but take it to the limit." As Austin punk Donna Rich put it, "Gary Floyd and Biscuit are heroes to me—they showed me how to be authentic and strong."

Gary Floyd: I believe I first saw Biscuit on the Drag in '77. We caught each other's eye. I looked hippyish—bored but holding on to a world of cosmic cowboys and watching paint melt in the heat. The next time we crossed paths, we spoke. He looked cool in a lot of ways. He had long hair, as did most of Austin . . . but wild clothes too. He was funny as hell. We were both sick of the relaxing, take-it-easy atmosphere. We liked to get stoned, though, and we got together now and then to get baked and laugh about the heat, the boredom, and the future we didn't know was near at hand.

> Gary and I have been friends since 1974 when we first met. So that's like half a decade before punk rock was really happening. We've always been kind of nutty and having fun.
>
> BISCUIT INTERVIEW, *COOL BEANS* FANZINE, NO. 5, 1996

Adriane "Ash" Shown (writer): For me, it was about them both being older gay men. The Big Boys might have been up there playing [Kool and the Gang's] "Hollywood Swinging," but there was an undercurrent to it because you had to think about what Biscuit and Gary were facing coming up. Like, what happened to teenage Randy? What happened to twenty-year-old Randy?

Gary Floyd: After punk had descended on Austin, Biscuit and I ran into each other again outside Raul's one night. We rejoiced in seeing how we were both eating up the excitement of this new happening—punk rock. It was new, and we were ready to get in deep. Soon he had the Big Boys, and I had the Dicks. We loved playing together and showing off and people loving it. He and I remained friends forever.

> Yeah . . . we borrowed [the Big Boys'] equipment . . . it was kinda shitty.
>
> BUXF PARROTT, THE DICKS, LINER NOTES, BIG BOYS, *THE SKINNY ELVIS*, 1993

Beth Kerr: Tim always said he was glad the Dicks were our friends. You wouldn't want them to be your enemies.

Punk meant different things in different places. It didn't always translate perfectly or transplant well. Many English punk songs were coded with class conflict, but Americans don't believe in class—they just hate the poor. So in American punk, the political was personal.

But stripping class consciousness out of punk without replacing it with *concern*—about racism, sexism, homophobia, and other injustices—is to turn the music into a cavalcade of naughtiness, a theater piece of shock and affect. This was the mistake that too many of the first Texas punk bands made. Some of them even sang with English accents, but more of them recreated the short, aggressive song structures of punk minus its agonized, indignant lyrics. They wrote sarcastic words and catchy neofifties tunes, but they wielded irony and wit instead of drawing from personal pain or a desperate confusion about the world in 1980.

The second wave of Texas punks, led by the Big Boys and the Dicks, took their lyrical cues from American protopunks like Iggy and the Stooges or New York punks like the Ramones. These predecessors wrote from a perspective of *personal* abjection, a feeling of wretchedness. Iggy Pop crooned—eerily—"I've been dirt / And I don't care." The Ramones were more cartoonish, but even they occasionally channeled pain into song, most famously with Dee Dee Ramone's autobiographical account of male prostitution at the intersection of "53rd and 3rd." Perhaps singing about feeling like trash or giving blowjobs for bucks is a form of class consciousness, but it needn't be expressed with that sort of rhetoric to be powerful, even transcendent. The Big Boys and particularly the Dicks understood this.

At first, the Big Boys didn't really stick out. At Raul's, they were not as infamous as the Huns or as musically skilled as the Skunks. Unlike Ty Gavin of the Next—who appeared to be half panther—the Big Boys didn't look or act like rock stars. But they were the first band in Austin who were listening to as much punk rock as they were playing. They loved the minimalist postpunk funk of Gang of Four, and they were gobbling up hardcore punk singles by Black Flag and Bad Brains. The Big Boys also perceived something deeper about punk: The audience was part of the show. They blurred the line between the two, telling their live audiences, "Now go start your own band!"

This positive empowerment was stitched into the Big Boys' records. In their short career, they recorded three albums, two EPs, and a single—more vinyl than almost any other Texas punk band. Across their discography, whether on a frantic, minimal song like "Self-Contortion" or a build-and-explode number like "Manipulation," Big Boys were practicing a funk inversion: Chris Gates's bass lines are melodic loops, while Tim Kerr's parts are slashes and karate chops—guitar played as a percussion instrument. In other words, the Big Boys were a dance band. They reached their peak with the 1982 *Fun, Fun, Fun . . .* EP, a fiery mix of aggression and joyous, body-moving anthems. The Big Boys had stretched punk like a rubber band, and taken it deep into the heart of American Black music.

For people in Texas and beyond, a punk band playing straight-up funk grooves was surprising and even heretical because many US punks regarded disco and funk as mindless party music. On their records and tours, the Big Boys played to audiences who had a choice between music that sounded "punk" and music that was alive with its spirit. They presented themselves as a fierce and eclectic band, fronted by a singer who wore a Mexican wrestler mask one night and a pink tutu the next. They were asking their listeners, "What is punk?" "What is masculinity?" "What is a Texan?"

Tim Kerr: Biscuit and Chris and I had been skateboarding at the Pflugerville ditch since 1976. Steve was there too. Biscuit had hair down to his butt, and then his hair just started getting shorter, and all of a sudden, it was *real* short. And he was talking about this place called Raul's.

Chris Gates: We were coming into the Reagan era, coming out of the chaos of Vietnam and Watergate. The vast majority of society was locking itself down and becoming rigid and codified and preppy and all the rest of that shit. Which left people like me thinking, "Where the fuck do I fit?" For me, the first place was skateboarding. And the second place was punk rock. Those people way out on the edge—whether they're artists and free-thinkers, people who were abused in childhood, drug addicts, or some combination of the three—that's largely the population we attracted.

Steve Collier: We went to see Devo at the Armadillo. I knew Chris Gates and his brother Nathan from skateboarding, and they were there, wearing homemade hazmat suits.

Tim Kerr: One day, Chris and I decided that we should try and form a band to see if we could play at Raul's one time. Since we both played guitar, we flipped a coin to choose who would play bass. The next day, Chris went to Raul's, and he asked the people there, "What does it take to play here?" And the guy said, "When do you want to play?"

Steve Collier: Chris had talked to me while we were skating, and around the fall of 1979, he told me about a couple of bands he was in. One was this prog rock cover band, and the other was the Big Boys. And the whole idea of the Big Boys was that we would play at Raul's *once*. The plan was definitely *not* to become professional musicians. But then [that first show] went pretty well.

Beth Kerr: The Big Boys were such an odd group. Biscuit was so much older, and Tim was older too. Chris was younger. Steve was, like, from the suburbs. They also came from all different kinds of music. Biscuit had been here during the cosmic cowboy days and the seventies, with crazy bands like the Uranium Savages. Tim and I went to Friends of Traditional Music concerts. Chris was more into metal stuff, like regular rock and roll. They seemed really super eclectic. It's a typical Austin thing—you wouldn't expect these four people to know each other, much less get along as well as they did, but it's because of skateboarding. The uniter was skateboarding.

Steve Collier: Big Boys seemed to become Raul's pet band. Everyone wanted to play with us. Biscuit was already a known character—everyone was just waiting to see what he would do every time we played. For every show, he had a unique outfit or theme or something going on. And we played almost once a week.

Sally King (fan): I don't think I paid much attention to the queerness of the scene. It wasn't like I ever met Biscuit's boyfriend. It was like, "Yeah, I know the guy who's wearing an entire suit made of bologna sandwiches." [*laughs*] *That* was a lot more noticeable.

Dotty Farrell (Technicolor Yawns): Biscuit would always have a pocket full of surprises. Like a little earring or a flip book or a tiny fanzine that he'd made, something to give you just to make you laugh. He just loved to see the look of delight on your face. And he remembered my name. This is before people [in the scene] were talking to me. Once I went to see the Big Boys at Nightlife, and I was wearing a Big Boys T-shirt that I had made myself. And Biscuit saw me and said, "Dotty?" He was so thrilled that I had made that shirt.

Steve Collier: At the time, I didn't think about whether the Raul's scene was gay. I hadn't spent much time in downtown Austin, and I just thought, "Oh, that's how things are here—everything is very *adult*."

Chris once told me, "I think Biscuit's bi." Maybe that was Chris trying not to freak me out. Then a week later, Biscuit said, "Steve, I just want you to know I'm gay." And I thought, "Okay! Like, you didn't think I knew that?"

Chris Gates: Half the reason we asked Biscuit to be the singer was because he was always singing when we were out skateboarding. And it was always old Motown songs or stuff like that. Within the first three or four songs we wrote was [one] called "Heartbeat," where the guitar and the bass are very much in a funk mode—the bass is carrying the song with the drums and the guitars doing that thing over the top, which is sort of what funk does.

Tim Kerr: We never went around and said, "We're a hardcore band." We never went around and said, "We're a punk band." We were just this band, and that was it.

Chris Gates: I got introduced to funk in middle school because I was the only kid that played the guitar. There were a bunch of Black guys on the football team who wanted to do a band for the talent show. They showed me the guitar part because they all wanted to play bass and drums and congas and shit. Kool and the Gang's "Hollywood Swinging" was one of the songs we played at the talent show.

Once the Big Boys got going, I remember suggesting, "What if we got my brother Nathan and some of his buddies from high school to be our horn section?" We wrote horn parts to existing songs. And we did "Hollywood Swinging" because Biscuit loved that song, and I already knew it.

Sally King: Hearing funk through the Big Boys opened up a whole genre that I had really discounted before because we loved to dance, and we would just lose ourselves. It was exciting. After that, my friend Albert and I used to go to Antone's for Funk Night because they let in minors. We'd go and dance and just act like fools.

Teresa Taylor: I had so much fun dancing to the Big Boys' "Fun Fun Fun." I saw them at the first Woodshock festival at a park downtown, and they had a whole horn section. I'd fall down and someone would pick me up. Just bouncing around, singing along to the Big Boys. We were so lucky, weren't we?

Ty Gavin: I could see that younger people were starting to come to Big Boys shows. They were doing the corniest, goofiest disco shit, but we grew up antidisco. They saw a gimmick, which was the skateboard stuff, and they took advantage of that angle. I loved everybody, but it didn't mean that I liked your band.

Steve Collier: A lot of people at Raul's and Duke's were coming from little places in Texas where you couldn't be gay or do some crazy art band. Austin is this liberal oasis in the middle of Texas where you *could* do that. Biscuit was from Gladewater, Texas, some *little* place. He could never have been *Biscuit* where he lived. He had to move to Austin to be Biscuit.

Once, he and I were driving by Hyde Park Baptist Church. He had on a homemade Biscuit shirt with a bunch of holes in it. Our hair was all waxed up. We were in his '58 Chevy boat car. And crossing the street in front of us were all these church ladies with bouffant hairdos. One of them looks at Biscuit and points him out to the others, and they were just laughing and shaking their heads.

So Biscuit leans out the window and yells, "I see your bra!"

They were mortified. I think Biscuit was always at war with the old Texas, small-town people. But he was one of them.

Adriane "Ash" Shown: I did love the Big Boys. I also loved the Dicks so much because of Gary Floyd. My father was queer, and he was born and raised in San Antonio, so I already knew about gay history in San Antonio—it was still an arrestable offense! To be a gay man cruising—whether it was in the park or at a bar—had an element of danger. [You had to think,] "Am I getting mixed signals? Is that guy interested in me? Is he a cop? Or does he want to kill me?"

The three of us—my dad, Biscuit, and myself—were all collage artists. Collage is a little world where you're seeing these tiny little pieces and thinking, "Oh, this is part of a bigger picture." I think Biscuit loved that I loved my dad being out. And that it wasn't an issue for me. For Biscuit, I think it was like, "Oh, there is a glimmer of hope for the future."

Chris Gates: The Austin scene was *way* more diverse than pretty much anywhere else we went. Most cities—like DC and LA—had a "sound" . . . and most were pretty much dominated by hardcore bands. In Austin, the music was *so* varied . . . everything from the Big Boys to the Dicks and later Scratch Acid, Glass Eye, and Doctors' Mob. And the audiences were generally more open to different things than some other places. . . .

The Big Boys got a lot of stares when we went on those early tours because we were playing with bands like Black Flag, TSOL, and the Necros, but we didn't *sound* anything like those bands. It wasn't until *Thrasher* magazine started writing about us and *Fun, Fun, Fun* . . . came out that audiences outside Texas started to understand what we were all about.

Beth Kerr: I was with the band the first time they went to California. They really only had one show set up. I saw how massively bigger the LA scene was—it was all about black leather, and it was a little scary. We also went to a giant show at Santa Monica [Civic] Auditorium. I think both Black Flag and the Descendents played. Darby Crash was all dressed up like Adam Ant and lip-synching to Adam and the Ants songs. His audience didn't appreciate that. It was mind-boggling. The cops came through, and there was a big punk riot.

Then we went up to San Francisco. I had written a letter to the *Thrasher* people saying, "Hey, we're coming and we're all skateboarders and can somebody show us the good places to skate?" That's how we got to know Mofo, one of the original *Thrasher* photographers. Mofo wound up doing this series in the magazine called "The Wild Riders of Boardz."

The Big Boys, Liberty Lunch, Austin, September 23, 1984. Misfits/Samhain singer Glenn Danzig is at the side of the stage, near Poison 13 singer Mike Carroll (RIP) and former Big Boys manager Beth Kerr. This was to be the Big Boys' last show ever.

It was fictional and really outlandish, about this skate punk band going around the country and skating and playing shows. But it was based on the Big Boys.

Bill Daniel (photographer, filmmaker): The Big Boys practiced reciprocity. They told other bands, "When you come to our town, we'll open for you, we'll give you a place to stay, we'll make the flyers, and we'll take you skating. And then, when we come to your town, you'll fucking put us on a great show, you'll open for us, give us the best slot of the night, and then show us your town." And that reciprocity is really, really core to the whole DIY thing. It's actually way bigger than punk rock—that's how graffiti culture and avant-garde improv music scenes function as well. That made a huge impression on me, and I incorporated that into my practice as a photographer and filmmaker.

AL FLIPSIDE: Are you gay?
BISCUIT: I don't know if I want to answer that or not because it doesn't make any difference if I'm gay or not. I'm a human being and my sexual preference doesn't play into my lifestyle. It comes from my heart and I want people to look at me and say I'm a human. . . .
AL: Where's your skirt, Tim?
TIM: It's in the wash tonight.
BISCUIT: He's a different human being. Ever since I was a little kid, I've been at the other end of the world. I play on that and enjoy doing it. . . . We have been the KKK on stage, Africans . . . I've been in drag. I don't care what you think I am. I'm gonna be an entirely different person the next time you meet me, so don't classify me as a drag queen. Tomorrow, I'll work in an oil field. The next day I'll cook eggs in a restaurant. I'm a hundred people and I'm the one person you saw tonight. That's what I love.

BIG BOYS INTERVIEW, *FLIPSIDE*, NO. 32, 1982

While the Big Boys practiced reciprocity and inclusion, the Dicks were all about confrontation. Direct action. On May 16, 1980, they played their first show as part of the Punk Prom at the Armadillo World Headquarters, the flagship of Austin hippie culture. Bassist Buxf Parrott and drummer Pat Deason were still learning their instruments, but the Dicks already knew what they were doing. A ragged blues underpinned their songs, and Gary Floyd may have had a green Mohawk. I can't be sure because the anger leaping off the stage—about fake punks, racism, homophobia—was so white-hot I thought my face was on fire.

Underneath the stage that night, an Armadillo staff engineer was recording the evening's program, and one of the things he captured in the Dicks' set was an improvisation called "Saturday Night at the Bookstore." In another era, this piece could have been called "Blues Jam No. 8," but here, as the band blared and bashed their way through it, Floyd roared about glory holes and shame in the male cruising scene at an adult bookstore. "Saturday Night" would become one in a series of astonishing Dicks recordings—the song is a furious assertion of visibility and an attack on the hypocrisy of men who stay in the closet so they can pass in conservative Texas society. At a crucial moment, the song's narrator sees one of his anonymous sex partners in the light of day: The man is at a grocery store with his family and won't even acknowledge the singer. This encounter explains something important about the Dicks: Underneath their rage, politics, and theatrics, it's all about betrayal.

Like the Big Boys, the Dicks were many things at once—punk and blues, gay and straight, revolutionary and even romantic. Gary Floyd was front and center—out, loud, and proud—but guitarist Glen Taylor was the secret weapon. He poured a passion for everything from Muddy Waters to the 13th Floor Elevators into his serrated, distorted riffs and dirty, undeniable melodies. Not everyone noticed, but Taylor—who was gay, but not quite out—connected the band to a legacy that was older than rock music itself. The Dicks played their own kind of Texas blues, but they built it with bricks from Stonewall.

Jeffrey "King" Coffey (Butthole Surfers): The Big Boys and the Dicks go hand in hand, and they were the two most important bands. The Big Boys created the scene and set such a good example. The Dicks were just about nasty, raw punk. The irony is that Gary Floyd was the best blues singer Texas ever produced, and *Kill from the Heart* is the best American punk record.

Tom Huckabee: I didn't see the Dicks at the Punk Prom, but I addictively listened to recordings of their set at that show. It was a perfect debut. Every song is a monster. I couldn't believe it—I never thought the Dicks would play—it was just a joke. Gary was brilliant, but I thought Pat Deason and Glen Taylor were just Beavis and Butthead. At Raul's, they would just stand aloof and snarl at everybody. I had completely written those guys off as idiots.

Steve Collier: I don't remember seeing [the Dicks at the Punk Prom]. But I do remember the show at Raul's where Gary Floyd was dressed as a Divine-like character, and he had stuffed raw liver into his panties. The liver was coming down his thighs. He threw it at people.

Gary Floyd: Of course, I was influenced by John Waters and Divine. But I made that my own thing.

Teresa Taylor: The Big Boys and the Dicks were polar opposites in sound, but they defined the scene, and they were linked in several ways. They both had these big, crazy-ass gay men. The Dicks' posters were just pictures of big, hard penises. When I started traveling around the US and seeing other punk scenes, those other places didn't have *that*.

Carlos Lowry: About 80 percent of the band members of the first wave of Austin punk bands were Radio, Television, and Film students at UT. The Dicks were all working-class. They weren't college kids—they were so different. Buxf Parrott and Glen arrived from San Antonio, and they scared everyone. They were so rough-looking.

Tom Huckabee: I once recited a Charles Bukowski poem onstage at Raul's. I knew that poetry wasn't allowed—it wasn't on the list of permissible things. But Pat and Glen from the Dicks were yelling at me the whole time to shut up. And then, when I got offstage, they both got in my face, yelling, "Don't ever do that again!"

Gary Floyd: I was able to get by with a lot of the bullshit that I did because I had Buxf, Pat, and Glen in the band with me. They didn't mind going out and beating the hell out of somebody. I, of course, was a pacifist.

Steve Collier: Buxf *was* scary. He knew me from the Big Boys. I was out in front of Club Foot once, and I was wearing this old vintage shirt. Buxf reached over and just ripped off the front pocket. I didn't know how to react. I thought, "I don't really want to fight *Buxf*."

Gary Floyd: Buxf made me look meaner than I was because he could be mean enough for two or three people. He *still* fucking scares me. To this day, he and his wife, Laurie, are some of my best friends, and when I go back to Austin, I always stay with them. But every once in a while, ole Buxf can throw a face, and I think, "Okay, I've gone too far."

Teresa Taylor: On the other hand, Glen Taylor was one of the bluesiest hardcore punks you could ever have—he was brilliant. It was the first time you could hear swampy blues thrown into the music, but it was punk as shit!

Laurie Greenwell: I once brought up Stevie Ray Vaughan with Buxf. I asked him, "Would Glen be able to play guitar [like Stevie Ray]?" And Buxf said, "*Yeah*. But he wouldn't want to." Glen played all the wrong notes. Only Glen could make all the wrong notes sound right.

Teresa Taylor: We had the kind of gay men that people saw in *Deliverance*. Glen and [his boyfriend] Santiago lived in a trailer park. And one time, my friend Dee and I went out there and climbed through their window. Me and Dee were sitting there drinking all their beer when they came home. They didn't care because they were already drinking beer too. Glen said, "Oh, I'm glad you're here—did you fall through the window?"

Glen looked like a regular cowboy, and Santiago adored him. They would say, "We have to fuck *a lot*."

Gary Floyd: How many queers were there in the Austin punk scene? If you named almost any band back then, there were some gay people in it. I have *no idea* why. You had Chris Wing [of Sharon Tate's Baby], Biscuit, me, and I could keep naming people. Those were three pretty popular bands. And they were mostly out—I mean, nobody was hiding. I don't know what made it that way, but it worked for *me*. That was a very liberating thing. I felt free and so on, but I didn't realize at the time how *important* that was.

Laurie Greenwell: *Tortured* is not a word I would ever use for Gary. He's happy with who he is. He's always had a kind of quiet self-confidence. I think *Glen* was kind of a tortured person. Maybe he was too smart for his own good.

Gary Floyd: I was always amazed when people who were gay or bi seemed to make such a deal out of not letting people know it or playing it down. I never wanted to be "in your face." I just wanted to be doing what I was doing, without getting a bunch of shit for it. I've often said to people I'm sort of a redneck fag. It's like, "You don't like it? Fuck you."

Carlos Lowry: Little Mexico was this apartment building a couple of blocks behind the Varsity Theatre. Some of the Dicks lived there, along with their inner circle of friends, like Santiago, Dolores, and Manolo Lopez. I was painting the mural on the side of the Varsity, and Manolo walks by one day, and he says, "Hey, I have these friends that have a single coming out, and they want someone to do the art."

Gary always had a pretty clear idea of what he wanted, and when I met him, he told me he wanted a hammer and sickle on the label of the single. Then I came up with the idea of having Marx, Engels, and Lenin on one side of the cover and the Dicks in that same classic formation staring back at them. It aligned right up with the politics I had. Gary loved it. It was all done using a Xerox machine down at the post office.

Pat Doyle: I first heard "Dicks Hate Police" on cassette before they released it. I had met Pat Deason, and one night, we were driving around Austin all night, and he just kept playing that tape over and over—I mean, it only had three songs on it. I knew what the name of the song was, but I didn't dwell on the lyrics too much. I knew immediately that it was gonna piss a lot of people off. And it did.

Gary Floyd: We were singing songs about what was going on: Policemen were throwing people into the bayous of Houston and drowning them. And unfortunately, a lot of that police violence is still bad. We were singing about the US presence in El Salvador and Nicaragua. Because we were pissed off about that.

Diane "Muffy" McGee Hardin: The first punk rock show I ever saw was a May Day party at the New Guild Co-Op. The Dicks were headlining. Gary Floyd was wearing a Mao tunic and proselytizing for the Communist Party. I loved them. Everything impressed me, including the audience.

Gary Floyd: Yeah, Austin was one of the cities that took it seriously, that old punk rock ethic: Just because you're onstage doesn't mean you're the entertainer. The audiences—when I was onstage singing—they were entertaining me as much as I was entertaining them.

Jeffrey "King" Coffey: When I was seventeen, I took a bus from Fort Worth to Austin. I saw the Dicks at the Ritz. There was a sea of people leaping from the stage. And I thought, "Okay, this is my life. This is the life I want to live. I've got to be a part of this." So as soon as I could, I got the fuck out of Fort Worth.

The Big Boys had formed and then toured outside of Texas well before the Dicks had done either. This may explain the differences between their sounds, approaches to audiences, and recordings. Big Boys' songs were fractured, but (slightly) more formal; the Dicks' songs were ragged and raw. Big Boys shows were celebratory and perhaps more rooted in older ideas of bringing people together with music; Dicks' shows were a challenge, a fist in your face. But Biscuit and Gary themselves were so different: The former was a uniter who contained multitudes, a show man, a father figure; the latter, a provocateur and instigator, with no fucks left to give.

In any case, both bands reached a turning point when they released a split LP in December 1980. The title of it was graceless—*Big Boys and the Dicks Recorded Live at Raul's Club*—but the music was harder and harsher than anything yet recorded (or even played) by other Raul's bands. The Big Boys would go on to make more records, but it was their tours and live shows that made a greater impact on US punk and hardcore music. By contrast, the Dicks' side of *Big Boys and the Dicks* still sears people worldwide whenever they hear it. Floyd uses his big, brawling voice like a hammer. ("Like it?" he had taunted the audience during "Saturday Night at the Bookstore.") Taylor's guitar is like a paint-by-numbers picture of punk, only it's missing some numbers: The parts barely connect, but the solos still sting. Parrot and Deason drive it all over a cliff. The music unerringly expresses the kind of disasters that anyone can relate to: lies told by someone you once trusted, cruelty at the hands of someone you once cared for, friends who are really haters, and, worst of all, the prison of self-loathing. Even the Dicks' political consciousness is expressed in a wrenchingly intimate context. Among other things, "The Dicks Hate the Police" is a portrait of a white supremacist family, framed as a dialogue in their living room.

In Texas, some English punk sounded great but felt a little detached. Dicks songs were at the opposite end of the affective spectrum: For anyone who'd ever had their heart broken, "Lifetime Problems" and "Shit on Me" were realer than real. Even the song titles—"Dead in a Motel Room" or "Wheelchair Epidemic"—were redolent haikus from a fucked-up life at the margins. These were existential crises and punk miniatures, all set in an unmistakably American landscape. Like the band themselves, Dicks songs were terrible and beautiful to behold.

Big Boys and the Dicks Recorded Live at Raul's Club became a flash point in Austin. It didn't help that the record's subtitle was similar to an earlier, less interesting, but more inclusive compilation recorded at the club. Some Austinites believe *Big Boys and the Dicks* drove a wedge between local punk and new wave groups. The Dicks began their side with a song called "Fake Bands."

Gary Floyd: What inspired me? Part of what is a great inspiration in Texas is the honesty. There's something about Texas that makes you be honest with yourself. That's one of the things I always loved—and hated—about it. It could have been my own heart, beating in the way that it beats . . . a Texas beat. It's a brutal honesty, but in the end, it's always best. I think the honesty in Texas forced me to be honest. That's why I moved—I had to get out! [*laughs*]

Beth Kerr: When the Big Boys first went to LA, that was the first time we'd seen skanking and mosh pits. And when the band came back to Austin, they actively tried to create that—without hurting people, of course. It was just this different way of dancing, which turned into the whole mosh pit thing. But I don't think any of those older Raul's bands appreciated it, you know?

Tim Kerr: The first mosh pit [in Austin] was instigated by Mike Carroll when we had just got back from California. Duke's Royal Coach Inn. The Cramps were playing.

Beth Kerr: The Big Boys were also trying to conscientiously get kids into shows. Chris Gates—probably because he was younger—realized that if you catch somebody at age sixteen, you've got a fan for life. Whereas I don't think some of the other Raul's groups paid that much attention to who was in the audience. I don't think the Standing Waves cared if you were under eighteen.

Larry Seaman: Part of the end of the first wave of punk in Austin was that the scene was getting so big. And moving into venues besides Raul's and Duke's. Club Foot was a big shift. And along with getting bigger, the scene started to "niche up." So, instead of having three pretty different bands on a bill, you'd have three bands that were alike on a bill. The Big Boys were so wonderfully playful. [But] I can remember David Dictor hitting me up to let the Stains play with us, and having seen the Stains, I thought, "This is gonna turn off our people."

And I had been at a party with one of those young hardcore guys—he was just *poison*. The attitude was, "If you're not hardcore punk, fuck you!" So *negative*. For me, that was a turning point. It kinda killed the fun of the Big Boys and the Dicks shows.

Dave Dictor: We saw a few bands blowing through town—Black Flag, Subhumans, DOA, Fear—they all played Raul's. They weren't playing "Rock Lobster." They were like, "We're all gonna die!" We wanted to go in that direction. But I wasn't totally sucked in until I met Gary Floyd. Then we got Al Schultz in the band, and he was a jazz-influenced, Gene Krupa–type, energetic drummer. We just started [*knocks the table with his fist*] picking up *the pace*. And people were responding to that energy.

Rob Buford: Some of the British punk bands had fairly sophisticated political lyrics. Gang of Four were talking about H-blocks in Long Kesh, and the Sex Pistols were talking about what a monarchy was . . . as a high school dropout, I didn't understand what any of it meant. Those albums were kind of like history class for me. Most of the American punk bands were not politically sophisticated. I gravitated to bands who featured themes I identified with: rage, self-destruction, drugs. Fear's first album is a masterpiece. And I still love Flipper.

Steve Collier: Big Boys played a show at Raul's with Fear. Glen Taylor's boyfriend Santiago was there, and he had a broken leg. All through Fear's set, Santiago was poking his crutch up at [Fear singer] Lee Ving. Then after the show, when we were packing up our stuff, Lee Ving just kicked Santiago in the chest—*hard*.

It was so negative and violent, it just made me sick. I thought, "I don't know about this scene." It all seemed like it was going that way.

Tim Kerr: The thing that attracted me to punk rock to begin with was that there wasn't any barrier between the band and the audience. When "new wave" started, or when that tag started to be used, those were the bands who were more serious about their careers. When people started to use the term *hardcore*, all of a sudden, you were either new wave or you were hardcore. And new wave kinda meant you were selling out.

Chris Gates: "Fun Fun Fun" was inspired by Oi! music. And by the fact that the Dicks had decided to plant their flag in an us-versus-them mentality inside of the scene. They had just written "Fake Bands." They were drawing a real sharp distinction between bands *within* the scene, between us, and new wave bands like F-Systems that weren't like "us." But F-Systems *were* us.

Gary Floyd: I was so anti–new wave. A lot of that was posturing. We did seem to draw the line. Who the hell was I talking about in our song "Fake Bands"? I don't know. I was so into making sure things were hardcore. The

Dicks took it upon themselves to be the great dividing line, to say, "We're *really* punk."

Larry Seaman: Yes, and I was on the other side of the line. So I thought, "Okay, I'm out!" Which was weird, having felt fairly central in the scene and now thinking, "Okay, now it's kinda *two scenes*."

Beth Kerr: It was [later Raul's manager] Steve Hayden's idea to make the *Big Boys and the Dicks Recorded Live at Raul's Club* a split album. I think other bands were upset that the Big Boys and the Dicks were the only two bands on the record. I think that started an us-versus-them attitude. I lay that on Steve's shoulders—he might have also started giving the Big Boys more shows, and some of the other Raul's bands might have thought, "Hey, we want a night [to play] too."

Gary Floyd: We were thrilled to record a live album together. The Big Boys were well-rehearsed and sounded great. The Dicks . . . well, we drank and drank more. We had different ways of approaching the project.

Laurie Greenwell: I mean, when you're in your twenties, you don't have enough life experience to know that you're part of something special. I thought [the Austin scene] was very egalitarian. Plus, it was a lot of smart people. Later on, when it got to be more hardcore, that seemed pretty male and . . . *icky* . . . to me.

Sally King: Fred Hawkins was a student at McCallum High, and he played with [his hardcore band] Toxic Shock at the school talent show. He was jumped by some of the kickers, and they beat him up. So Chris Gates organized a little "replay." The Dicks and the Big Boys showed up at McCallum at lunch the next day. Okay, nothing happened. But two three-hundred-pound gay guys—with scary-looking skinny dudes—was enough to nip that kicker problem in the bud.

Laurie Greenwell: I met Buxf, and I wanted to go out with him. I'd seen the Dicks, but only maybe twice. Maybe that's a good thing. The Dicks had a persona. But when I met him, Buxf was a person. I was at Brent Grulke's house, and Buxf was practicing next door. When they finished, he came over with David [D Angus] Macdonald, and they were talking about the Cowardly

Gary Floyd, the Dicks, Voltaire's Basement, Austin, April 1984. In the crowd are Jim "Straightedge" Koppenhaver, Roger Manriquez, Bonnie Cook-Kassens, and Mark "Chico" McCullough (RIP).

Lion's song in *The Wizard of Oz*. They were trying to remember the lyrics of the song. I just thought that was so funny. And I thought, "I like this guy."

Dotty Farrell: I met Buxf at the OAF House. I had heard tales of Buxf getting in a knife fight, getting arrested for a terroristic threat, and stabbing a frat boy, which he did. But it was Glen's boyfriend Santiago who was terrifying. Everybody endured Santiago because they loved Glen. But Santiago would lick you and then bite you. I saw him and Glenn go at it. I saw Santiago beat people. I saw him get beaten. He bit my friend Bonnie when she was giving him a ride home. I was in the car.

Laurie Greenwell: Glen and Santiago had an intense, abusive relationship. There were definitely times—in fact, like, every night—where Buxf and I just had to leave because they'd get too drunk and start fighting. It would turn into a physical fight. And why did Glen stay? I mean, it takes two to be in an abusive relationship. I never really understood why Glen would put up with it. He must have been tortured. I mean, he died when he was forty. He essentially drank himself to death.

The Big Boys and the Dicks had all been regulars at Raul's, although they were beginning to pay attention to hardcore bands from California while other performers at the club were still enthralled with Talking Heads. That is to say, they formed during the first wave of Austin punk—which was already front-loaded with queer punks like those in Sharon Tate's Baby and Reversible Cords—but caught fire and became more influential during the second wave. In the crowd and onstage, some punks in Austin presented as freaks first, and queer (maybe) second. Others, like the folk-punk-art activists of Meat Joy, were more upfront.

Ken Hoge (photographer): I grew up in Waco—it was like *Leave It to Beaver*, but with more music. My older sister taught me how to dance the Mashed Potato when I was about eight. Waco had a big dope scene, and by fourteen, I was smoking pot and taking acid. I had a Prince Valiant haircut when I graduated from high school in 1977 and was accepted at UT Austin. I ran away as fast as my little legs could carry me. I knew I was gay from very early on, so I had that cross to bear.

Lynn Keller: One of the things that gay men allow for women—and for straight guys, if they're open to it—is that they hold the space for anything to be acceptable. These guys [at Raul's] were not snarky or judgmental. These guys were earthy. They weren't highfalutin' types, like, "Oh, I'm the queen of England." That was none of these guys. That wasn't the vibe. And they weren't hating on women. Except maybe John Burton from the Huns. But it didn't matter—he didn't even know what a woman was.

Tom Huckabee: The only time my mother ever slapped me was when I was nine or so, and I said, "Queer of the year." I didn't even really know what I was saying. But she slapped me.

When I graduated from high school, I went directly to Hollywood. And the only people that were nice to me were gay men. Very, very nice. I mean, I got hit on a couple of times, but it was always very polite. With David Bowie, Lou Reed, and Elton John, it became hip in my world to be gay. When I started adding up who my literary heroes were—William

Burroughs, [Arthur] Rimbaud, Walt Whitman—they were mostly gay men. . . .

Raul's was where I lost most of my residual homophobia from being a straight kid who grew up in Fort Worth. I lost it by accumulating so many gay friends: Dan Puckett, Joel Richardson and John Burton from the Huns, Lynn Keller and Doug McAninch from the Re*Cords. Doug was getting his wild thing on. Doug's family was very, very prominent—his dad was head of the Republican convention of Houston. Then word got back to him that Doug was seeing an older gay man.

Gretchen Phillips: It was scary to be an out musician in Texas. I felt like I could be a target, which I most assuredly did not want to be. But I was willing to risk that to make being queer just a bit easier for others because I was singing my little heart out for all the world to see. The Big Boys and the Dicks and Sharon Tate's Baby did help me feel more brave. They created a safer environment when I really needed them.

Sally King: We'd go to the drive-in and watch bad Roger Corman movies and do mushrooms and just hang out and be teenagers. I don't remember what movies we saw, but we saw definitely some queer stuff. I know that I saw [John Waters's] *Pink Flamingos*. I don't remember if I saw it at the drive-in, but we went on Gay Night and we went on Horror Night. We went all the time.

Lynn Keller: I think I was struggling with my own identity at that time, with what it meant to be gay. I was more used to gay guys because I had a lot of gay male friends. In high school, I used to go to the gay bars in El Paso, but in the women's scene, in Texas—well, I went to one club in Houston, and it was really about role-playing, and I wasn't very comfortable with that. I thought, "This doesn't represent me." I was totally comfortable at Raul's because basically everybody that was gay was guys.

Dayna Blackwell: I think the queerness of the scene made it safer, at least for me. My mother had always taught me that if you ever feel unsafe, find a queen somewhere. I was raised by queens and drag queens and faggots—that's what mother always called 'em. She said they're always the life of the party and the more fun individuals. She said the wonderful thing about queens is that they've already overcome their difficulties. They've had to come out and tell their parents—they've already crossed the Rubicon into a mentality of "Here I am, I'm queer, get used to it." I think that carried over into the music and gave it a sense of freedom that straight music didn't have.

Lynn Keller: I'll be honest with you—it was not even discussed. I'm gay, and a lot of other people in the scene were, too, . . . but nobody said, "Oh, I'm gay." Nobody was talking about *gayness*; nobody said anything *directly* about it. Everybody knew it. It was just accepted. Because everybody was a weirdo. Everybody was just, like, an interesting person. I think the punk scene in Austin was a place for everybody who was an outsider, and in Texas [*laughs*] that's a pretty vast group.

Gretchen Phillips: I started going to punk shows in Houston in 1980, then in Austin in 1981. I saw the Big Boys in drag opening for the Go-Go's at Club Foot. They called themselves the Short Girls, and they blew the Go-Go's off the stage. I was hooked.

In Houston, there were the mydolls, who had a dyke bass player. And in Austin, we had Whoom Elements, which was, to the best of my knowledge, [made up of] two out of three lesbians.

I was also going to see plenty of folkie women's music at the time. Meat Joy was my attempt to bridge these two worlds. I knew that folk and punk shared the aesthetic of the protest song: "Something is wrong here, let me tell you all about it."

Kathy McCarty: Meat Joy were seminal, revolutionary. They were very, very cool, very ideological. They did this one entire show nude.

Gretchen Phillips: Two different lovers introduced me to punk: Kat Mims, who was a bartender at the Island, the punk club in Houston; and Teresa Taylor, who, before she went onto fame in the Butthole Surfers, was our first drummer in Meat Joy. In 1982, we met Mellissa Cobb, and I bought Teresa a red Ludwig drum kit from some lesbian friends for $150. [Our first band] the SufferJets jammed occasionally with [future Meat Joy members] Tim Mateer and John Perkins [the actor now known as John Hawkes]. I really wanted to have a band that had men in it because I was also very influenced by Martin Luther King and his writings about a dream day when we will *all* be included and equal. I am a major lesbian feminist, but I don't want to live without the men in my life.

Dotty Farrell: Meat Joy remains one of my all-time favorite bands, and I was always thrilled that our band got to play with them. They were one of the very first queercore bands. Their songs ran the gamut from snarky, pointed satire to the spooky ethereal, and they laughed in the face of everything—including our punk scene itself. They were, in a word, *brilliant.*

Gretchen Phillips: Teresa and I rented a room in the Buffalo Gals' warehouse on Fifth and Red River. It was above a wood shop, so lots of noise and sawdust would drift upstairs to our rooms. Meat Joy practiced there, along with other bands, including the Butthole Surfers. It was hot and airless and fertile. We recorded there during one of our album-cover-decorating parties.

Sherri Canon (Technicolor Yawns): I was at the album-cover-decorating party. We hand-decorated stacks of LPs with Day-Glo paints and other stuff. That was a fun night.

Dotty Farrell: My friend Darcee invited me to do the artwork for a gigantic stack of Meat Joy album covers. She had been spray-painting covers like mad, and the place was like a giant glue-huffing bag.

Gretchen Phillips: Eventually, a bit of wife-swapping went on, and Teresa and I broke up in June of 1983. When it got to be too stressful between Teresa and I, she quit Meat Joy. The Buttholes asked her to join their band, and we asked Jamie Spidle of the Buffalo Gals to join Meat Joy. Somehow, we got a gig at Club Foot, and that began our next phase of greater fame and visibility. The Twilight Room in Dallas became a regular spot. We shared the bill with the mydolls in Houston a fair amount.

Tim Mateer (Meat Joy): We did sing-alongs with printed songbooks, showed movies, and ended every show with a rhythm improvisation.

Gretchen Phillips: Meat Joy was greatly influenced by Tim and John's work as actors with Big State Theatre. Every single Meat Joy show began with some sort of improvisation or spoken-word piece before we burst into a song. We were always talking about ways to break down the fourth wall—so on the night Reagan was reelected, we decided to end our show at Voltaire's in the most vulnerable way possible: naked.

Tim Mateer: That was November 6, 1984, the second time Reagan was elected. Louis Black claimed that we saved his life with that show. It was a glimmer of hope on a dark night.

Gretchen Phillips: We did a dance portion of the show, and that entailed eventually disrobing. We formed a straight line once we were naked. The music was over, and the room was quiet. We stood there and just said whatever popped into our heads.

Then we ran back onstage and played a regular set. It was so fucking *great*. It felt amazing to be a lesbian in the 1980s who felt perfectly safe being naked in front of an audience with my band.

But like the rest of Texas (and the United States as a whole), Austin wasn't *really* safe for gay and lesbian punks. Bands like Meat Joy and the Dicks and performance spaces such as Voltaire's Basement had established conditions that allowed queer people to be *more* safe, but those conditions were subject to change. Just months before Meat Joy's naked show at Voltaire's, Offenders drummer Pat Doyle witnessed a gay-bashing incident at that same underground venue. Two rednecks attacked Butthole Surfers drummer King Coffey at a burger joint outside of Dallas that year too.

Some punks were just as hateful as Texas cowboys. The Bad Brains, from Washington, DC, were four Black men who had smashed the mostly white male landscape of hardcore punk with their supercharged, unpredictable songs and explosive live performances along the East Coast. When they began touring with Texas hardcore band MDC, some of whom were queer, explosions started happening backstage as well. When the Bad Brains and MDC got to Austin, they set off the most traumatic episode of homophobia in American hardcore punk history.

Tim Kerr: MDC called us up in 1982, and they said, "Hey, we're with this band, can you put together a show?" I had never heard of the Bad Brains, but Biscuit knew all about them—he had read about them somewhere, in some fanzine—so he was all excited.

Teresa Taylor: MDC set up a nationwide tour with Bad Brains. When they began the tour, some of the Bad Brains' wives were with them. And the Bad Brains would say things to them like, "Stir up that soup, bitch, and give me my dinner." MDC were like, "You talk to women like that?" And the

Bad Brains said, "Oh, these bitches, they're just good for feeding you and fucking." And MDC were feminists. They said, "You can't talk to women like that." And the Bad Brains were like, "Fuck you, too, bitch." And the whole tour went like that.

Tim Kerr: When they got to Austin, the Bad Brains stayed at our house. In our bathroom, there was an infamous Big Boys poster that Biscuit had made, and it said, "Hot and Bothered Young Men." It was a picture from *Colt* magazine, with a guy with a cowboy hat and a big dick hanging down. Well, when I walked in the first day that the Bad Brains were here, I noticed that somebody had taken some toilet paper and stuck it on the poster to cover up the guy's dick.

Darryl Jenifer (Bad Brains, interviewed in 1995): We came to their town—they was on our jocks 'cause we're the Bad Brains. They respected us, you know what I mean? These dudes in the Big Boys—one of them was kinda gay. We were just comin' up into Rasta, and we'd been taught that it's not natural to be homosexual.

Tim Kerr: The show that night was Big Boys, the Dicks, MDC, and the Bad Brains at Esther's Pool. The Bad Brains were one of the best live bands I had ever seen.

Bill Daniel: All of my images from that show have a white blur in the middle of them because [Bad Brains singer] HR swatted my camera like it was a bug. I was onstage, and HR was like the Tasmanian Devil, just spinning like a tornado, and on one rotation, his hand simply went out, smacked my Nikon, and then kept going on with the song as my Nikon went flying off into the audience. Luckily, I had a long, springy flash cord, so I just reeled the camera back in and kept shooting. And I thought, "Dude, that is so cool."

Sally King: I was at the show. The Bad Brains were *fucking amazing*, man. But there was a subtext to their message, and it was antigay. They said some shitty stuff during the show.

Tim Kerr: When the show was over, Biscuit and HR were hugging each other. Then HR stepped back, looked Biscuit in the eye, and said, "Oh, are you—but are you gay?"

And Biscuit said, "Yeah."

HR grabbed his head and just started screaming and hollering, "Oh man, this is Babylon! All these faggot bands!" They'd seen MDC preaching all this stuff onstage, and they'd seen pictures of Gary Floyd singing in a nurses' uniform, and they realized that all the people down here in Austin didn't care, you know?

They're yelling at each other, and all of a sudden, Biscuit realized how useless it was. He looked HR straight in the eye, and he said, "Yeah, this is Babylon, and I'm the devil."

Darryl Jenifer: What happened was, the singer pressed up on HR—came on to him—and HR got really fucking freaked out. But HR was also a young man. He was definitely homophobic and definitely judgmental, you know what I mean? But you don't size up a whole man like that. You know, you gotta live, and you learn.

John Slate, a.k.a. Control Rat X (editor, *Xiphoid Process* fanzine): The Bad Brains were spectacular that night. It's one of the very best shows I ever saw. [But what happened afterward] was a sucker punch. I was completely in the middle of it because I interviewed the Bad Brains after the show. And to look back on it and just say, "Oh, well, it was a long time ago"—that's *not good enough* for me. Sometimes, all you gotta do is say, "I did it, and I'm sorry." But the Bad Brains have never apologized for it.

Dave Dictor: We worshipped the Bad Brains. They were phenomenal. But . . . the next day, we went over to Tim Kerr's house, and we told them, "We just can't go on this tour with you."

> They called us "blood clot faggots" and tried to make us feel ashamed because we have gay friends . . . they're really talented musicians, and their message, on the surface, is real cool. The idea of "positive mental attitude." But they don't live up to it. They said to us that they were using punk to lure people to gigs, and then hit them with "jah's message."
>
> MDC STATEMENT ABOUT BAD BRAINS, *MAXIMUM ROCKNROLL*, NO. 1, AUGUST 1982

Bill Daniel: That story [about the Bad Brains] is absolute bullshit. It's just so wrong. It's a virtue-signaling thing, like a straight person sticking up for their gay friend who they didn't like while not even talking about the race aspect of the incident. The path that leads you to become Rastafarian is so completely different from any of the paths in our little scene in Austin. And to judge those guys—from a completely different world, with a totally white, politically correct perspective—is just really shallow.

Darryl Jenifer: I know I was a little foolish. I've just learned recently that you can't judge anybody, you know what I mean? I was maybe afraid of homos, whereas now it don't make no difference to me. By no means is HR or any of us [still] a homophobe or any type of -phobe, for that matter. But I never talked to the Big Boys again. No happy ending there. We became enemies.

Sally King: That was definitely talked about for years. It had a deep effect on the scene—we were all on Team Biscuit, and we were shocked by the homophobia. Biscuit was *ours*. Yeah. *Don't mess with our people.*

Tony "Autoharp" Arena (artist, *J.D.s* fanzine): As a gay punk teen on the other side of the country, I had no clue that Biscuit or Gary Floyd were gay. The first time I saw the Big Boys on video was in a *Flipside* VHS compilation. I was astonished—the singer looked like John Wayne Gacy—like a clown in drag. It was scary and fascinating. I think the first Texas punk guy who I learned was gay was King Coffey, and I remember thinking that was incredible that someone was actually out and in a hardcore punk band. Unless someone actually came out and declared it very publicly in the major zines, you could see someone in drag, looking and acting queer, and think, "They're just being punk and outrageous!" I eventually realized that Texas should've been considered the forefront of "queercore."

3 | FRONT AND CENTER

Punk rock is a contact sport. Physical stamina, a willful disregard for accepted norms of hygiene, the ability to dodge airborne teenagers—these are all helpful, but more than anything, punk rock demands participation. Playing in a band or making a stink in the mosh pit are popular options, but other positions are available. Poster artists, photographers, and fanzine creators have been crucial to every punk scene, from NYC 1975 to Vienna 2023, and so it was in Texas.

Before they were playing shows, both the Dicks and Scratch Acid were "poster bands"—that is, they were no-budget Xerox publicity campaigns for bands (and even clubs) that didn't yet exist. Besides singing for the Big Boys, Biscuit was one of the most gifted and hilariously innovative punk poster artists in the United States. He also worked at Kinko's, the campus copy shop, which was helpful if your band needed fifty posters on electric pink paper.

Visual shock tactics were the coin of the realm, so Texas poster artists rifled through porno magazines and Vietnam War images to patch together their flyers. Several posters became more infamous than the shows they advertised, including one with a naked, well-endowed cowboy and another, later in the 1980s, depicting an unusual Nativity scene. The latter was an opening salvo by Frank Kozik, a Butthole Surfers fan who would go on to change US rock poster art forever with his gorgeous and scandalous silk screen posters in the 1990s. Another notorious Texas punk poster began life as a simple IRS 1040 tax form.

Clair LaVaye: The first and probably best punk-inspired publishing was the band poster: hand-drawn, copied on colored paper, often individually colored with Magic Markers, and stapled to utility poles on Guadalupe Street to advertise performances.

Lynn Keller: [Re*Cords keyboardist] Bert Crews got the idea to do the IRS tax form poster. We were having the fifty-cent show—charging a fifty-cent cover—and I think putting it on a tax return was interesting unto itself.

Tom Huckabee: Bert and Doug were traveling around Austin picking up all the 1040 forms they could find—they'd just go into a post office and take the whole stack. That was par for the course with them. Their reasoning was, "Well, they're free."

And they had a fantastic printer at what was called the Sluggo! House. An offset printer—that was a wonder to behold. Bert had become a master at using it. And they printed up *so many* copies of that poster! I distinctly remember them driving around, just throwing fistfuls of the poster out the window onto the streets of Austin. So they did get around. It was a beautiful work of art.

Lynn Keller: We were just stupid. I didn't even know that this was a federal offense. Bert probably knew because he was smarter than us, and he was a few years older than us.

Caroline Estes (fan): I'm hanging out with Nick Modern [at Sluggo! House], and all of a sudden, this big dark sedan pulls up, and four men in black suits get out and walk up and start banging on the door. We're like, "Holy shit, who are these guys?" We opened the door, and it's the feds. They're looking for Burt Crews because he stole all these IRS 1040 forms, made Re*Cords posters out of them, and put them up all over the Drag. The Re*Cords were my favorite band back then—I just loved everything they did, and I really loved that poster. But the *men in black* were after us. We said, "Bert Crews? Don't know him! Never heard of him!" And they left.

Tom Huckabee: We were at sound check on the night of the show, getting set up. Of course, the poster said where and when we were gonna be there—you know, the culprits that had committed the crime. We didn't have that in the front of our minds.

Bert and Doug were late as usual—and maybe . . . not coming. These two really square, three-piece-suit guys come in. They were Treasury agents—that's how they introduced themselves. They asked us our names, and then they said, "Are you members of this band?" And we said, "We are." And then they said, "Well, do you have any knowledge of how this poster came to be?"

Lynn Keller: They were starting to ask us questions about Bert. And I was like, "Yeah, I don't know his last name."

Tom Huckabee: Lynn told them that we had a lot of really serious fans who would do posters for us. She was just lying through her teeth. They asked, "Who's Bert Crews?" And we said, "Well, he's a member of the band; he's the keyboard player."

"Well, where is Bert Crews?"

"Gosh, he *should* be here at sound check, but we don't know!"

I asked them if I was under arrest, and they said no. I said, "Then I'm gonna leave."

And they said, "Okay, nobody's stopping you, but if you see Bert Crews, tell him we're looking for him."

Lynn Keller: He did get arrested.

Tom Huckabee: I think they picked him up at his house, and he was taken to jail. They had a hard time coming up with a charge. They settled on defacing or destroying government property. I think the case was thrown out.

Lynn Keller: In any case, he ended up getting probation.

> AUSTIN CHRONICLE: Your artwork is unlike anyone else's.
> BISCUIT: I feel like my stuff has merit. It's more of a cartoon slant—as is my life—and yes, it is junk, but it's intricately put-together junk. It's all subjective. I don't expect everybody to say it's cool, because a lot of people may just not like that style of art, the same way there's some things I just can't stand. Whatever. I don't direct people's lives nor their minds, and if they don't like it, I'm sorry, but I'm sure trying hard.
> INTERVIEW WITH MARC SAVLOV, AUGUST 26, 2005

Bill Anderson (Poison 13): In 1987, Poison 13 were booked to play this show at the Texas Tavern at the UT Student Union. We asked Frank Kozik to make a poster for the show. We were calling it Barbecue Baby Jesus because the poster was a picture of Joseph and Mary, wearing sunglasses, and they've got Baby Jesus on a barbecue grill. They're poking him with this long fork. So we put the posters up around town. Then, the next thing we know, there's this big controversy in *The Daily Texan*, with Christian students writing to the paper about the poster! So the Texas Tavern cancels the show! I mean, I didn't really understand the point that Frank was trying to make with the poster, but we all thought it was pretty funny.

> Frank Kozik: I don't know what art is. Art maybe is some dude that's fucked and cuts his ear off and lives on crap in a hole somewhere and is insane and pukes all his shit out onto a canvas and dies and 100 years later people decide it's cool. Is that art? I don't know. Or is art like some elaborate renaissance guy with a big studio who is patronized by the Pope and has all of his assistants doing his stuff. Is that art? I don't know what the fuck art is, dude. All I know is that I like to make stuff.
>
> INTERVIEW WITH BLOGGER AND JOURNALIST JEREMY BRAUTMAN, A.K.A. JEREMYRIAD, PUBLISHED AS "FRANK TALK WITH MR. KOZIK," *NEON MONSTER*, MARCH 11, 2010

When I arrived at the University of Texas in the fall of 1979, I didn't know what I wanted to be when I grew up. But I was already a photographer, so I took photo classes in the journalism school. One of my professors, a great documentary photographer named Dennis Darling, told us we should take pictures of our own lives because those photos would mean more to us later. My life at the time was all about punk rock, so I began taking pictures of the bands and my new friends at Raul's.

Steve Anderson was one of the first people I met at Raul's. All his opinions were a mile high and barbed. He was skinny as a rail and fearless: He was once walking across West Campus with his girlfriend, Maria Cotera, when a pack of fraternity boys surrounded them and began closing in. Out of nowhere, Steve produced a bicycle chain and began swinging it at them. The frat boys evaporated.

Even as I started dipping my toes into the scene, Steve invited me along for adventures. Maybe he sensed that I wanted to photograph something more intimate than Big Boys gigs. One day he took me over to Chris Wing's house. Wing was the far-out-of-the-closet singer for Sharon Tate's Baby, and I was still pretty nervous around gay men, especially slightly sleazy older ones like Chris. But none of that bothered Steve. At Chris's house, he and the STB singer stripped their shirts off and dyed their hair blue-black while I took pictures. These were just the sort of casual, offstage moments I had been looking for. After they rinsed out the last of the Clairol, Steve and I returned to the UT campus, where Steve posed for several more portraits. Just because.

Of course, I wasn't the first one documenting the scene: Both David Fox and Ken Hoge had been taking pictures of Texas punks since the Sex Pistols show in San Antonio. And I soon met the most radical and innovative photographer in town: Bill Daniel. As DIY photojournalists, we weren't unique: In the late seventies and early eighties, something similar was happening in Dallas and other cities all over the world.

Ken Hoge: I hooked up with [Austin journalist] Margaret Moser when I started working for the *Austin Sun* in May 1977. She aspired to be a music writer, and I wanted to be photojournalist. We were both heavily involved in covering the music scene in Austin and excited about emerging punk rock music, so my interest was both professional and personal. We had been playing *Never Mind the Bollocks* in our house a lot. . . . We couldn't believe our luck that the Sex Pistols were playing in San Antonio! I was excited about how visual the band was, particularly Johnny Rotten and Sid Vicious. I had never looked forward to photographing a show as much. We arrived pretty late, and Margaret and I bulled our way through the crowd to the front of stage right. Fortunately, that was Sid Vicious's side of the stage, so I was happy with the shots I got.

John Spath (photographer): When I got out of high school, I took a year off and then started going to junior college in Dallas. I decided to take a photography course, right as this whole punk thing was happening. And I started bringing my camera out to the shows, and then ultimately to a lot of skateboarding stuff, and just started taking a shit ton of pictures. I thought, "Oh, nobody else is documenting this stuff." I was becoming the guy that's in a band, takes pictures, runs the door, sweeps the floor. It was just full engagement.

Bill Daniel: I wanted the future to see what *this* [Texas punk rock] looked like. I thought, "Nobody's gonna know what Black Flag is, so I have to get these pictures!"

Ken Hoge: With Margaret, I could waltz into any music venue in town and get backstage. I did a lot of promotional work in trade for access and as part of the DIY ethic we all had within the scene. Money was never on the agenda because nobody had any. Although free beer was always appreciated! At the time, I managed our apartment complex, so Margaret and I had free rent. We collected Coke bottles for the five-cent refund, and she worked at Piercing Pagoda in the mall, so we had some money. We certainly didn't make much from our published work. I would get five dollars for a quarter-page photo, twenty-five dollars for a cover. I graduated from the UT RTF program in May of 1977, and by then, all I wanted was to build a career in photojournalism in the Austin cultural scene. We *loved* what we were doing—everyone was skinny, poor, and happy.

Bill Daniel: My theory is that Austin punk got a good part of its aesthetic and energy from [legendary street photographer and University of Texas professor] Gary Winogrand. Because not only did [punk poster artist and *The Western Roundup* fanzine creator] Michael Nott take his classes, but so did Tim Kerr from the Big Boys. I think Steve Marsh [Terminal Mind] and [*Sluggo!* fanzine editor] Nick West did too. In those days, people thought Winogrand didn't look through the viewfinder when he was shooting, but now, because of the miracle of YouTube, we can see rare, 16 mm footage of Gary working in the street. And he looked through the viewfinder—for a *millisecond*. He would get right where he wanted to take the picture, then the camera flies up to his face, he takes the picture, then the camera flies back down again!

John Spath: I grew up with the Daniel family, with Clay, the youngest brother. But I knew Bill and Lee [Daniel, later the cinematographer for *Slacker*, *Dazed and Confused*, and other Richard Linklater films]. Bill was in Dallas a lot, and I remember really fucking loving his pictures, specifically those in *Western Roundup* fanzine. There are some photos that just blew my mind. I was watching him and how he held the flash off camera. We would often pontificate on Tri-X film, so I started mimicking that.

Bill Daniel: I'm not really a documentary photographer. I never shot pictures of the outside of the clubs, for example. I wish I did. I only shot, like, 364 rolls of film—that's not very many pictures. Every week, I would develop the film and see what I had shot in the last few days, and I would go, "Aha! The farther I move the light this way, the more interesting things happen." By overexposing and overdeveloping the film, and then printing hard, I thought I could make my photography look like Xeroxes, like the pictures in fanzines. The photography that I wanted to do was kind of my performance. I started creating this triangulation with my camera, my Sunpak flash, and the subject.

John Spath: I eventually got a 24 mm Nikkor lens because that's what Bill used. And I started running the flash off the camera with a little sync cord. And that worked for a while, until my flash cable broke. And I remembered that I could continue taking pictures if I used the bulb setting. I'd just keep the shutter open and pop the flash off and then release the shutter. That turned into a couple of accidentally decent pictures. Then I started doing that all the time.

Bill Daniel: There's a direct analogy between analog waves of photochemical exposure and analog waves of amplification. [In a music recording,] when an audio signal hits the end of the scale, it just flattens out and creates distortion. And all of the punk music that we love so much was created by smashing so much energy into the upper limit of the equipment. So I was definitely interested in that analogy, specifically about wave deformation at the end of the scale, but also in getting this feeling of, "Oh yeah, it's *in the red*. It's raw."

John Spath: There were certain situations where I would purposely blur stuff. I wasn't terribly mathematical about it. I learned later that Bill *was* mathematical about it, especially in the lab when he was processing the film. He actually did pay attention to stuff like water temperature. [*laughs*] I was just popping off pictures, getting the best I could, hoping that there was something there.

Bill Daniel: That Misfits show at the Ritz was absolutely the loudest thing I'd ever experienced. They were so theatrical and so much in control of their whole space. We had all been reading about them in the zines, about how one of them hit somebody with his bass. And yet, I was on the stage, taking pictures two feet from [Misfits singer] Glenn Danzig's face. Dude, they wanted their picture taken. They wanted to be in magazines. They understood the camera's not your enemy.

People were crowded into the lobby to escape the sound pressure waves, and they were peering around the door to watch the show, but also trying to take shelter from the blast, like the military people and scientists in those atomic bomb test films.

But punk became such a cliché. The hardcore scene just became stupid and boring and repetitive. So when I went to shows, I would take a couple of pictures of the band, but I was mainly taking pictures of bodies in space. I was photographing this energy in the gestures of these bodies. In fact, the last roll of film I ever shot, I have three pictures of the band and three *rolls* of people dancing. And that band was . . . the Minutemen! The beloved Minutemen!

Bill Anderson: Those photos are indispensable. Bill Daniel was right before you, Pat, but you documented my favorite time in the Austin punk rock scene. Nobody had an iPhone back then, of course, so it was either really shitty snapshots with a disposable camera or somebody with a camera who knew how to take pictures and be invisible. Like Pat Blashill. When I looked through those pictures recently, I thought, "I don't remember Pat taking any of these pictures, and he must have been *right in our faces*." That's like a superpower that you have. Punk photography is basically like battle photography.

My favorite photographer superpower is the ability the extraordinary ones have to zoom out even as they zoom in, to capture a scene or detail that explains something much, much larger. Somehow, Texas was blessed with at least a half dozen real masters, including Russell Duke and Carolyn "Wild Lady" Woolfork in Austin and Ben DeSoto in Houston. And even though I could never pick my favorite Texas punk picture, there is one that seems like a secret window onto everything you need to know about US punk in 1982. It's a Bill Daniel shot that captures the audience at the aforementioned Bad Brains show in Austin. In it, about ten or eleven young people are bopping and shoving and skanking past the silhouette of Daniel's Sunpak strobe unit, which resembles a flashlight thrust into a cavern. Looking at it is like witnessing a strange subterranean tribe, deep in its own rites and celebrations.

Fanzines are the five-dimensional chess of punk art: Poster art skills, strong original photography, found imagery, collage, savage or funny prose, and

The Western Roundup fanzine cover, published and bound in Austin, 1982. Design and concept by Michael Nott; photo of a Dicks show by Bill Daniel, featuring David Dictor of MDC and David Yow of Scratch Acid in the crowd.

a great concept are all crucial for the most unforgettable zines. The title of this book itself is from the cover of the one and only issue of the *Austin Vanguard*, published by Nick West, a.k.a. Nick Modern. West later partnered with E. A. Srere to create *Sluggo!*, still regarded by some as the best Texas fanzine ever.

The themed issues of *Sluggo!* may have inspired California fanzine *Search and Destroy* to morph into the RE/Search Publications book imprint, but in Austin, a few *Sluggo!* contributors went on to publish *Contempo Culture*. The pack of fanzines that followed included *Xiphoid Process* and *Idle Time*, and even lured Lester Bangs, the most infamous music critic in the United States, to Austin for an extended season of couch surfing. A more nihilistic crowd cherished the brutal humor and comics of *Buttlikker Comix*, while hardcore punks lapped up the live reviews and raw graphics of *Duck Butter*. For me, the apotheosis was *The Western Roundup*, a clever mash-up of cowboy clip art and punk rock renegade mythology.

Ty Gavin: *Sluggo!* was punk rock without a band. Their band was the magazine. It really was. They were creative. They spurred on so much stuff.

E. A. Srere: I went to some in-store record party at Dobie Mall, and that's where I met Nick Modern, whose real name is Larry Dickson. And he had a pile of these [magazines] with the headline, "Someday All the Adults Will Die!" I said, "What the heck is this?" And he said he was trying to get together a punk fanzine. And we started talking about it. He said, "I'm just trying to find money and people to donate paper—the biggest cost is going to be printing." And I was actually working at the telephone company as an operator back then. We met some people who saw [the *Austin Vanguard*], and they just gave us this Multilith 5000 printing press. But I was just the money woman at *Sluggo!* I'd go with Larry to the graphics store, and he'd get everything he wanted, and I'd pull out my checkbook. I was never a writer.

Caroline Estes: I had a few articles in *Sluggo!*, and my roommate E. A. worked on it with Nick Modern. We had a *Sluggo!* party one night, where everyone took acid, and we made covers for the magazine. Everybody handmade different covers, so every single magazine had an original cover. The one that stuck in my mind is one that I still have. I loved Patti Smith; she really moved me. But someone took a Patti Smith single that was worth a lot of money, and they broke it on purpose and glued the pieces onto the cover they made for *Sluggo!* I just thought that was so cool. Even though I wish I had the single! [*laughs*]

Ty Gavin: Yeah, I was a centerfold model for *Sluggo!* They came over early in the morning, and I was still in bed. It wasn't a planned-out photo shoot. I was laying on the bed with rumpled-up sheets; my hair all messed up. And Dottie Swenson, my girlfriend, she had her legs over where my cock is—her legs were in front of it. It was a cool picture because it wasn't just, you know, "Look at my dick."

Lynn Keller: There was an intellectual group that was in the punk scene—people like [filmmaker] Brian Hansen and Nick West. Nick did have a kind of misanthropy. But everyone expressed it in an ironic, cynical fashion.

E. A. Srere: The *Sluggo!* guys could be vicious. And that's one thing that drove me away. You can be vicious if you want, but if you get vicious with me *in print in the magazine*, I'm gone. With my checkbook.

Lynn Keller: *Sluggo!* was huge in the scene. All those fanzines might have led Lester Bangs into the scene. I didn't know who Lester Bangs was. I guess some people did, and that's why they were being nice to him. But we were like, "Fuck you!" 'Cause he was an asshole.

John Slate: I saw a copy of *Contempo Culture* at Inner Sanctum, and I felt very compelled to introduce myself to the editors, Stewart Wise and Ellen Gibbs. So I knocked on their door and said, "Hi, I really like your fanzine." Lester Bangs was sleeping on their couch. I didn't know who he was. He was super encouraging to me. He just said, "Go for it. Run with it, man!" The *Contempo Culture* folks invited me to contribute a page or two to their fanzine, and I did that for two or three issues. Then Stewart and Ellen said, "Well, John, maybe you should do a fanzine now."

I started calling myself Control Rat X, which was more of a nom de guerre. In a world of great punk names, I needed one that was distinctive but didn't betray my youthfulness. Not so much an alter ego as much as a fun name—the same way that Lux Interior and Lydia Lunch are fun names.

Scott Stevens (member, Butthole Surfers, and fan): *Idle Time* was a great zine—Dixon Coulbourn knew composition, and he knew art, and he knew how to make an interesting package of it all. I met him at a Black Flag show at the Twilight Room in Dallas. He was a Renaissance man: He had his fanzine. He took great photos of bands. He made his own music. He was *not* a cook! He drank a lot. He was great with stencils. He made great T-shirts. He knew that I liked Nancy, from the comic strip of the same name, and he made a T-shirt with a wicked stencil called Nancybug. It was Nancy's head with a cockroach body. I made a photocopy of it, and it's hanging in my studio to this day.

John Slate: I like what I like, and I don't like people telling me what I'm supposed to like. With my fanzine *Xiphoid Process*, I had no interest in objectivity at all—the plan was to be completely subjective. That meant writing about the Dicks, but also James Brown and Grandmaster Flash. I felt that I needed to fill a void in the Austin music scene. Music critics like Louis Black [*The Austin Chronicle*] and Ed Ward [*Austin-American Statesman*] really didn't like a lot of the Raul's crowd. Louis once wrote, "I don't think the Dicks are ready to be recorded. I'm not sure they're worth recording."

Gretchen Phillips: A very important idea for [our early band] the SufferJets was the notion that people should branch out into other art forms they weren't necessarily proficient at, but should explore for the sake of expanding their creativity. So somehow this zine called *Iconoclast* was formed. There were a few meetings where we got together with all these other people and put this sort of arty fanzine together. There was no curation; you paid yourself for each page. We put out two copies.

John Slate: One ulterior motive for doing my zine was to get access to clubs while I was underage. I had to beg my way in, to ingratiate myself to Joseph Gonzalez. I told him, "I'm just here to review bands and enjoy the music." And he said, "As long as you stay in the back and don't try to buy alcohol here, I'm totally cool with it." Then all the Austin High kids got caught buying alcohol, and Raul's got shut down for a day or two. That really, really irritated me. I was trying to set a good example for high school–age people, and they were spoiling it for everybody.

Roy Tompkins (artist/author, *Trailer Trash*): These fanzines were incredibly inspiring to me, a freeing of the young mind, a removal of limits in creativity and publishing—like a step beyond the underground comics that I was checking out in the late 1970s. This was the next step, a Xerox revolution where you didn't need a publisher. You suddenly realize you can do whatever the fuck you want.

Bill Anderson: *Buttlikker Comix*? I loved that rag.

Rob Buford: Whitney Ayres was an original member of our band, Crotch Rot. He went on to create *Buttlikker Comix* with Richard Mather. He also stayed in school, unlike us, and ended up on the staff of the student paper. The Austin High mascot was a stupid maroon pom-pom with eyes, so Whitney surreptitiously published a cartoon of the pom-pom masturbating on a toilet. There was a big kerfuffle. They weren't going to let him graduate—he had to hire a lawyer.

Buttlikker was modeled after the *Highlights* magazines that you'd see at the pediatrician's office. *Duck Butter*, by contrast, lived up to its name. It was slapstick humor at its best. The polar opposite of the competition. And it was about *our* scene. [Editor] Lonnie [Layman] had a spot-on sense of comedy. Besides [his band] the Fudge Tunnels, *Duck Butter* was his biggest contribution to the scene. He should get a medal for that.

Bill Daniel: Michael Nott saw me taking pictures all the time, and one night he said, "We're starting a zine called *Western Roundup*, and it's gonna be this dude ranch thing. Will you be the photographer?" He wrangled all of his friends to help put it together. A zine doesn't happen without people coming over and stapling and collating the pages, and somebody's got to shoot the pictures. But Michael Nott was the genius behind *Western Roundup*. It's really a conceptual thing, almost a design exercise. And he really nailed it—this mash-up of 1950s cowboy art and 1980s Texas punk. But that idea must have been irresistible to other people because then came all these other fanzines like *Cretin Bull*, *Throbbing Cattle*, *Cattle Prod*, and *Peligro!*

Jane Fletcher (writer, *The Western Roundup*): I stitched [the spine of] nearly every issue of *Western Roundup* on the Kenmore sewing machine my dad gave me for my high school graduation.

4 | LADIES AND GENTLEMEN

I remember this: Ralph was always there, wherever I went. She was at Raul's and Duke's and Club Foot. She was at the Ritz and Studio 29 and Sparky's. She was at Texas Student Union happy hours and every after-party. She knew all about the Misfits and Black Flag and Roxy Music and Bryan Ferry. She was often too drunk to talk about any of them. But *she* remembers it all today.

Ralph was in the car when I chauffeured a bunch of younger punks and runaways to Thundercloud Subs late one night. We didn't have anywhere else to go, and I guess some of the kids were hungry. In the middle of this sad and funny scene sat Martha, who had a bright blue Mohawk. Ralph took a bite out of her sub, sat down in Martha's lap, and gave her a big sloppy French kiss. I grabbed a photo of it, and it's still one of my favorites because Ralph wasn't just ever-present, like a hardcore Everywoman; Ralph was always there, *enjoying herself.*

Lisa "Ralph" Armstrong (fan): We moved to Texas from Boston in 1978. School was horrible. Every time I opened my mouth, people would laugh, including my teachers, because of my Boston accent. So I'd go home, and I'd just be crying in front of the mirror, saying, "Par-tee, par-tee. I *can* pronounce my *r*'s. I'm gonna learn this, 'cause I am miserable."

My name on my birth certificate is Lisa Katherine Armstrong. But I just wanted to be someone different. I started using the name "Ralph" on my first night at Raul's.

Sally King: If I close my eyes, I can see myself with a big smile and a polka dress, dancing at Duke's Royal Coach Inn. The polka dress was my favorite by far. I sometimes wore petticoats under it, but I didn't give much thought to the entire ensemble at the time. Years later, I was reflecting on the influence of my dad, who died when I was twelve, and the image of that polka dress came to me. I thought that perhaps as I was looking for an identity, I unconsciously dressed in a way that brought back happy memories. My dad very much identified with his central Texas German roots. My sister and I knew how to schottische from a very early age, and I remember loving the crazy matching polka outfits that the dancers wore. At Wurstfest in New Braunfels, my family were often guests of Myron Floren. He was the accordionist from *The Lawrence Welk Show*, and we knew him through my cousin Cissy King, who was a ballroom dancer on the show. So Lawrence Welk at the Dicks shows? There was an earnestness mixed with irreverence that made perfect sense to me.

"Texas" Terri Laird: I got my dirty mouth from Fort Worth. I remember once I called my brother a "butthole," and my mom started chasing me around with a washcloth and a bar of soap. Another time we were playing kickball, I got called out, and I wasn't out, so I called this girl a "fucking bitch." Everyone in the game looked at me at the same time—they couldn't believe I'd said that.

I remember we used to go hang out in the sewer pipes, and there was all this graffiti and drawings and bad words written on the drainage pipes. And I thought, "Oh, I like this." The bad boys weren't there themselves, but I knew then and there that I liked bad boys.

Alice Berry (member, Texas Blondes, and fan): I'd been an artsy, theater kid in high school, like going to see *Rocky Horror Picture Show*. I saw it maybe, like, twenty times in Houston. So fun. And I've seen numbers of people in punk rock scenes all over who said, "Oh yeah, I did *Rocky Horror*." It's like the gateway drug. This idea of wearing outlandish clothing out in public and just kind of embracing who you are. Don't dream it, be it? That was definitely a gateway for me. Even though I was just as straight as you can get. I was, you know, a good girl.

Trish Herrera (mydolls): I found out about punk when I was singing with Kinky Friedman and the Texas Jew Boys. We played Randy's Rodeo in San Antonio, and the Sex Pistols had played there the day before. We were like, "What the hell?" They were talking about beer bottles being crashed everywhere and *spitting* and everything. I'd already had Elvis Costello and Blondie records. I didn't really understand or know what hardcore was. But I knew it was political. And I knew that I had a huge interest in it. So when we got to Houston, I got off the tour bus and just said, "Hey, I'm gonna go open my salon, and I'm gonna have, you know, a life."

Diane "Muffy" McGee Hardin: When I was fifteen, I would have my father drive me down the Drag so I could look at people with Mohawks. He wasn't scared at all. Then I started using makeup, and my first look was really Goth. I painted my face white, dyed my hair blue-black. I looked like the singer for the Cure. One time, my dad borrowed a wig from my mother, and he put on a necklace, and he carried a purse! He looked like a man in drag who hadn't put enough effort into it, although he did *swing* the purse. He was trying to embarrass me like, I guess, I embarrassed him. And I just thought it was the greatest thing ever. I felt like he was . . . participating.

Adriane "Ash" Shown: I have been dealing with molestation and rape since I was a child. [Within punk,] I was finally in a space where I was allowed to have a voice, so I was not about to give that up. And I had more language to use to fight back, rather than continuing to be gaslit. It was hugely important to me to try to help other young punk women find their voice and their power. That started one day when I was driving around three gals who were all talking about sex, and they were all thirteen or fourteen. So I said, "That's it—we're going to get you all appointments at the People's Clinic. For your gyn." They were all like, "No, no, we're just *talking* about sex." And I told them, "Right, but if you don't learn about your anatomy *right now*, the next thing I'm going to hear is, 'Oh, well, I'm pregnant.' I didn't want anybody else to feel disempowered the way I had felt at that age.

It may be a paradox, but when people write about women in punk, they're usually also writing about men. Talking to Texas punk women often means talking about the hell of gender. No matter how much we may have wanted to be better men and women, we couldn't escape a culture of ladies and gentlemen. Or as Exene Cervenka and John Doe of the Los Angeles band X once sang, "The world's a mess / It's in my kiss."

Some women reinvented themselves within the white light and white heat of punk; others seemed to find a second family there. But unlike men in punk (or the myth of them), life didn't become simpler for women once they started listening to Fear and Big Boys. It got more complicated, as if they'd just added another role, another way of presenting themselves: good girl *and* hell-raiser, femme *and* butch, rebel *and* heroine.

Sally King: Our persona was transmitted through our appearance. There's a cultural rigidity in Texas that we were making a stand against, and it served to glue our scene together. If you were going to buy some Doc Martens at Blue Velvet or Atomic City, you planned on it for months, and you saved, and you picked them out carefully. You wanted to look different from everybody else. It was a way to work out who I was. From a young age, I was crafting a persona. It was important to me to make my own jewelry out of bits of old broken rosaries from Catholic school. I was a teen from an unhappy home, and there was a reason that I was out on the streets. My mom and I had a dysfunctional relationship, and . . . nothing at home was safe. Nothing felt safe. But for all of the negativity and self-destruction of it, the *music* saved me. It kept me sane, and it kept me going.

Lisa "Ralph" Armstrong: I had gotten kicked out of high school and kicked out of the house on the same day. On my first night at Raul's, after a couple of beers, I got over my social anxiety and just started walking up to people and poking 'em in the chest and asking, "*Hey*, who are you?" And they'd be like, "Oh, I'm so-and-so. Who are you?" And I was like, "Oh, Agatha. Clyde. George. Ralph." I was just doing that to get attention, to get people to talk to me. I thought that was punk rock because I had no clue.

And then I started asking people, "What's behind that curtain?" They were like, "Oh, that's backstage. You can't go back there. Tuck, that big scary guy at the front door, he'll throw a fit."

So I kept my eye on the door, and when Tuck had his back turned to me, behind the curtain I went. And I was sitting back there, hanging out with the Reactors. And [singer-guitarist] Mike Runnels kept saying, "Come on, tell me what your real name is." And finally, he said, "Okay, I'm just gonna go with Ralph because that's my dad's name." And that's the name that stuck.

Rene Miller and Lynda Stuart at home, Austin, fall 1984. Hair gel by Knox.

Diane "Muffy" McGee Hardin: Ralph was my navigator. She told me about the Dicks show at the New Guild Co-Op, which was the first show I saw. At first, I went to every show Ralph told me to go to.

Lisa "Ralph" Armstrong: When I first started hanging out, man, I was just in awe of Texas punk women. They were inspiring. Most of them scared the shit out of me. They were just, you know, fierce, independent, beautiful. Didn't take any shit. They were everything that I wanted to be and didn't think I was or could be. They were just their own people. They were real. You know, if you said something stupid, they were gonna tell you [that] you said something stupid. They weren't being insulting. They weren't trying to start a fight. They were just speaking their honest opinion. Which I wasn't used to. They really helped me to get over my social anxiety and learn my worth.

Cindy Melbie was *the* scene queen. I thought, "Oh my God, you're Buxf's girlfriend. You spend 24-7 with the Dicks." Yeah, Cindy and the Dicks backup singers, the Torn Panties. I was like, "Oh my God, they love gay men as much as I do."

Cindy Melbie: Roxanne and Bird and Dolores were the Torn Panties. We laughed all the time—they were so freakin' funny. They were raunchy. But I didn't trust them because they were the biggest gossips I'd ever met. As for other girls—a lot of them would ask me, "How can you feel safe when you are alone with Buxf?" But he wasn't the problem. I didn't trust the *women*.

Lisa "Ralph" Armstrong: Helen McDonald and Dottie Swenson dressed like fifties pinup queens and never, never seemed to have a hair out of place; their makeup was always perfect. I'd never known too many people like that. I was always with the outcasts. And then you meet them, and you start talking with them, and these women are fucking smart and funny. But yeah, I just don't remember meeting too many stupid women in the scene.

Beth Kerr: I was most impressed with a bartender at Raul's. The only other thing I remember about her was she was studying Russian; like, she wanted to be a translator for the UN or whatever. I thought that was pretty impressive. She taught me that if a beer is too foamy, stick your finger in it. That's a trick I still use.

I liked [Texas journalist] Molly Ivins a lot. She liked *Texas*; she just didn't like what was happening to it. That was true for me too.

Laurie Greenwell: I thought Alice Berry was really cool. I liked her hair. She had star quality.

Alice Berry: My mother's father, Beauford H. Jester, had been governor of Texas. And people would assume that the governor's family must be rich, but trust me, we weren't. I started off as a sorority girl—I think there was an expectation that I would be in the same sorority that my sister, my mother, and my aunt had all been in. But at the same time that I was going through [sorority] rush, I had also gone to my first show at Raul's, which was the Inserts. And it blew my socks off. I thought, "Okay, this is amazing. Okay, *Billy Problem*." So I did the sorority thing, but it was half-hearted because I wasn't buying into all of it, especially because the guys that were supposed to be my future mates just weren't interesting at all to me. I saw too much of a disdain for *everybody* from the frat boys.

Lisa "Ralph" Armstrong: I met Terri Laird pretty early on, within a few months of hanging out at Raul's. We became friends. We used to rassle. We'd do mud wrestling at parties. There was one show at Inner Sanctum—they built a half-pipe in the parking lot, and the Big Boys played. There was a skateboard competition and, you know, it was summer, so it was hot as fuck. We're all up there in the pit. And Terri just goes, "Fuck this shit," and strips off her T-shirt. And I was like, "I want to be her."

"Texas" Terri Laird: Every time Ralph saw me, she wanted to rassle. I was always game. We were pretty evenly matched. She's a little bit shorter than me, but she's as strong as a bull. I would go to a party, see Ralph, and then we would wrestle just so I could check it off my list and get on with my night. I don't think it was about winning or losing, really.

Lisa "Ralph" Armstrong: Yeah, I think we wrestled in my backyard, [in my house] on Depew. [*chuckles*] There was a little bit of a hollow—[the ground] got wet from the ice or something. Bang Gang played at that place once too. I also wrestled [Bang Gang singer] Jeff Smith every chance I got.

Maria Cotera: We were a bunch of nerds, trying to be badasses.

Karen Ruth Getchell (fan): Ha! That's totally true. We were! But at the same time, you did have to be a little bit of a badass because you were gonna be tested. That was part of the ritual. I remember being at a party when I first got to Austin, and Terri Laird was just a few feet away, talking to James Frank "Prince" Hughes about me, really *loudly*: "Oh, look at this new one! Well, where'd she come from?" Meaning, like, "Who's this poser, this college girl?" It was scary. I thought, "She's out to kick my ass." I just tried to be really cool, and I kept talking to the person I was talking to. I tried to pretend I didn't hear her, and luckily, she stopped.

Alice Berry: I don't think I missed a single Big Boys show. [Even though I was in a sorority,] I was not treated as an "other" by people in the punk scene. But I was leading a double life. I was sneaking out and changing clothes in the parking garage and going to Raul's, then sneaking back into the sorority house late at night, at 3:00 a.m., in my weird clothes. The girls at the desk would stare at me, but I wasn't really running into anybody else because it was so late at night. And finally, I thought, "This is ridiculous.

I'm not doing that anymore." I never *quit* the sorority; I just stopped going to the meetings.

Play the first fifteen seconds of any punk song ever, and you will probably hear two things: It is angry and it is critical. That's one of the reasons punk is so exciting to young people who are trapped in a world they never made. But punk fury is super malleable. The singer may be angry about a thousand things, and their lyrics may very well attack something that many other punks cherish. The initial wave of British punk directed much of its rage at systems and political realities. Early American punk—from Patti Smith to Black Flag—was typically more pissed off about parents, cops, and lovers. US punk hated the way that the world lies to us about who we are.

In the late seventies and early eighties, Texas punks thrashed in the undertow of some very different waves of thought about gender. They were scornful of 1950s myths—the double-martini, role model prisons of Ward and June Cleaver—but suspicious of flaws within the later feminism of Betty Friedan, Gloria Steinem, and *Ms.* magazine. Punk sneered at all of that, but it didn't always offer an alternative.

Sally King: I don't think the dick swinging was any different from any other rock and roll scene—guys join bands to get laid. I didn't know that at the time, of course, and certainly learned the hard way.

Kathy McCarty: I was a feminist. Ideas like "your body isn't a commodity" just seemed like sanity. I was very much a Reagan hater, and I made posters about how he was a devil. Most of the women in the scene were feminists, and most of the guys said they were too.

Lisa "Ralph" Armstrong: Well, we were feminist up to a point. But at some point, it's like, "No, I like men. I like having sex. I like having a man hold the door open for me, you know?"

Alice Berry: I didn't feel like I was a gal in the scene. I just felt like I was a person in the scene. I did not feel sexism. I did not feel misogyny. I didn't feel any difference. You were encouraged to go out there and do it and explore all the things that you wanted to do. And I just so appreciated that fact. I loved the Big Boys / Dicks *Live at Raul's* record, and Biscuit signed my copy with "Welcome to weird world. Start your own band."

Sally King: Would it have been different for me if there were more female musicians in Austin? Since the few that existed were fucking my boyfriend at the time, no.

Adriane "Ash" Shown: I was angry about sexism and misogyny. I just created a barrier, and part of that was [a barrier against] the constant bombardment of sexual attention. That type of shit is what I am still angry about. Why do men think that it's okay to just grab a woman? Yech. This has been my entire life, and I don't dress provocatively. I'm covered from under my chin to my ankle but still, it's like, "What the fuck?"

Maria Cotera: If you look at the intersection of race and gender, that's where you can often see what the actual values [of a scene] *are*, and I will say that all of the punk rock goddesses in our scene were typically beautiful white women. That's the undercurrent; that's what you don't see when you hear people calling someone "spic" or the N-word . . . but when you come down to it and ask, "Who are the people who are most valued?" and you look at aesthetics and sexuality, that's when scenes expose themselves in interesting ways.

Sally King: Well, I think there is more here that is tied to teen girl low self-esteem and how rebelling against a masculine popular culture is a way to reclaim yourself. One reason I rejected popular culture then was the hypermasculinity in arena rock in those days. I didn't find the local punk scene to be predisposed to misogyny, although it wouldn't take long to find questionable lyrics.

> The spray on your hair it makes your head look frozen
> Girls like you—they're a dime a dozen
> I wouldn't fuck you with another guy's stick
> Girls like you, they make me sick
>
> THE SKUNKS, "CHEAP GIRL," LYRICS BY JESSE SUBLETT

Alice Berry: I just considered "Cheap Girl" to be a funny song. I never considered that [Skunks singer and lyricist] Jesse Sublett and the boys were being misogynistic. I mean, I didn't think that guys should be sleeping around with every single girl, in the same way that I don't really think that girls should be sleeping with every single guy. I think it's a little more special than that. So I just separated *the song* from *them*. And I didn't think that he thought that way about all women.

Kathy Valentine: Jesse is a very clever songwriter, and he loved Lou Reed, John Cale, and the Velvet Underground. So I don't think "Cheap Girl" is out of line with his sensibilities. I don't remember the Skunks getting called out for sexism. [But by then] I was in a band with a hit album. I wasn't really paying attention.

Sally King: Oh, I loved "Cheap Girl." I played it at high volume in my bedroom. Yeah! [*laughs*] That and "Too Young to Date" by D-Day. Loved them—absolutely. I didn't care. I was fourteen. I mean, I also liked Adam Ant.

Austin teenagers were sneaking into punk clubs since the earliest days of the scene—I was underage myself when I first strolled into Raul's. Some of us had liberal or overwhelmed parents who couldn't keep track of everything we were doing. As American punk shifted into hardcore, all-ages shows became a way for bands to reach the young people who needed the music the most. In Austin, the Big Boys were particularly keen to play shows for minors, and they sometimes performed at assemblies in area high schools. But the downside of all this was that young and vulnerable kids—particularly underage girls—sometimes got in over their heads. Runaways began turning up at shows, and some older punks preyed on them.

Dayna Blackwell: We know now that we shouldn't let our thirteen-year-old children go to clubs and sleep with rock stars and do drugs and stay out till two or three in the morning. Years later, my mother and I did therapy together, and she told me that at the time, I threatened to run away [if she told me to stop going out]. She said I told her that I would leave, and she would never find me. And she said, "I was scared you would do it."

Sally King: We went to Duke's once—we had to sneak in to see the Dicks. Buxf saw me by the bathroom, and he remembered me sitting outside of Raul's, and he said, "How'd you get in here?" He knew we were underage. But [after that,] he was really looking out for me, making sure that older men weren't bothering us and that we had a way home.

Dayna Blackwell: There were people in the scene who pulled guys off of me. Ty Gavin was one of them. I can't tell you how many times he would

A fallen dancer at the Ritz, Austin, summer 1984.

drag me out of a back bedroom at the Next house and tell me, "Go home, go home." "Hey, somebody needs to get a cab for Dayna!" All I know is that I always felt safe if Ty was around. If anything happened, I knew he would be there.

Sally King: There were a couple of those guys—older guys in the scene—who looked after the younger kids: Buxf, James "Prince" Hughes, Biscuit, Clay Allison, Glen from the Fudge Tunnels. On several occasions, I remember Prince telling me, "You're not getting in that car." And then *he* would drive me home from the party.

Maybe that helped create a bubble effect where we felt safe: As much sexism and stupidity and violence as was going on, it really didn't feel *serious* because we knew people had our backs. No one took advantage of me when I was young and out all night partying, but I know it happened.

Adriane "Ash" Shown: When I met my friend Bethany, she was twelve, and I was seventeen. I could see that she was a child—she was this beautiful, extremely talented young woman in the sixth or seventh grade in junior high school, just beginning to be able to form her own opinion about herself. And to have that squashed—ruined—by some asshole who grabbed her, I wasn't going to let that happen to these younger, twelve-year-old gals.

Was I really able to protect Bethany? Um, yes, but she was her own person and was still trying to explore and push back. She did enjoy meeting different band guys. She did call me mom for a while. I was still a teen myself, and her own mother wanted me to become her guardian. I said, "No, absolutely not. I can't even take care of myself."

What happened to Bethany? Oh my God, she's had a full life. She went to Boston, then she was working in a nightclub in Manhattan while she was still underage. She ended up at the Chelsea Hotel. She traveled quite a bit, all over Europe. Ended up on a lot of fishing boats and whatnot. She's still continued writing and painting and drawing. She's a fabulous artist to this day. She's more than okay.

Punks from Poly Styrene to Kathleen Hanna have tried to reclaim and reinvent all the shitty things people say about girls. But the project to redefine a *groupie* dates back to the 1960s to Miss Pamela Des Barres and the Plaster Casters. That seems reasonable, especially since the word for a man who likes to hang out with musicians is not *groupie* but *journalist*, *manager*, or, if you're just mean, *drummer*. Brian Eno has suggested that the listener is just as important as the performer; Des Barres argues that groupies are fans who take it one step further. But, as with mosh pits, it is possible to get too close to the musicians you admire.

Lisa "Ralph" Armstrong: I remember the Misfits show at the Ritz mainly because I got kicked in the head by Glenn Danzig. All my illusions were destroyed because I loved that band. I was standing in front of the stage like everyone else, and he would just occasionally kick out and nail someone in the head with his combat boot. I've talked to people all over the country, and they say, "Yeah, that's what he does." That was his thing. He was an asshole. After that, I thought, "If I buy a Misfits record, I'm buying it used."

Teresa Taylor: I got to meet Debbie Harry later. I looked her in the eye and said, "I'm Teresa, I'm the drummer for the Butthole Surfers." And she says, "I *know* who you *are*." I was so flattered. I told her, "I admire you so much. What you did changed the course of my entire life."

Lisa "Ralph" Armstrong: The Black Flag show at the ALA Club was infamous for me. I ended up going out to Black Flag's van with [Black Flag drummer] Robo and fooling around with him. In the middle of it, [Black Flag roadie] Mugger comes out and pulls back the curtain and goes, "Hey, Robo, hurry up. It's my fucking turn. I want some."

I was so furious and humiliated. So that pretty much killed the moment. We got dressed and went back inside. [Black Flag guitarist] Greg Ginn starts saying, "Ha ha, you have crabs—Robo just gave you crabs." And he started calling me names. I was drunk, and on acid, so I kept punching him, or *trying* to punch him, in the face—he's really tall. And he just knocked me on the ground. And I'd get up and punch him again. [Black Flag bassist] Chuck [Dukowski] was there, too, adding his two cents. It was basically just MDC and Black Flag who were there. And MDC were just too much in awe of Black Flag to come to my rescue. And I seemed to be [*laughs*] holding my own, I guess.

So I grabbed Robo and said, "What the fuck?" And he was such a sweet guy. And he's like, "Yes, it's true. I'm so sorry. We go to get medicine tomorrow."

We go back to the MDC house, and by the time we get there, the couches and every bit of available floor space is taken. Under the dining room table, there's somebody in a sleeping bag. I finally go over to [Black Flag guitarist] Dez [Cadena] and tap him on the shoulder. And he was the only one that was nice to me. I was like, "Could I share your sleeping bag? I have nowhere to go." And we did. And we just cuddled, and we've been good friends ever since.

Then the next morning, me and Robo walked hand in hand up to the pharmacy.

Alice Berry: There was a period where I was out every single night of the week. Eventually I was scheduling my UT classes to never be early morning classes because I was gonna be at the after-party after every single band, every single night of the week. Even a Tuesday 10:30 a.m. class was pushing it—I'd choose an 11:00 class instead. And again, not because I was up drinking and drugging all night long. I was *pogoing*.

E. A. Srere: Margaret Moser was three years older than me, and I guess we both had the same kind of experience with going to see bands. What did you want to do? You wanted to get *backstage*. You wanted to get in free and get backstage. And learn how to smooth up the roadies and learn the tricks of the trade. But it was . . . it was a different time.

Alice Berry: I admired how Margaret Moser worked really hard and made things happen for herself. Not that she was a perfect person. I mean, she worked hard as a writer. She went after it. And she embraced everything she'd been in the past, admitted it, was proud of it.

E. A. Srere: The "Margaret loves John Cale" graffiti [seen on walls at Raul's, Duke's, and other Austin clubs] came after Margaret *met* John. I remember when she met him. I was actually backstage at the Armadillo as a reporter from *Sluggo!* Margaret was there and had obviously met him, and she was giving him these looks. And she was really pissed off at us because he was giving us a really long interview. I didn't really know who Margaret was [at that point]. I couldn't understand why she was giving us these dirty looks. And I'm like, "Okay, whatever, girl. We were here first, thank you very much."

Alice Berry: [Margaret and John] were in kind of a relationship through the years.

E. A. Srere: I mean, Margaret met John and then just fell in love with him and fell out of the whole groupie thing. Or, well, she wanted to be a groupie, but for John. She always felt hope in her heart that they could be together. Even though she knew they couldn't.

I mean, I was once a teenage girl. And there's a lot I have to say about that, but you don't want to hear it—about being a teenage girl and how cool it was when you had a twenty-five-year-old boyfriend. Trust me, they weren't coming looking for us. We were going out looking for them.

Dayna Blackwell: I knew exactly what I was doing. And at fourteen, do you really? But I was different. I was very, very different. I knew a lot of things. I grew up really fast.

E. A. Srere: Margaret and I would use Dayna as our wedge to get backstage.

Dayna Blackwell: Did I know that Margaret and E. A. would let me walk in front because they were sure that we'd get backstage if the crew saw me first? No . . . [*sighs*] Probably. That's kind of the MO that they would use. I mean, Margaret and E. A. were beautiful in their own ways. But I'm sure that's why Margaret grabbed me when I first met her. "Oh, hey, come on. We're going backstage."

E. A. Srere: We did something once that cracked me up. Dayna lived across the street from the Opera House, and Margaret and I would come pick her up when we were going to a show. So one day we came around in my car, and Dayna's standing out in front of her place looking just cute as fuck, you know? A brick house. And I look at Margaret, she looks at me, and we both shook our heads, and I drove right past Dayna. Like, "I'm not following that one inside." Because being with Dayna could be like being the band playing after the Rolling Stones. We came back immediately to pick her up, of course. But it was pretty funny.

Dayna Blackwell: I don't remember exactly how I met him. I was fourteen. It was on the street or at a record store, something like that. It was just before he played at Club Foot. I had no idea who the fuck he was, and I was just being my regular snarky, bitchy self, and he thought that was hysterical. He goes, "Come on, you're coming with us." And I did.

Then he told me it was almost his birthday. I said, "Oh, we should have a party for you at Inner Sanctum." [Then] I called up Joe Bryson at Inner Sanctum and told him, "You should have a party for this guy I'm with." And Joe said, "Go away!" And I said, "No, you should—hold on—Jim, what's your stage name? Oh yeah? Okay, Joe, his name is Iggy Pop. You should have a party for him. It's his *birthday*."

So we had a party for him.

Then I went to the show at Club Foot with him. I got really mad at him because he stole my blue spandex leopard-skin leggings from me and wore them onstage. I really liked those tights. He said, "Don't worry, I'll buy you another pair!" I said, "Yes, you will!"

And then he said, "Come to Dallas with me!" so I did. At one show, I was sitting out in the back, and Iggy got offstage and came out on the floor and kneeled in front of me and sang the song to me. That was Dallas or Houston, I don't know. We hung out for a month or two.

E. A. Srere: I think that whole Iggy thing was a little bit much, even for me. Iggy and Dayna Blackwell. She traveled with him a couple of times. She *was* awful young. It was a different time. I felt sorry for some people. Some people grew up very fast.

"Texas" Terri Laird: I love that Dayna was having those adventures. If I had tried, maybe I would have had those adventures too. But I was happy with my little punk rock boys from Raul's.

Dayna Blackwell: I'm curious if he even remembers me. He did a lot, a lot, a lot of drugs.

Alice Berry: Margaret was the leader and founder of the Texas Blondes. The Texas Blondes were somewhat based on Pamela Des Barres's group of groupies, the GTOs. Bands [who would be visiting Austin] contacted Margaret—she never contacted them. And word got around. So, if it was a band, Margaret used to, like, get all the folks in a row. It was like, "Okay, the drummer, he's faithful to his wife at home. Okay, well, he wants her." And she'd point to me because I would not be one that he would be encouraged to sleep with. She would kind of parcel off, like, recommend which girl would be a good, fun, late-night companion for that person.

Dayna Blackwell: The Texas Blondes owned this town. Owned it. We were not just fuck buddies; we were more than just someone backstage to put your dick in. Anybody can do *that*. No, we'd pick bands up at the airport, get them to the club on time, get them some Texas food. It was about *hospitality*. No wonder promoters and club people wanted us there!

E. A. Srere: I was technically a member of the Texas Blondes, but I was not part of what they were doing. I was just . . . I always felt like I was not that attractive so I didn't try to do that kind of stuff.

Alice Berry: A lot of it was southern hospitality. And definitely some schtupping of rock stars.

Dayna Blackwell: Hell, Alice Berry was a fucking virgin. And she was one of the best Blondes ever.

E. A. Srere: Alice is an interesting case. She was not one of the Texas Blondes that "dated" the guys. I remember she really got into U2 and had a really good conversation with them over religion and being saved or whatever.

Alice Berry: Mind you, I did a lot of hanging out on my own without Margaret or the Texas Blondes. I was also a chick in a band, so I had my own groupies. I'd say it was a very short time period for me where I felt like I was a groupie. I'm sure some people thought of me as a groupie—I'm sure some people thought we were horrible trash. But I don't know, and I don't care.

For way too many people, "good" punk rock means a man onstage screaming and performing anger. Women who perform anger generally inspire far more ambivalent reactions, as Texas punk women discovered when they began forming bands, and especially when they ventured beyond the normal boundaries of their scene. In 1980, the sight of a female drummer or a woman with a microphone seemed to short-circuit otherwise rational human brains. Their male allies flipped out, overcompensated, and gave them bad advice. Even the most progressive DJ in England thought a female punk band from Houston was a novelty, but at least he gave them a chance.

Sherri Canon: I just always wanted to play drums. I had been fantasizing about being a drummer since I was a little kid. My mom made my sister and [me] take piano lessons, and I loved it, but I always asked my mom, "Now can I play drums?" When I moved to Austin to go to UT in 1981 . . . I was going to Club Foot almost every night of the week. . . . The Jitters were one of the first bands I met. And they had a female drummer, Terry Lord, who was definitely an inspiration to me.

Trish Herrera: In Houston, there was this club called Paradise Island. It was a strip club owned by a Mexican guy. And he [got rid of the strippers] and started having punk bands. We started going there every night. One night there was this band—they were just so bad, just the pits. We laughed. And Diana Ray looked at me and she said, "You know, we could do this."

So I tried to help her find the notes on her bass—for a while, she had them marked with Magic Marker. Then Linda Younger decided she wanted to be part of it. She'd never played guitar.

Then [early Houston punk band] the Hates asked us if we would open for them at the Parade Disco. Linda's husband was Ronnie "U-Ron" Bond, the singer from Really Red, and he was so nervous that we were gonna get on stage that he was nauseous. He was like, "Now you need to play loud. You need to play really loud, really loud." He was so *worried* for us. There weren't women doing this at the time.

Karla Eppler, fan and singer for Toxic Shock, on the stairs of Halcyon student co-op, West Campus, Austin, fall 1982.

We said, "We're doing it. We're gonna play with a punk band at a gay club." And it was a great success. Everybody loved it.

Kathy McCarty: In Austin, it was totally normal for women to be in bands. Most bands in Austin—Meat Joy, Standing Waves, Stick Figures, Butthole Surfers—had girls. And the ones that didn't had gay guys.

Lynn Keller: We played in Killeen, at Fort Hood. We got bottles thrown at us. A lot of times, people were very freaked out about seeing a woman singing. And during our shows, I used to stand up on the tables. I remember one biker guy in Raul's came up to me after one of our shows. He told me [*drawls*] "I don't want to see no woman up on the table." I was like, "What?" It was weird. You know . . . Texas.

Trish Herrera: mydolls had a male road manager, [which] helped a lot, especially in Philadelphia. Whoa, so much sexism—they wouldn't even pay us unless they could hand the money to a male! I mean, just ridiculous machismo. We thought, "This is too violent. It's too toxic." Toxic masculinity lived in Philadelphia. So we never went back there after that, as much as we loved the people.

Kathy McCarty: I never experienced any gender hatred in Austin, but I sure did in other cities. When we toured, we saw that in a lot of towns, they thought that it was weird to have girls in the band. That shocked me. People would interview you and just want to ask, "What's it like to have girls in the band?"

Caroline Estes: In one of my last semesters at UT, I took Jerry Grigadean's rock and roll history class. And he told us that if we made a band, we'd get an automatic A in the class. So [I started a band] with Karen Morgaloff, who was Brett from Scratch Acid's girlfriend. Frank Kozik made a poster for us. We played at Club Foot, and I was the bass player, but I really didn't know shit. I couldn't play anything, so I played topless, because I figured no one would notice I sucked, because I was twenty with my boobs out. They loved us. We were called the Gay Politicians.

Trish Herrera: mydolls were still very much owning our femininity—putting on makeup. George had this drum kit with a big reflective vinyl dot in the middle of the bass drum—we would use it to put on our lipstick. There was a lot of little girl things going on there.

Laurie Greenwell: Seriously, one of the best things about punk was the inclusiveness—a chick with a guitar or on the drums became less and less of an anomaly. And just because you were female and wanted to see music, it didn't mean you wanted to fuck the band.

Trish Herrera: I don't know if mydolls had any ambition. We had *a song* called "Ambition." We were so disgusted with how people let it overcome their need to read the room, as we would say now. We did play Rock Against Racism, and we were very political. But I don't think we ever had the ambition to, like, have a logo. Although we ended up with a logo.

Laura Croteau (Rabid Cat Records): I was playing bass in a band, and I decided to record some songs. I ended up putting it on vinyl and releasing it on a label I had formed. I called the label Frodo Records, but that was poorly thought out. When the record arrived, the rest of my band moved to San Francisco, and at the same time, I received a cease-and-desist order from Tolkien Enterprises. They demanded that I stop using the name Frodo Records. So that record pretty much just gathered dust. But it was a valuable learning experience, and it left me with a desire to take it further.

Beth Kerr: As the Big Boys manager, I would work the door and work with the people who ran the bar, and that actually gave me an ability to talk to strangers or to talk about business. "Oh, what's the guarantee?" Stuff like that. Men had to deal with me—it forced them to see me as an equal.

Laura Croteau: Honestly, I was never very focused on sexism. Stacy Cloud was my best friend. She was seeing Mike Chester, the bassist of Not for Sale, and I was seeing Tony Johnson, guitarist for the Offenders. We wanted to share their music with as wide an audience as we could reach. So we pooled our meager resources and started Rabid Cat Records. [Eventually,] there was one band on our roster that did not give us credit because we were "just a couple of chicks." But the rest of our bands just wanted to get their music released.

Basically, we were driven by our love of the music. We were naive; we had absolutely no idea how to do this; we had zero financial backing and no business experience whatsoever. But we were rabid! So we did it anyway! Rabid Cat Records was always just Stacy and myself. Our first releases were on 45 rpm vinyl with cardboard sleeves. We literally sat on the floor of my house with Elmer's glue and folded the covers, glued them, and piled books on top till the glue dried. Then we put the records and paper inserts inside. We drove around to the local record stores and sold them on consignment. We would trade records and T-shirts for ad space in little fanzines that kids all over the country were printing out on the Xerox machines at their moms' office jobs! We were DIY, hand to mouth. It wasn't until we started doing twelve-inch vinyl that we were having actual shrink-wrapped records delivered to us. That felt very *big time*!

Trish Herrera: The reason that we made a record was because Really Red's drummer, Bob Weber, started a record company: CIA Records. Then we decided to go to England because we wanted to be on the BBC.

We went up to the BBC studios on the day [legendary DJ and punk influencer] John Peel was doing his show, and these people were lined up around the block with asymmetrical haircuts and props and wild colors. We walked right up to the front desk and said, "We're here to see John Peel."

They said, "You see all these people here? They're waiting to see John Peel."

We said, "Well, we're from Texas."

So she called John Peel and said, "There's some women here from Texas, and they say they have a record."

And he said, "Okay, send one of them up."

> JOHN PEEL: It's curious, because there's an enormous number of records being issued in America, an enormous number of independent records like yours, and only a few of them actually get through to this country. . . . I'm supposed to know what's going on, but my knowledge of it is fairly sketchy and imprecise and prejudiced. But where do you see mydolls going from here? I mean, what are your aspirations?
>
> LINDA YOUNGER (MYDOLLS): Well, our first aspiration is to make enough money where we don't have to work full-time jobs and do the band after work and on weekends. All of us really enjoy writing and playing music.
>
> JOHN PEEL: Does that mean that you're going to have to come to terms with the idea of signing with a major record company?
>
> LINDA YOUNGER: We would be willing to sign with a major record company, provided we can maintain some of our freedom, as far as what we write and what we play.
>
> JOHN PEEL: This is what everybody says.
>
> LINDA YOUNGER: I think it would be more important to us to play what we want to play. We were offered a chance to do another song on a compilation album, and we didn't want to play the kind of music they wanted. . . . Obviously, we're very naive, thinking we're gonna come to London and get on the radio, but *we did it*. [*both laugh*] But we don't particularly want to play the kind of music that they're playing on FM radio stations, or even worse, AM radio in Houston, Texas.
>
> FROM AN EDITED TRANSCRIPT OF THE *JOHN PEEL SHOW*, BROADCAST ON BBC RADIO 1, JANUARY 26, 1982

As I did research and then interviews for this book, at least half a dozen friends and acquaintances gave me credible accounts of suffering sexual abuse and assault both inside and outside the Texas punk scene. Some of them went so far as to suggest that abuse was a common experience for most people in our circle—why else would people be so drawn to the "second family" aspect of punk communities?

Unfortunately, I'm not so sure punk was exceptional in this regard. Sexual violence, like police violence, was and still is endemic to American life. mydolls guitarist Trish Herrera discovered as much one night when she was pulled over for a traffic violation in Houston.

Texas punk was an extreme reaction to religious, political, racial, and cultural repression in the Lone Star State. Did that leave us vulnerable to violent reprisals that were sometimes sexual in nature? Absolutely.

Adriane "Ash" Shown: [The concept of] consent was not in the vernacular, really. I don't think consent was a big topic of conversation. When I saw a guy manhandling or just groping someone, I would be physical. I'd shove him against the wall, grab his junk, and say, "Oh, you think that's cool? Is this cool? Keep your fucking hands to yourself! Who do you think you are?" It was every single show.

Marcy Buffington: I only got groped once in Austin—by a frat guy at a Joe "King" Carrasco show—but in Houston, the harassment was ubiquitous. It was constant attempts, including by [Omni club owner] Joe Starr, who seemed to think copping a feel was reasonable, since I worked for him. And oh my god, the Valium, the Dilaudid? Everywhere, including *in my tip jar*?! To me, Austin punk was a little family—even if you were a stranger, it felt safe. Houston? No way. Not much scared me, but there was more than one night [when] I had a coworker walk me to my car because someone had gone from harassing me for my phone number to calling me a stuck-up bitch who deserved what I was gonna get, as he got drunker, bolder, and meaner over the course of the night.

Trish Herrera: In Houston, [the problem] was just . . . the police. I was scared because I'd gotten arrested for not putting on my blinkers when I changed lanes, and then strip-searched and put in jail. It made *Time* magazine, and Phil Donahue wanted me to be on his show because this was happening all over the United States. A lot of women were being pulled over and strip-searched, so I was like, "Fuck that," and I sued [the City of Houston].

I had an ACLU lawyer, and he wouldn't let me do the Donahue show. He was like, "No, we just need to keep focused and go straight for the police chief." And I won: I got a police chief apology and $5,000. I used the money to start my hair salon.

At one point, the Houston Police Department raided [Houston punk club] the Island and took people to jail just for being drunk, just to bother us. It wasn't that we minded the police—law and order was fine with us—we just didn't want them to beat the fuck out of us and kill us.

Sally King: I would say that in that era, we endured unbelievable sexual harassment from men *outside* of the scene. Explicit propositions, followed by a stranger trying to yank you into a cab? Check. Gropers on Sixth Street? Yep. Rapey frat boys? Uh-huh. Bikers want to kill your boyfriend to get to you? Well, next time, go to the Black Cat. They don't allow that there.

Lisa "Ralph" Armstrong: I had been at a party at TV Ranch—we'd been doing peyote and mushrooms all day. I went down to Sixth Street. I think my flip-flops got left behind at the house. I ended up getting separated from my friends, and this guy offered me a ride and asked if I wanted to smoke a joint. I was like, "Oh, cool." Black guy—dreads and glasses and a stack of textbooks on the passenger's seat, you know? So you're thinking, "Oh, this is a cool dude."

Maybe [he was looking for] drunk, fucked-up girls who looked easy, who weren't horrified at the idea of jumping in a car with a Black man with dreads. I had no money, no shoes. I didn't know his name; I didn't even know what street I was on. And he takes me out to this house in East Austin and overpowers me and rapes me.

The next day, it was like 110 degrees. I mean, you couldn't have your feet on the sidewalk for five seconds. He had no phone. That afternoon, he finally let me go. After raping me several times. He finally gave me a ride back to the Drag, just dropped me off on a corner. I accepted the ride because, without shoes, I didn't know how I was gonna walk a mile to I-35 and then walk home from there.

A while later, through talking to her, I found out that my friend Lisa had had the same experience with the same guy. He had nothing to do with the punk scene. He picked us both up on Sixth Street. I guess he would troll Sixth Street. And he would offer you a ride.

Sally King: I was good friends with Karla Eppler, Richard Mather, and Harry Wilson. I had a car. So one night, we had pulled into Players on MLK. And some frat boys pulled in next to us. Karla got out of the car, and they started aggressively propositioning her. There were two or three guys, but they were big. And Richard stuck up for her—like, "You can't say that to our friend." And Harry got out of the car, too, and the guys jumped on Richard.

Richard Mather (Criminal Crew, *Buttlikker Comix*): Some redneck guy said something rude to Karla under his breath. The next thing I remember was Harry and the redneck fighting. They were really going at it—hard fighting. Harry can really hold his own.

Sally King: This was when Richard got hit with a crowbar. I ran inside to Players, and I told the people working there, "You gotta call the cops! They're gonna kill him." And they didn't call the cops.

When I ran inside, Harry was already on the ground. When I came back, Richard had gotten back up. And I jumped on the back of the guy that was on top of Richard.

Richard Mather: The guy had a crowbar or a long tire tool, so Harry and I pulled out weapons from his trunk. I had a four-way, a very sucky weapon, and I was drunk. But I was not angry enough to brain someone with a weapon.

The redneck hit Harry and myself, and we both went to the hospital. I was told I collapsed, so they called the ambulance.

Sally King: I went to see Richard when he was in the hospital. He didn't know who I was. He couldn't speak. It was upsetting for him. He was trying to tell me something, but I couldn't tell what it was.

Richard Mather: I had a head injury, and I ended up with an S-shaped scar on my head. I had to learn the alphabet and how to read, all from scratch. Before that, I was a champion speller, ha ha. I lost all that, and I took a "Who cares?" attitude for another twenty years.

Sally King: I didn't talk about it afterward. It was something that was really difficult. Even though I was housemates with Harry, we didn't talk about it.

The scene felt much darker after that. When Richard came back, the music happened to be moving in a harder direction anyway. We weren't in our little bubble anymore.

As it happened, of course, hardcore and postpunk laid the groundwork for "alternative," grunge, and the riot grrrl movements in the late 1980s and 1990s. Bands like Bikini Kill articulated some of the gender trouble we experienced but couldn't always verbalize in Texas. By the time the #MeToo movement reached critical mass in 2017, many of my female punk friends were mothers or grandmothers, teachers or computer systems consultants. Some of them are activists these days, which may account for one of the most frequently seen signs at street protests in 2023: "I Can't Believe I Still Have to Protest This Shit."

Alice Berry: There was a woman in the scene who hated me. She used to say I was a Barbie doll. She used to attack me occasionally—burn me with cigarettes or shove me into mosh pits. Then, years later, she apologized and admitted that she was out of it and going through some psychological things at the time. So the only time I was ever mistreated was by women.

Lisa "Ralph" Armstrong: [Scene regular] Becky Balboa once thanked me on MySpace for teaching her how to pee in the bushes. I thought, "Very good, young Jedi." I mean, that's an important thing to know, especially in the heyday of cocaine, when you're trying to see a band, and there's thirty people in line for the restroom, waiting to powder their noses, and you can't get in to pee before the set's half over.

But I was also like, "Hmm, I hope I taught her more than *that*."

Trish Herrera: Our scene was playful in the beginning, kind of skipping around and having fun. But then it started getting violent. And that's when we started backing off. The last tour that we did was pretty intense. Even though we weren't hardcore, people treated us like we were, and it just gets a little frightening sometimes, you know? If you're a female, they don't really care. The mosh pits were like a football game. I thought, "This is just so *male*. It's not even fun. It's not inclusive. It's not even what punk rock is about."

I still love hardcore—there's a place for it. I just wish there was a place for women in it.

Dayna Blackwell: My favorite band? Terminal Mind. Period. [Singer-guitarist] Steve Marsh was the one guy in Terminal Mind I never nailed. I always told him, "I'm gonna get you one day." I'm romantically retired, and I came out as queer years ago, but . . . *I will get Steve.*

Sally King: It took me many years to forgive that young, angry me and to untangle my emotions surrounding religion and death. It occurred completely unbidden, as I was driving alone down a two-lane country road, behind a young woman with crazy pigtails in a beat-up pickup truck. As the sun set on the back of her wild blonde hair, I smiled—she was a vision of myself from twenty-five years ago. I was smiling because I understood how wonderful it was to have lived my youth doing whatever I damn well pleased—beat-up pickup truck, crazy hair and all. I don't regret a minute.

I passed the young woman, rolled down my window, and waved, tears rolling down my cheeks. "It's gonna be okay," I said to her. "It's going to turn out just fine."

5 | WHITE RAGE?

The title song of the Big Boys' 1982 *Fun, Fun, Fun . . .* EP ends with a very telling and overdetermined moment. "Fun Fun Fun" falls apart with a snarl and a clash of cymbals, but when the noise clears, a chorus of punks in the studio is singing "The Eyes of Texas." Hearing this—both then and now—evokes a sense memory that isn't pleasant for everyone, because "The Eyes of Texas" is traditionally sung by the huge crowds at University of Texas football games. Accordingly, a few seconds into this seemingly impromptu punk rendition of the song, a lone voice screams, "Texas sucks!" Then, "Fuck Texas!"

Bassist Chris Gates wrote "Fun Fun Fun" as a knockoff of the anthemic English Oi! punk rock he loved, and the lyrics suggest that punk culture itself is open-minded and inclusive. After its release, the song became both an anthem and a commercial enterprise. (In 2006, several Austin producers borrowed the name of the song for what would become a successful music festival.) Gates actually orchestrated the "Eyes of Texas" singalong in imitation of Oi! recordings that ended with soccer chants. He may have known that some Oi! fans and bands were involved with UK white supremacist groups, such as the National Front. However, he may not have known that "The Eyes of Texas" was first performed as part of a minstrel show. It has been interpreted as an expression of the Lost Cause ideology, which argues that slavery in the United States was a fine and ethical thing.

People like me luxuriate in onionskin moments like "Fun Fun Fun" because they seem to explain everything across disparate cultures and historical periods. It's all there in a single recording: the legacy of racism in Texas and punk, our ambivalence about our home state, plus football and the word *fuck*. At its most poignant, an antiracist band was singing about inclusivity, from a position between layers of exclusion and hate. Texas punks, as a chorus and a community, may have called out bigots, but we were often unable to confront our own privilege and white supremacy.

Chris Gates: At the end of those Oi! songs, they all start singing a football song because they were all soccer hooligans. So I thought, "That's awesome. I want a bunch of people in here yelling anyway, but let's sing 'The Eyes of Texas.' That'll be funny." But also, yeah, fuck Texas. Because outside of our tiny little bubble, when we would drive from Austin to Houston to play shows, and we would get out in La Grange to get gas? It was a little scary. People in towns like that had never seen anything like us. And if you start rubbing people's noses in a world they don't know exists, they get real busy killing it.

With a few notable exceptions, American punk has been a white thing. And regardless of what else is in play—humanism, political idealism, violence, or drugs—punk is always about fury. If we shine a light on race and rage in Texas punk, it makes sense to start with "The Dicks Hate the Police" by the Dicks. The song refers to the 1977 Houston police murder of Chicano laborer and US Army veteran Joe Campos Torres. The Dicks released the song as their debut single in 1980, and it is still one of the most progressive and deathless blasts of punk ever recorded.

Diana Garcia (fan): I *loved* "Dicks Hate Police"! [*sings*] "Mommy, Mommy, Mommy / Look at your son!" I could totally relate to all of that. I didn't look at the bands and think, "Oh, look at those white people making music." I thought, "We all speak the same language—the punk language." The lyrics, the anger, the energy, *the wanting something different*. There was a *reason* to be angry. I saw that the music brought all these diverse people together—from different classes and different towns.

Roger "El Borracho" Manriquez (fan): There was something untouchable about Gary Floyd. He was promoting a lot of pissed-off anger. His songs were deep—like "Dead in a Motel Room"—like, super heavy.

Gary Floyd: Anger is a part of everything. When you suppress it, you get an ulcer, or you're vomiting blood. Or you're a big fucking phony.

Trish Herrera: [The Torres murder] happened right before our band came together. I can't even speak Spanish, but when I got arrested once in Houston, the police started calling me Hispanic slurs because of my last name. They pulled me out of the car and hit my head. They hurt me. They tied my hands behind my back so that it left bruises on my thumbs. I was put in jail and then strip-searched. It was horrible.

Brecht Andersch (fan): I grew up in Brooklyn, and I first came to Texas when I was about ten years old. My parents had bought some land outside of Denton because they were trying to found an ashram for their guru. My parents were a mixed-race couple—my stepfather was Black. I'd heard a lot about Texas and seen cowboy movies, and I knew it might be difficult for a family like ours. And we were pulled over by the police in some small town. My stepfather was driving, and he didn't have a license. He got out of the car and talked to the policeman, and we went to the police station, but everything was okay. Nothing happened, and I was paying attention to all of that.

Sally King: Racism was definitely endemic in Texas. It was part of our culture. It was everywhere. It was no big deal to call someone a "wetback." And that bled over to us when we were punk rockers.

Maria Cotera: We were part of a movement that rejected movements. I think we all participated in a big fuck-you to liberal convention. One of those challenges to convention was calling people "spic" and the N-word—punks were using those words. And you could say that people of color like me accepted this racist discourse as part of the price we had to pay to be involved in this movement. And I have to ask, "*Why* was that acceptable?" At what level did we have to submerge feelings of hurt?

I grew up with racism in the suburbs of Austin. I remember classmates, bullies, and relatives using the N-word, and it became clear to me that those people were *assholes*. So, if growing up is a process of defining yourself, and punk rock is a process of defining yourself *against* something, I came to think of myself as a white kid who liked cool music and hated racists. Like a lot of white liberals in Austin, I thought I was above bigotry. I thought I knew better.

In 1980, as I became a regular at Austin punk shows, I listened to the songs, looked at the gig posters, and assumed that all of us in those places hated the same things. "We" hated blonde Barbie people and Reagan. And even if we loved our parents (and some of us did), "we" still hated the idea of parents. "We" were angry, but only some of us were white and racist. We didn't see the bigotry that we layered into our fanzines and music, just beneath the irony. This "we" didn't always realize that people of color in the scene may have been angry about different things, or, to be more precise, they may have been pissed off about extra things.

Most Texas cities were (and still are) rigidly segregated, and the faces at punk shows reflected that reality. However, unlike most other punk scenes in the United States, Mexico was in the mix here. Joe "King" Carrasco, the first truly Texan new wave star, was a white fella who combined cheesy Farfisa riffs with Mexican pop and Latin rhythms. Carrasco was also evoking the key role of Chicanos, such as Sam the Sham, in 1960s garage punk, which was itself a major influence on early US punk rockers like Patti Smith Group guitarist Lenny Kaye. These loops of influence and feedback—sometimes deracinated—tend to submerge in a scene only to show up again unannounced and by surprise.

Raul's, the first punk venue in Austin, began life as a Tejano music club. From the influence of José Guadalupe Posada's Día de los Muertos prints and the ubiquity of Santeria candles in every punk bedroom, to the sheer number of Latinos and Latinas in bands, poster-making, and the mosh pit, Lone Star punk scenes were less Texan than Texican.

Carlos Lowry: In the sixties, the US was coming out of segregation, and the seventies weren't that much different. I went to college at Southwestern University—there were two thousand students, and nineteen of those were Black. In Austin, white people were scared to cross [to the eastern side of] I-35. I think the punk scene here was a by-product of that segregation. On the other hand, in Texas, Mexicanos have just always been here.

> Visit Raul's, a small club on Guadalupe. Depending on the night you go, you will (a) be met by a round of determined looking Chicanos who, at the slightest lapse of social grace, will lift your body up and attempt to hurl it all the way back to the North Dallas suburbs . . . or (b) be immediately in the midst of an array of the finest specimens of humanity. This is Raul's on a Punk Night, where sleek, golden-tanned bodies accompany poetically perceptive, yet razor sharp minds.
>
> NICK WEST, ". . . TO BE A PUNK IN AUSTIN,"
> *AUSTIN VANGUARD*, 1978

> JOE "KING" CARRASCO: It really freaks people out when we sometimes play polkas. We're trying to educate people. . . . When we first started playing Raul's—if you want to get out of there quick, play a polka.
> BRAD KIZER: The punks really had a hard time with polkas.
> JK: I love seeing people try to polka. It's funny you know?
> CONTEMPO CULTURE: Do people ever really try to polka?
> JK: Yeah. You play for Chicanos and they know how to do it right.
>
> INTERVIEW WITH JOE "KING" CARRASCO AND BASSIST BRAD KIZER, *CONTEMPO CULTURE*, NO. 3, 1980

Carlos Lowry: Raul's was a Chicano bar, and Joseph Gonzalez was the manager. I was doing artwork for the Brown Berets and the Austin Committee for Human Rights in Chile. There were at least four events that the group had at Raul's, on Sunday nights. They were called Pena Folkloricos, and this was in 1978 and 1979, way before hardcore punk and the Dicks. My friends and I got those events together because we had started to go to punk shows at Raul's, and we'd met Joseph Gonzalez there.

Garinè Isassi (writer, musician): Walking through the punk scene in Austin was a completely white-person experience. Not only no Black people, but also nobody Middle Eastern, and no Asian Americans. We didn't think about it because we didn't have to—we were not living the Black or Hispanic experience. As a "not exactly white" person myself—I'm Armenian American—I experienced bias and weirdness in the Texas punk scene because I would be mistaken for Mexican all the time.

Diana Garcia: I don't think the Austin scene was just angry white boys. I was angry, and I don't consider myself white. I'm Mexican American. I had a very Chicana culture. I hung out with Minnie, and her mom is Nicaraguan. Minnie was Latinx; Tara was Black. So two of my best friends were not white. I hung out with Harry Wilson—Harry wasn't white. We all had issues; we were all revolting against something.

Trish Herrera: I always identified with being Mexican, even though I couldn't speak Spanish. My parents would say, "We're not going to teach you Spanish because it's not good for you." My mom told me, "Don't go out in the sun." She did not want me to suffer racism. That made me feel some shame. And I thought, "What are we so ashamed of that we have to hide this? Fuck it. I'm going out in the sun. I'm gonna run around without a bra." So yeah, I felt some shame, and punk rock helped me break out of that shame.

Teresa Taylor: [Shortly after I started listening to punk rock,] I had the most vivid dream of my life. In the dream, I saw myself putting the needle down on a 45, and it was MDC's song "John Wayne Was a Nazi." And I saw this giant, beautiful Indian chief standing over our suburban swimming pool. He cut himself, then dove into our pool. All the water was bloodred. When I woke up, I thought, "This is a *racist* country."

Roger "El Borracho" Manriquez: I grew up in fucking Vidor, Texas. I worked at a steel plant with all these rednecks, and I'd play my Psychedelic Furs shit [for them], probably Joe "King" Carrasco or some new wave shit. But I had a Mohawk, and they were like, "Why don't you dye it purple?"

Diana Garcia: Joe "King" Carrasco was fun. I went to a couple of his shows because I loved that song "Party Weekend." It was really catchy. I liked Rank and File. I thought [guitarist] Alejandro Escovedo was such a babe. He's good-looking in an unusual sort of way.

Maria Cotera: I grew up in a revolutionary movement centered on Chicano nationalism and the idea that Chicanos in Texas had been treated like shit because of racism. My parents helped found a radical third party called La Raza Unida. They contested Democratic and Republican control of the electoral process . . . until the Texas Rangers and other white supremacist forces destroyed the movement.

But like most kids, when I was eighteen, I was not invested in my parents' history, or in replaying it, or even thinking about it. At that moment in the early eighties, radicalism *was* the punk rock movement. There was the anti-apartheid movement, but that was not a movement that spoke to me in the way that punk spoke to me. But it had these contradictions. [*laughs*] We just weren't thinking in sophisticated ways about this stuff the way we do now!

Diana Garcia: I come from San Antonio, from the West Side. Went to high school with kids that sold drugs, kids that took guns to school. I thought, "I don't wanna live in the barrio—I want to go to college and have other

David Yow sings for Scratch Acid, egged on by Harry Odel Wilson, Voltaire's Basement, Austin, July 1984.

opportunities." And that's what brought me to Austin. By the time I was in college, I was really angry. And when I first heard Flipper and all this punk rock music, unconsciously, I felt like it was about anger at the system. But punks in Austin didn't understand what *really* tough neighborhoods were like. That also formed part of my rage. And the fact that I was in class at UT, and everyone in my class was white except for me. The only Hispanics I could see were the custodians. I was always very polite to the custodians. My mom was a custodian.

Sammy Jacobo (fan): I used to go to Club Foot for hardcore punk shows on Sunday nights, circa 1983. Because I needed a break from studying and because I was bored. I became friends with Joseph Gonzalez there. We spoke Spanglish with each other, and I only hanged with him at the front door because I never liked dancing with boys. Some of the music was great. Some of it was horrid. But I never felt threatened by the punks there. I felt more threatened walking on the streets of Austin.

Trish Herrera: Everybody in the punk scene had this attitude that we were all the right size, we were all the same. [But] I kind of related Catholicism to being Mexican. And then I realized that I was not really fighting against being Mexican; I was fighting against the *corporation* that runs Mexico and all these Catholic countries. I mean, I still respect people that really practice their religion. But that's what it is—Catholicism is a corporation, and the people that are running it use it as a hierarchy.

Well before punk rock took a Greyhound bus to Austin, racism and anti-Semitism tainted the music. The Ramones spooned up Nazi imagery in "Today Your Love, Tomorrow the World" on their debut album in 1976, and later that year, Siouxsie Sioux wore a swastika to a Sex Pistols show in London. In 1979, Lester Bangs wrote "The White Noise Supremacists," a *Village Voice* piece about racism in the New York punk scene.

So it made sense when some of my funny friends started wearing swastikas to Austin punk clubs. They were just trying to get a rise out of people! And it worked: Several of the older music writers in town, including *Austin American-Statesman* music columnist Ed Ward and future *Austin Chronicle* founder Louis Black, wrote passionate editorials taking punks to task for dabbling in fascism. "The squares just don't get it," I thought . . .

Steve Collier: In the beginning, I didn't know David Yow that well. I thought he was funny. I saw him at Club Foot once, though, and he was wearing the full-on Sid Vicious swastika armband. I thought, "God, that is so offensive!" I could not see the humor in it.

David Yow: Do I regret wearing swastikas? I wouldn't call it a regret. I wouldn't mind if it never happened. I didn't know what I was doing. I was so ignorant about Nazism and Hitler. I was just doing what Sid Vicious had done.

Polar Bear (anarchist): I told several people dressed up as Nazis in Austin that they were being stupid. But I knew they were not actually Nazis, so I did not punch them in the face. I had encountered real Nazis in the mid-seventies, and I knew they had to be stopped from organizing and murdering us.

Dave Dictor: I'm old enough to remember seeing civil rights marches where people were attacked by police with fire hoses. I once said the

N-word—because I'd heard it at school and had no idea what it meant. My mom told me to go stand in the corner and think about what I'd done. I never said it again.

Diane "Muffy" McGee Hardin: My friend Harry Wilson was the god of high school. He's one of the most charming people I've ever met. I remember walking down Twenty-First Street with Harry and Brett from Crotch Rot, and this car stopped. This redneck with a beard and a stupid hat gets out, and he was *really* mad. He asked Harry if he knew whether he was Black or white. Like Harry couldn't be Black *and* punk—he had to pick one!

Cathy Criss (singer): [Do Dat singer and guitarist] Byron Scott told me one club wouldn't pay him for a gig—they'd only agree to pay a white member of his band. I got used to being the only Black girl at punk shows, and mostly nobody bothered me. But my band, the Negros, broke up after skinheads took down some of our posters and wrote *niggers* on others. I got the message that I should just be a fan and not ask for trouble. We weren't very good anyway.

If punk rock has been made chiefly by entitled white men, San Antonio is the exception that proves the rule. The true working-class (and Chicano) rebel music in San Antonio has always been hard rock and heavy metal. Naturally, one of SA's finest punk bands, Marching Plague, began their career by trolling metalheads. Their side band, the Fearless Iranians from Hell, would become nationally infamous later in the decade, partly because they declared a half-serious jihad against white "American" institutions like 7-Eleven and sports cars. And still another San Antonio group embodied the rivalry and comingling of heavy metal and punk rock: the tough Chicana group of three sisters known as Heather Leather.

Jeff Smith: San Antonio isn't about downward mobility. A lot of people move there for a better life; they're not there to be bohemians. Marching Plague were a good San Antonio band. They took a lot from the Angry Samoans, but they were sort of prehardcore.

Brad Perkins (Marching Plague / Fearless Iranians from Hell): San Antonio is known as the Heavy Metal Capital of the World. There were all these metalhead guys that would try to beat up [punks]. That's how we came up with the title of our song "Rock and Roll Asshole." The cover of that record had a drawing of a big bat biting off Ozzy Osbourne's head. We just thought it was funny. [We weren't mad that] Ozzy had peed on the side of the Alamo. We thought that was funny too!

Jeff Smith: The first version of Fearless Iranians from Hell—the version of the band with an actual Iranian guy in it—that version of the band was basically Team Marching Plague.

Brad Perkins: Fearless Iranians from Hell all played in ski masks, except for Amir, the singer, who was Iranian. Amir's family had fled Iran after the shah [was deposed]. So some of our songs were serious and some of them weren't.

One of the first Fearless Iranians shows was at this hotel. And when we got there, we found out that there was gonna be a party at the hotel that night for a bunch of US Army Rangers. And we thought, "Oh, this doesn't sound good."

But we played anyway, and everyone had fun, and everyone got along. I mean, there was one ranger who started to get kind of aggressive, but someone pulled him aside and said, "We're all just having fun." And it turned out okay.

> Direct from Tehran, by way of San Antonio, Texas, the Fearless Iranians from Hell have come on a mission to bring American imperialist dogs to their knees. . . . American women, American Trans-Ams, even American Seven-Elevens; nothing is sacred to the human wave pouring forth from the middle eastern desert. . . . Yes, the great Persian empire will rise once more, and Boner Records is proud to be a sponsor of the cause. . . . We pity those who, for failure to provide radio airplay or critical support, must eventually face their brutal Islamic justice.
>
> BONER RECORDS, PRESS RELEASE, CIRCA 1988

Brad Perkins: After 9/11, someone put a bounty on the heads of the guys in Fearless Iranians from Hell. So they had to get a court order against this person. It got to be where the guys in the band didn't want their identities to be known.

Jeff Smith: Heather Leather was maybe the most punk rock of all the SA bands, even though they sounded more like heavy metal. I say that because they were Mexican and female. Before that, out of the eighty or so arena concerts I'd seen in San Antonio, only one or two of them had women onstage. Heather Leather were there *to rock*. I gave [bassist and lead singer] Ruth [Garza] a ride home once, deep into the West Side, where it was pretty rough. That part of San Antonio didn't have paved streets yet—it was still gravel roads where Heather Leather lived.

Brad Perkins: Heather Leather were great. I mean, they weren't so proficient on their instruments, but a lot of the punks loved them. I saw a Heather Leather show at Uncle Sue-Sue's in Austin once—that place was wild. Their father was up in front watching them play—he had this really big smile on his face.

Hindsight being twenty-twenty, it's easy to speculate that some early US and UK punks were simply showing us who they were when they wore Nazi regalia or complained to Lester Bangs about Black people on the subway. The list of protopunks and punks who later sincerely embraced radical right-wing and racist positions is depressingly long and includes the Velvet Underground's Moe Tucker, Johnny Ramone, Johnny Rotten, and both Exene Cervenka and Billy Zoom from X.

It's also easier today to see that back in 1981, white privilege allowed us to "play" with the language and totems of white supremacy. This is how Fort Worth's Hugh Beaumont Experience could name one of their songs "Zyklon B" (after the cyanide gas used to murder people in Nazi concentration camps) and then show up to protest at the Ku Klux Klan's 1983 march in Austin. I went to that KKK march as a lark—just something to do on a Saturday. The stakes were higher for the Chicano activists of the Brown Berets who were there that day. Many of them were brutally beaten by the police for simply being in the wrong place, for the crime of standing while being brown.

Diane "Muffy" McGee Hardin: When King Coffey moved to Austin, he and his friend Phil Flowers were still in the Hugh Beaumont Experience. There was this big KKK rally, and a bunch of us marched against it. It was just a social time—a way to meet up with our friends! Even though we hated the Klan.

Richard Mather: The city trucked down hundreds of cops from Houston or Dallas. At the last minute, I guess the Klan got nervous—there was a very large crowd of protesters—so they rerouted the parade to avoid the crowds. I remember like ten fat guys in robes walking in a sad formation. The grand Poo-Bah had a bullhorn, and he was saying things like "Ku Klux Klan, number one!" with a heavy Texas accent.

Diane "Muffy" McGee Hardin: We yelled at the KKK guys and harassed them. Becky Balboa and I stole one of their signs. It said, "Stop Gay Pride Day."

Richard Mather: They assembled on the front lawn of the Capitol building, and the leader started to speak. He was quickly drowned out by thousands of people chanting, "Fuck you!" in unison. Then something happened, and the Klan got hurried to their vans by a bunch of cops in riot gear, and people threw stones, and I saw some bloody Klansmen.

Pat Doyle: Tony [Johnson] was there waiting along Twelfth Street. They were tossing rocks at the Klan. I asked him about it, and he said, "I was throwing bricks." It's hard to believe, knowing that Tony eventually became one of the Sons of Confederate Veterans.

Carlos Lowry: I was at one of the KKK's big marches before that one. I remember walking by this Klan truck, and the front seats were just filled with weapons—rifles, pistols, and probably machine guns. A scary amount of weapons.

> The Klan thrives in Texas. . . . When they had a public demonstration at the Capitol, only 33 members had enough balls to come out in public and half of them wore hoods. I would say the organization is much larger than anyone really knows, because with all the neo-Nazi groups that have been exposed lately (Posse Comitatus, The Convent, Aryan Nations) no one really knows who is who anymore. I wouldn't want to make any predictions about just how vulnerable the public will be to all this insanity of late, but we can all try to change things on a one to one basis by making people aware of their ability to work for a better world.
>
> INTERVIEW WITH PAT DOYLE OF THE OFFENDERS,
> *SUBURBAN VOICE* FANZINE, 1984

Diane "Muffy" McGee Hardin: I was raised to not be prejudiced, and I never thought my parents were prejudiced. Until they saw evidence that I'd made out with Harry. I came home with him one night, and my parents reacted in some very weird ways. My dad was looking at the ground; he couldn't look me in the eye. He said, "I just think Harry needs to find a Black girl, and you need to find a white boy." I thought, "This goes against absolutely everything you've ever said." My reaction was, "Okay, Harry's gonna be my boyfriend!" So we did that for a while, but that's a pretty shitty reason to make someone your boyfriend. It was more racist of me.

Maria Cotera: Like every other space in America in the 1980s, the Austin punk scene *was* a white supremacist scene. It wasn't overtly political that way—we didn't have a *politics* of white supremacy, except in some small niches. I wasn't calling anyone out. But of all the people, I should have. I knew better.

Writers from Frantz Fanon to Isabel Wilkerson have explored how Blackness was constructed, setting up an important question for punk: How, and by whom, is "whiteness" performed? The bizarre and popular group Devo, from Akron, Ohio, were, among other things, a parodic performance of whiteness, and they acted as a gateway to punk rock for many of us; Nazi skinheads in the US and UK gave another performance, insisting on another, more sinister definition of whiteness.

Perhaps punk—as an aesthetic—lives somewhere between these two extremes. One English record label codified whiteness with its name: Stiff. David Byrne of Talking Heads performed whiteness as a clueless, spastic man in a suit. In the 1970s and 1980s, even as right-wing figures such as Anita Bryant performed Eisenhower-era white "respectability," punk art and music responded by delving into the dark side of America's recent past: the rise of zombie consumerism, killers like Ed Gein and Charles Manson, nuclear horror, and paranoia. The aforementioned Hugh Beaumont Experience was named after an actor in the television show *Leave It to Beaver* because, for us, the high avatars of grinning conformity, horrible parenting, and white middle-class culture were Ward and June Cleaver. In American punk posters, images of Ward Cleaver, Ronald Reagan, and dads from 1950s Chrysler advertisements were interchangeable, and the message was clear: Don't be (white) like this.

Meanwhile, in antebellum mansions just across the street from punk clubs like Uncle Sue-Sue's, the fraternity brothers and sorority sisters of the University of Texas reigned supreme as the racist, homophobic junior royalty of central Austin. The Greek community—the sons and daughters of the richest families in Texas—were nightmares of whiteness and had a long history of disrupting campus life with bigotry and assault. Fraternity bros wore starched Izod shirts and hunted punk rockers for sport.

Big Boys singer Biscuit responded with a poster he plastered up and down the Drag. It depicted a frat boy and a sorority girl, complete with arrows and helpful captions like "Too much makeup" and "Lots of Daddy's $." At the top were the words, "HOW TO RECOGNIZE THE ENEMY!"

Maria Cotera: Racism just didn't seem to be the biggest issue. The biggest issue was Reagan and frat boys and fucking *sweaters*. It was a culture war. We talked about fighting with frat boys. And who are frat boys? They are the bastion of white supremacy on campus. There was some displacement. Like saying, "Fucking frat boys!" may have been, at some deep level, like saying, "Fucking white boys!"

> In 1982, the *Texan* reported three Jewish fraternities withdrew from Sigma Chi's Fight Night after the fraternity printed anti-Semitic advertisements for the event. Two years later, the *Texan* reported Alpha Tau Omega and Zeta Psi were penalized when they modeled Roundup floats that then Interfraternity Council president David Sheehan said "could be perceived as being racist."
>
> Walter Buenger, a professor of Texas history, said this behavior occurred in part because participants sought enjoyment from degrading already marginalized groups.
>
> "I suspect that the crowds who watched appreciated having their racial stereotypes reinforced and perhaps also enjoyed demeaning others," Buenger said. . . . In 1990, the *Texan* reported an unidentified individual painted racial slurs onto a car Delta Tau Delta used in the Roundup parade. During the same weekend, Phi Gamma Delta distributed t-shirts portraying Michael Jordan with ape-like facial features.
>
> "ROUNDUP'S LONG HISTORY OF RACISM," *DAILY TEXAN*, MARCH 29, 2019

David Roach (Junkyard): You must remember the parties off the Drag? Sometimes they would happen too close to a frat house, and we'd intermingle. One night, some frat boy talked shit to Tomas [who was Black]. So Tomas came back with a wooden railroad tie! I have no idea where or how he got it. Tomas chucked it at these guys, and then he ran. They chased him across the street, but one of the frat boys got hit by a car.

> There was the time that . . . [Dicks bassist] Buxf Parrott was standing outside Raul's talking to me and without missing a beat caught the flying beer bottle hurled at us from a frat car and threw it back at the car smashing the back window, then finished his story.
>
> TIM KERR, QUOTED IN *THE DICKS* (TEMPORARY SERVICES, 2008)

David Roach: One night, me and Spike and Mindy were in the drive-through at Jack in the Box. Some drunk frat boy walks up to our car. One of us had a Fear shirt on, and he says, "You got Fear on your shirt, but y'all look scared."

Spike gets out, pulls out a switchblade, and the dude ran away so fast he left a shoe.

> As a sort of ultimate protest against right wing political extremism [Big Boys] performed during rush week last year wearing white robes and conical hats, announcing the band as "Kappa Kappa Kappa." Members of UT fraternities were said to be unamused.
>
> CHRIS WALTERS, *AUSTIN AMERICAN-STATESMAN*, OCTOBER 6, 1982

Diane "Muffy" McGee Hardin: I came up with the name "Muffy"—it was my mockery of *preppy*. I had some preppy clothes, and I tore them up and that's how I came up with my punk rock wardrobe. I had this Neiman Marcus purse that I'd swing. I was mocking that style, that ideology: pure white girl.

> In the modern world today, forty years since World War II, a new breed of bigots have been raised. They are called fraternity members, or "frats." . . . Equating Nazis with Fraternities? The Izods, the Jordache jeans and the mirrored sunglasses

are the fraternity member's uniform just as the brown shirts, swastikas and high leather boots were to the Nazis. The customized jeep equipped with alcohol is just as much a "staff car" as the Volkswagen was to Nazi officials. . . . Many fraternity members take intense delight in "joyriding" while drinking alcohol, and then attacking people, very frequently cornering a single person.

TEXT FROM A BROADSIDE POSTED AROUND THE UT CAMPUS IN THE MID-1980S

Songs like "Gator Fuckin," "White Nigger," and "Baby Let's Play God" obviously define some sort of contemporary Texas lifestyle. The real hit though is "We Got Your Money," a fun, fun party song about ripping off frat boys.

BRUCE PAVITT, REVIEW OF BIG BOYS' ALBUM *LULLABIES HELP THE BRAIN GROW*, *THE ROCKET*, SEPTEMBER 1983

For the past five Sundays, punk rock musicians living in a small apartment complex on Rio Grande Street have obtained permits from the city to blast live music that neighboring students say makes studying almost impossible. . . . "My room opens up right next to them," said Mary Young, 19, a San Antonio business major. . . . "They even had a little sign up last week that said "Go ahead! Complain! We're legal."

ANDY MANGAN, *AUSTIN AMERICAN-STATESMAN*, CIRCA 1984

But our skirmishes with frat boys and nineteen-year-old business majors were nothing compared to the problem in our own house. Beginning in 1982, violent skinheads—racist and otherwise—became a problem at Austin punk shows. Some of them were homegrown, some were just passing through (or fleeing crimes in other states), and some boasted of connections to national white power organizations. This did not occur in a vacuum—it was just one corner of a national landscape of resurgent white supremacist movements. In the 1980s, the Ku Klux Klan combined David Duke's aboveground political activism in Louisiana with its armed underground criminality, marking the beginning of its so-called Fifth Era. The Posse Comitatus, a racist states-rights group founded in Portland, built alliances with survivalists and quasi-religious Christian Identity organizations. The Order, a violent splinter group of the Aryan Nations, was making headlines with their counterfeiting operations, a string of armored car robberies, and murder. Viewed from the present day—as Donald Trump flirts with Proud Boys—this all sounds sickeningly familiar.

In Austin, when skinheads Roger "El Borracho" Manriquez and Tommy "Hogg" Pipes talked about their hometown, we all knew it wasn't just another Texas backwater. Vidor, near the Louisiana border, was a notorious base for the Ku Klux Klan. Tommy had an Iron Cross necklace tattooed on his sternum. Roger, a.k.a. Elbo (short for *el borracho*—the drunk), epitomized the contradictions and inexplicable nature of racism in Texas. He was often blotto and talked with his fists. He sometimes spouted white power notions. He was also Mexican American.

Roger "El Borracho" Manriquez: I left Vidor for Austin in 1982. I had a real bad experience. I found my best cousin dead on the Neches River Bridge. It was after we had gone downtown in Beaumont, and we were real drunk. So I was like, "I'm outta here."

Diana Garcia: Roger hung out with these white boys, and we gave him a hard time. We told him, "Elbo, why are you hanging out with them? They're all white supremacists."

Roger "El Borracho" Manriquez: I didn't grow up with my culture; I didn't grow up with the language. As a kid, I used to look at the color of my skin. I'd wake up, and I'd go, "What the fuck am I?" "Am I a white guy or what?" No, I'm not.

Diana Garcia: But the skinheads accepted him, which means they weren't really white supremacists. Otherwise, why would they be friends with Roger? He's, like, *so* Mexican American.

Tarbox Kiersted (journalist): I remember sitting outside at Les Amis café one night with Mimi Vitetta, and Roger walked by. He saw us and started chatting. I heard his long and rather involved explanation that Hispanics are actually white, and that they are, in fact, the most superior variety of white.

Roger "El Borracho" Manriquez: When I was a skinhead in Austin, to tell you the truth, I always thought I was white. Because I didn't grow up with

Roger "El Borracho" Manriquez, Buddy Boy, Tommy "Hogg" Pipes (RIP), and Jerry Paterson (RIP), Austin, April 1986. The attitude of some scene regulars was, "They might be fuckups, but they're *our* fuckups."

all that other shit, people speaking Spanish or saying, "Hey, *ese*!" I didn't see myself that way. I grew up around Anglos.

Maria Cotera: That makes a lot of sense. Roger grew up in Vidor, the homeplace of the Klan, which was profoundly dangerous for Mexican people and Black people.

Cathy Criss: Elbo was one of the skate punks who thought it was cool to sport Nazi symbols, although I don't know if he was one of the people who defaced our posters.

> Tom Metzger, a television repairman from Southern California and the leader of the San Diego–based White Aryan Resistance (WAR), appears to have infused the far right with new blood through the burgeoning skinhead movement. . . . The right wing of the skins are becoming the children of the

> Klan, and they may already be its future. . . . In Texas, the Confederate Hammer Skins have been tied to forty crimes since 1987; they are known for activities like smearing "Hitler was Right," "Get out Jew Pig," and "Yahweh our White God" on synagogue walls.
>
> JAMES RIDGEWAY, *BLOOD IN THE FACE* (THUNDER'S MOUTH PRESS, 1990)

Gary Miller (fan): One of the things I liked about punk rock music was that it didn't matter who you were or where you came from as long as you liked the music. That is, until the Hammer Skins from Dallas showed up in Austin. Until I got beaten up by a half dozen of them on a fire escape three blocks above Sixth Street. Not one of them would challenge me individually. I made it my mission to confront them every time I saw a stupid Nazi skinhead in my town. And it wasn't just me—lots of punk rockers in Austin resoundingly rejected that racist ideology. I got into a lot of fights. I don't regret it.

Polar Bear: The skinheads were never well organized as a racist group in Austin. They were more like lost kids who would have been happy as fraternity bullies if they had come from money. Some of the younger hardcore bands let them know they would end up with less beer if they were total dickheads.

Richard Mather: I saw Scott Oi and Nick the Dick meet for the first time. "Scott, this is Nick the Dick." They shook hands and simultaneously tried to kick each other in the balls. But instead, they kicked each other in the knee.

Jim "Straightedge" Koppenhaver (roadie and fan): A few of us were not scared of the Nazi skins, and they grudgingly listened in certain situations. It was hard to keep them from making things shitty. Most were just scammers and thieves, but they certainly made the scene end sooner than it should have.

Roger "El Borracho" Manriquez: I remember I got into a lot of fistfights. I think a lot of that was just inner stuff. I didn't really like myself. I provoked it out of my system. A lot of it had to do with a lot of drugs and alcohol. That just fueled it.

Jacob Mackey (fan): There was a period in the eighties when a certain skinhead was making life unpleasant. He spit on me at the Ritz when he saw my "Nazi Punks Fuck Off" T-shirt. He made life difficult for me and my friends. He had a platoon of little shitbird skins—a bunch of them beat up my brother and broke his fingers. I got so involved in anti-Nazi activism while I was working at [the memorabilia shop] Aaron's Rock and Roll that one skinhead came in with some KKK guys and took my picture. He told me, "Now, the Klan knows who you are. If you fuck with us again, you're dead." They ruined a shitload of shows, especially at Liberty Lunch and the Ritz. Other than that, no problems with racists in Austin back in the day at all!

Mikey T. Milligan Jr. (skater): I think a lot of that shit was coming out of the California prison system.

Maria Cotera: At some point, there was a "Which side are you on?" moment, where you could see the scene was getting fucked up. A Black band was playing at the Continental Club. And these skinheads, who had been slowly infiltrating the scene, showed up specifically to beat the shit out of people. Some guy tried to stab Buxf! These skinheads were from outside Austin. Some of them were formerly incarcerated, like *the real deal*—members of serious white supremacist organizations and gangs. And Roger was part of that skinhead group. He was there that night. It was clear they were gonna push this question in the scene. They forced people to contend with the fact that they weren't talking about race. It's not that people in the scene were racist; it's that they weren't antiracist. It blew up. We had ignored the infiltration of these racist skinheads, and then it blew up in our faces.

Roger "El Borracho" Manriquez: I ran with some of the San Francisco Skins. Some of them came through Austin. But they got to be more like Nazis. They got worse. After a while, I kinda got brainwashed by that shit. It got to where I couldn't even talk to Byron and Alvin, all my Black friends from the scene. And I thought, "Fuck this shit. I'm not even white. I don't want to be part of this shit no more." They got so radical. I'm not into no gangs and guns and all that shit.

One September night in 1984, all of this rage and antiracism erupted at once in the middle of a mosh pit at Liberty Lunch. But instead of the Dicks or the Offenders, Austin punk's most beloved party band was onstage. The Big Boys had just returned from a very long tour, and the opening band was Samhain, the new horror-punk group led by their friend, Glenn Danzig, the warped genius behind the Misfits. The evening got off to a good start, but then something happened out in the crowd.

Tim Kerr: It wasn't meant to be our last show. There was a lot of shit going on within the band, and the last couple of shows had been really intense. [Big Boys singer] Biscuit and [bassist] Chris were absolutely not getting along, which had nothing to do with the music. It was just human nature.

Dotty Farrell: This Nazi recruiter had been hanging around Austin for months, giving pot and pamphlets to some of the younger kids. Most of these kids were idiots, and they were already destroying the scene at that point.

Chris Gates: The Nazi part of it was almost irrelevant. This dude was only giving [Nazi literature] to cute young boys, little impressionable, thirteen-year-olds who were runaways. Biscuit was always so respectful and gentle about his sexuality, but he had a real problem with some of the folks around who were chicken hawks, who were targeting the really young kids at the shows. And this guy looked like a chicken hawk.

Tim Kerr: Biscuit saw the guy standing in the crowd, and he pointed him out, and he said to the crowd, "Hey, that guy down there is a Nazi. That's guy's trouble. There he is. Fuck him up." And standing by him was this smart-ass kid who had ruined so many places for us. And he was smirking and *Sieg heil!*–ing us, which pissed me off. I said something like, "Yeah, and there's Justin too. He's part of it" or "Get 'em." Then boom—we went into our song "No." And it was like throwing meat to a bunch of dogs. Everybody was trying to beat up this guy.

John Slate: I was way in the back. The Nazi guy looked like [actor] Paul Bartel in a beret, and he was lucky. I prefer peaceful resolutions, but racists deserve everything that's coming to them.

Bill Anderson: I was on stage left. The Nazi guy was undoubtedly an asshole, but I hate a mob worse than anything. I felt like [Big Boys' roadie] Jim Straightedge and I were the only people in the entire room who saw what was going on and tried to stop it. A brief whirlwind of violent insanity. I ushered the Nazi guy out—he looked dazed and glad to be alive. I wouldn't have cared if one guy went up to him and started something, but it was a melee.

> "This is what anarchy's all about. We decide what's right and wrong, not the rest of society," singer Randy (Biscuit) Turner said after the band finished the song during which the fight occurred.
>
> CYNTHIA BRODT AND HELEN MORONEY, *AUSTIN AMERICAN-STATESMAN*, CIRCA SEPTEMBER 1984

Tim Kerr: Afterward, I remember sitting in the hallway on the floor and just feeling sick to my stomach. And Glenn [Danzig] told me, "Aw, that shit happens all the time in New Jersey!"

Steve Anderson (Toxic Shock, Scratch Acid): I had the unenviable bad luck to be in the room after the show when the band met to decide its fate. I was crushed.

Tim Kerr: It was really disturbing that what happened happened, and it was really disturbing that Biscuit absolutely would not admit that he'd said, "Fuck him up." It was just that whole thing of not wanting to take on the responsibility. That was the straw that broke the camel's back. I'm really proud of all that the Big Boys were saying. But I thought, "Jesus, I just want to do something and not have to worry about taking any kind of responsibility at all."

Chris Gates: What happened that night was a shame. [But] the main reason the Big Boys broke up was lack of money. Like, if we would have been making enough money to afford hotel rooms a few nights a week or be able to pay our rent while we were on tour, so we wouldn't have to give up our houses, maybe it wouldn't have been so bad. Biscuit's rent was only one hundred bucks a month, but we were living on *five dollars a day*. He was worried about how he was going to keep his house while he was gone. Yes, the tour was too long, but there were all these stressors.

Gary Floyd: It was very sad . . . very, very sad.

Paul Crow Willis (Agony Column): It was like the whole scene was starting to implode. The Big Boys had always been the glue. Things were certainly different after that.

The Big Boys broke up that night, but the scene did not implode. In fact, Kerr and Gates formed the astonishing bloozobilly group Poison 13, which would become nearly as influential as Big Boys. One ironic footnote to this part of the story emerged in Austin later that year, as skinheads began wearing more bandanas and plaid. On the surface, this may have been a nod to Suicidal Tendencies, the Los Angeles hardcore punk band who connected with cholo culture and broke MTV with their 1983 masterpiece "Institutionalized." But this new/old style also may have inadvertently connected Chicano punks like Roger to some of the Mexican American culture he had ignored as a youth in Vidor.

In any case, violent skinheads continued to drift in and out of Texas, attacking my friends and ruining shows, but neither the KKK nor the Hammer Skins established a foothold in the Austin punk scene. In the early nineties, I interviewed Black Flag singer Henry Rollins, who had seen racist skinheads invade punk scenes across the United States. He told me that a lot of these white supremacists eventually ended up fucking with the wrong person. He told a story about a skinhead who knocked down a kid in a mosh pit in California. The kid got up and left to get his gang brothers. When they returned, they grabbed the skinhead, took him behind a 7-Eleven, and put a bullet in his head.

Tim Kerr: In the late eighties, Redd Kross came and played at the Continental Club. These three skinhead kids sneak in through the back door and start doing their dancing, parting the crowd, and making everyone get out of their way. When one of them came by me, I stuck my foot out and tripped him. When he came back around, he pushed me, so I kicked him in the balls. Then his friend jumped me, but by that time, the whole club was like, "Oh, Tim's in a fight!" So they pulled us apart and this, that, and the other.

Later on, in the mid-1990s, I'm standing at Emo's, and there's two really big guys on either side of me. They're drinking those huge beers, right? And I get this feeling they're staring at me. I look up at them and, you know, I grin. And the guy bends down and says, in this Texas drawl, "Ah remember you!"

He keeps staring at me, then he says, "You remember that kid you kicked at the Continental Club?"

And I thought, "Oh my God, I'm going to get killed."

The guy stood there for another minute. Then he smiled and said, "Ah probably deserved it."

6 | "I HATE MYSELF"

In the middle-1980s, it seemed like every punk in Austin—straight, gay, Black, white, and Latino—loved the Offenders, the fiercest hardcore band in town. Chicano rights activist Carlos Lowry made their posters, and the skinheads wreaked havoc at their shows. Unlike the art students in the first wave of Austin punk, the Offenders were working-class army brats from Killeen. And they roared. What they lacked in versatility, they made up with speed. The Offenders were one of the first US groups to weld hardcore to heavy metal, the only subcultural form of rock that was whiter than punk. Their fans wore Iron Maiden and Motörhead T-shirts, the first I'd ever seen. But some Black influences animated their classist rage: guitarist Tony Johnson had always been obsessed with Jimi Hendrix, and, quite improbably, the Offenders covered the Supremes' "You Keep Me Hanging On," with singer J. J. Jacobson flipping the pronouns and transforming a desperate soul classic into an agonized cuck anthem. This was grievance.

"The Offenders were good at distilling really large ideas into one-liners," remembers Butthole Surfers drummer Teresa Taylor. "'I Hate Myself' was profound. I could not believe that someone had condensed everything I was starting to feel into one line: "I . . . hate . . . myself!'"

Their sound was epitomized by one of their gig posters: a cartoon close-up of a studded, raised fist. With "I Hate Myself," the Offenders—a group of angry white men—evoked a classic dichotomy in punk. Bands like the Clash pointed a finger at the ills of the world. Bands like the Offenders pointed a finger at themselves: *We are the problem.*

Jeff Smith: The Offenders were at the nexus of hardcore and punk. Other people made the money, but they made the music. They were harder than hard.

Carlos Lowry: The Offenders were all from Killeen. Not necessarily working-class, but they didn't fit that mold of RTF students.

Pat Doyle: The Offenders first started playing together in 1978. Mikey [Donaldson] was the brains behind it. He was a big Kiss fan when he was a little kid, but when punk hit, he was just discovering all this stuff. He had a knack for writing songs that had a real heavy edge to them. Tony was the old-school, Hendrix-era guitar hero. He never played in a band before he got into the Offenders, so his timing was sort of unique and self-taught. And Tony was a real character too. The way he looked—you just never forgot that face. He kind of added the mystique and the flash. And I just wanted to be around cool people and talk to musicians. I was the one who was picking up all the equipment, making sure the van was running and getting the oil changed.

Before we got a singer, Davy Jones from the Ideals was sitting in with us until we could find somebody. He had this friend Mick Buck, who had spent a year in London chasing around the Clash. Davy convinced him to move to Killeen and try singing for us, the Clash being the common denominator. Tony loved the Clash.

Carlos Lowry: On the first Offenders 45, the band were more like hippies trying to be punks.

Pat Doyle: Eventually, in 1980, I moved to Austin, with no prospects whatsoever. I just crashed on Davy's couch for a few weeks. Mikey came down to Austin last, but eventually, the whole band ended up at Davy's house. After that, Mick's and the band's musical interests began to diverge. Rank and File came to town and stayed in 1981, and that was the same year Black Flag came to town. Mikey had been listening to a lot of Circle Jerks and Dead Kennedys and liked it way more than the first-wave punk stuff. Once, when the band got together to practice, Mikey proposed a couple of ideas that were real fast and loud, and we proceeded to get drunk on tequila and argue with each other about them. A few days later, Mick told us he was done with the band.

Carlos Lowry: J. J. was a street punk. And very young. But there was an incredible transformation of the band once J. J. became the lead singer.

Pat Doyle: My first impression of J. J. was that he was a little kid. Just another one of the fans. Mikey brought him into the fold, and he said, "We need to get this guy; he's bringing a lot of energy." And it just immediately clicked. J. J. was the streetwise, runaway kid that had a fistful of anger and a little bit of hell channeled into his delivery and stage presence.

Teresa Taylor: Onstage, J. J. was scary. In person, he was a jokester, such a happy guy. I was talking to him one day outside of their practice space. He had shaved his head and his eyebrows too. And then it started raining heavily. J. J. said, "Ah, shit! I got water in my eyes!" So I said, "That's why God gave you eyebrows."

Pat Doyle: J. J. built up a lot of self-confidence as a singer, but I think his hostility to societal norms was well-established before he met us. He would talk about how his dad threw him out and how he deserved it. He felt like all the shit that happened to him was his own fault. Little did I know that he'd been sexually abused. I didn't know that until long after the band had broken up. That can make for a fucked-up childhood. And a fucked-up adulthood.

Carlos Lowry: What did the Dicks, the Offenders, and MDC have in common? They were all hardcore, and they were all angry. By the time the Offenders got bigger, it was really speed metal, really thrash, really another evolutionary stage of hardcore. There's definitely a left-wing, antiauthoritarian thing in the Offenders—but it's less political, more personal.

Pat Doyle: Nobody in the Dicks and nobody in the Offenders had gone to college. I think we were all either working or trying to find a job or barely working or starving. I was literally living off one meal a day. I don't feel like we were angry. J. J.'s lyrics didn't leave space for much interpretation. "Fight Back" is a universal theme of resistance; "Like Father Like Son"—the familiar cycle of family and societal violence; "Face Down in the Dirt" . . . these are raw proclamations of power that strike a chord with anyone who's ever had their oxen gored. I think the anger came more from

J. J. The band just brought the power and the glory behind it. The speed that we were playing was kind of a competition amongst us to see what we could pull off that would still sound like music and not noise. Politically, I've always had the same outlook that I have today: shit sucks, and next year is gonna be worse than this year. Back then, I was looking at the possibility of getting drafted or of crazy Reagan firing off a couple of nukes to show his balls to everybody.

> We've never been a violent band, and Austin is not usually a violent scene, though it has happened. We had a gig at Sue-Sue's last week, and everyone knew each other, there was all this fake fighting—everyone was having a blast. I can see that if someone walked in and saw a big fat skinhead jumping up and down on a tall skinny skinhead they'd think it was too violent. But it would only be Chris Gates (of the Big Boys) and Straightedge (a Big Boys roadie) having a good time.
>
> MIKEY DONALDSON OF THE OFFENDERS,
> *AUSTIN AMERICAN-STATESMAN*, CIRCA AUGUST 1984

Larry Seaman: Of course, the irony is that this more aggressive punk was being played by some of the sweetest people I knew. Tony Johnson of the Offenders—just a soft-spoken, *nice* guy.

Laura Croteau: The Offenders were unlike anything I had ever heard before. They weren't straight, three-chord punk: Tony's guitar leads were metal as fuck, no one else played bass the way Mikey played, Pat was a powerhouse drummer, and J. J. had a desperation onstage that you could almost taste. I never saw a crowd react to a band the way they reacted to the Offenders. I wanted the *world* to experience what the Austin audience was hearing.

Carlos Lowry: The Offenders came out of early heavy metal, like Deep Purple and Mountain—that kind of world. And they weren't college kids, so they had less friends who were artists to do their artwork for them! [*laughs*] So I did the art for their first 45 and their first album. I had the skills to prepare the art to send to the printer, but I had the sensibility to not make it look like I wanted to compete with the latest Electric Light Orchestra album cover. When I did the album artwork, everyone liked it, but Tony wanted the sky to look more like a heavy metal album.

Tony Johnson plays guitar for the Offenders, encouraged by Mark "Chico" McCullough at left, Liberty Lunch, Austin, July 1984.

Teresa Taylor: [Buttholes guitarist] Paul Leary had a thing about Tony Johnson. He said, "Watch his big toe when he's playing a really intense solo." And I looked, and Tony's big toe came up through a hole in his boot. He'd worn a hole in his boot from playing guitar so intensely. Paul just said, "That's a really good guitar player."

For many years, I made a point of describing Houston as a hell on earth, an inexplicable petrochemical wasteland. Houston punks might have agreed, but they had more pressing problems: At least three local groups recorded songs protesting the 1977 police murder of Joe Campos Torres in a bayou on the edge of the city. The best one was the bleak, spine-tingling "Teaching You the Fear" by a protohardcore band called Really Red.

Like those in many US cities, Houston punks were broke and scattered across a vast junkspace metropolis. The city was cursed by a lot of the same problems that bedeviled hotbeds of underground music like Los Angeles and New York, which begs the question: If the cityscape had been even one ampere less apocalyptic, would the Houston punk scene have coughed up even more great punk music?

Brit Jones (skateboarder): Houston was a very racist, violent scene in the 1980s. I grew up in a lily-white, superconservative, racist small town thirty miles outside of Houston, and I grew up a superconservative, racist, homophobic kid. My punk experience opened my eyes to the ugliness of racism and homophobia, and it changed my worldview for the better.

Joe Nick Patoski: I first saw one of the Houston punk groups when I went to the Rock Island, which was a terrible club in a terrible part of town. The band was Really Red, and they were very angry. But they had a right to be angry. Texans know a few things about adversity. We know a few things about getting beat down.

Bob Weber (Really Red, Culturcide): Our first gig was at this icehouse outside of Houston. There were about two or three people there. We got paid with a plate of barbecue.

When we started out, we called ourselves "new wave" because there wasn't any other word for what we were doing. But we had a hardcore sensibility. I mean, we'd play shows with a band like [popular Houston new wavers] the Judy's, but it didn't really fit.

Brit Jones: In Houston, it often seemed that people went to shows to fight instead of enjoying the bands. I can only think of a few shows I attended where a huge fight *didn't* break out. Skins on punks, punks on skins, skins on skins, et cetera. It got worse when high school football players found out about shows and would show up simply to beat up punk rockers.

Bob Weber: [In Really Red,] the whole idea was that we'd save all the money we got from playing shows and put that into recording the band. Our thing was, "We're not gonna sign to a major label; we're not gonna sell out." But that was never really an option anyway—there wasn't much [record company] interest in what we were doing.

We did four tours, and one of those was in the Midwest in 1983. We called it the Cowpunk Tour—that was our lame attempt at marketing ourselves, at trying to set ourselves apart from the LA and San Francisco and New York punk scenes.

Some of our best shows were the Rock Against Reagan shows. We achieved our height in '83 or so. By 1984, I don't know—maybe our lives were getting too complicated. I was getting less interested in the music and hardcore punk, and [singer] Ronnie "U-Ron" Bond was drinking a lot. It was getting dark. We thought the world was gonna end. We thought there was gonna be a nuclear war between the Russia and the US.

Besides Really Red and the Dicks, the Texas band who challenged the US status quo most directly was MDC. They can also take some credit for focusing punks on corporate corruption: The group initially insisted their name was short for Millions of Dead Cops, then later for Multi-Death Corporations, and later still for Metal Devil Cokes. Before all of that, they were known as the Stains, just another Devo-influenced punk band, scrounging for gigs at Raul's. Accounts differ, but after the band discovered hardcore, three things certainly happened in quick succession: They changed their name to MDC, they recorded an astounding self-titled debut album, and they got the hell out of Austin. Some were glad to see them go.

Dave Dictor: When I first got into the scene, I was into Devo. I had one of those plastic suits, and I went to the Armadillo World Headquarters. I liked the Romantics. [*sings*] "That's what I like about you!" I liked Patti Smith, Elvis Costello. Talking Heads. So I didn't come out of the womb like Sid Vicious.

Pat Doyle: Dictor wore a Devo hazmat suit with wraparounds—Deadheads turned punks. Dave was the last to go hardcore. Al, Mikey, and Ron had committed to it months before—Dave was a lover, not a fighter. He used to *try* and break up fights all the time, ha ha, while the Big Boys were real brawlers.

Chris Gates: At one point, the Stains were just Dave and Ron. Then they got Al to move down from New York to play drums. Still didn't have a bass player. So they got Mikey Donaldson of the Offenders to play bass with them. At the first or second rehearsal, they're learning the songs, and it's boring as fuck for Al and Mikey. These slow plodding songs. They take a break, and Dave and Ron go outside to smoke pot.

As a joke, Mikey and Al start trying to see how fast they can play the songs before they fall apart. And Ron and Dave come back, and they [say], "Oh, that's *cool*."

Pat Doyle: I don't say this lightly, but Mikey Donaldson was pretty much responsible for MDC becoming hardcore. MDC were the Stains, and they were medium-tempo punk rock. Mikey got into the band to help them put out their new record, and they came out with this blazing fast suite of stuff. They sped up their song "John Wayne Was a Nazi" first, and then they just went from there.

Chris Gates: Sometime after that, the Big Boys were playing a show at the Cathay de Grande in LA, and the Stains were with us, at the show. And this lowrider car pulls up, with four East LA Hispanic dudes and this six-foot-four, three-hundred-pound, muscle-bound white dude that was part of their crew. And they get out, and they're asking where the Texas Stains are. They are the LA band called the Stains. They walk over to Dave and Ron and say, "We're the Stains—find another name." When the Texas Stains came back to Texas, they were calling themselves something else.

Dave Dictor: We went out to California and played some shows—one of them was with the Los Angeles Stains, so the show was billed as the Battle of the Stains. We knew we had to change our name—we were thinking Bloody Stains or Bloody Cops. Then Buxf said, "Millions of Dead Cops."

Teresa Taylor: The Butthole Surfers loved the Stains. But we thought Millions of Dead Cops was a *badass name*!

Cindy Melbie: I remember going to Rock Island in Houston with the Stains. We passed one of those railroad bridges, which are for trains, but not for cars. And there was this graffiti on it that said, "No War, No KKK, No Fascist USA." Dave Dictor saw it. The next time I saw the Stains, they were Millions of Dead Cops, and they were singing "No war, no KKK, no fascist USA." But Dave was only singing "KK"—just two *K*'s. So I told him, "You gotta sing three *K*'s."

Carlos Lowry: For MDC, I did the first single, "John Wayne Was a Nazi," and then the cover of the first album, *Millions of Dead Cops*, that image of the line of cops in riot gear. It's based on a mural by [Austin Chicano artist]

The Offenders, UT Photography Department photo studio, Austin, spring 1985. *From left:* Tony Johnson (RIP); Pat Doyle; J. J. Jacobson (RIP); and, *seated*, Mikey Donaldson (RIP). Donaldson also played with the Stains/MDC and was a catalyst for their evolution into a hardcore punk band.

Raúl Valdez. I designed the back cover, too, but Buxf did the picture of the guy who's half-KKK, half-cop.

Dave Dictor: To record our first album, we went to this place called Earth and Sky Studio in Houston. A guy there heard a tape of our songs, and he said, "I can do justice to this." Hippie guy. He got us such a good sound. When it was finished, I was surprised—I didn't know we were that good. And I never saw that engineer again.

When it came out, everybody loved it. Black Flag loved it; Dead Kennedys loved it. We went from being one of the top twenty bands in Austin to being one of the top ten bands in the US.

Yuri Campbell (fan): Up in Akron, Ohio, where my cohort had little knowledge of the history of the band, that *Cops* LP seemed to herald a ferocity for personalized politics that no other band had. It wasn't arty; it wasn't pogoing or new-wavy. It was the anger of someone that had been kicked while down and who seemed to reject everything mainstream. I used to have a small poster that depicted John Wayne in front of a pile of dead Native American bodies. The perspective that prompted that was kindled by MDC. It seemed next-level. Texas punk had that mix of unhinged derring-do, arty personal expression, and courage. I arrived in Austin in the fall of '88, and immediately, my love of the Dicks, Really Red, Big Boys, and, yes, MDC came into much sharper focus in the context of a prevalent culture that was a real threat. My eyes were popped right the fuck open.

Dotty Farrell: When I was still in South Florida, we loved MDC. That first album—*Millions of Dead Cops*—we couldn't believe how fucking amazingly great that was. They were gods on a pedestal for us. So when I came to Austin, I went to see MDC at Nightlife, and nobody was there. And I thought, "This is so weird." But then I found out later from Buxf Parrott that the band were all speed dealers, and they ripped people off.

Teresa Taylor: When MDC moved to San Francisco, we thought, "We want to go to San Francisco." Gibby had a really good memory for phone numbers, so he called Dave Dictor and said, "We're coming to San Francisco—where can we stay?" And Dave said, "Well, we all live in the [former Hamm's brewery then known as the] Vats."

Then, what we found out was that MDC was really political. And we weren't at all. We went to a taco place, and King ordered cheese. MDC saw him putting dairy on his taco, and they said, "Look, King, you can either be part of the problem or part of the solution."

Dave Dictor: It was different when we got out of Austin and started playing all over the US. California was scary. SF Skins and Suicidal Tendencies fans and gangs and all sorts of things. People *Sieg heil!*-ing me when we played "John Wayne Was a Nazi." We played with the Dicks at the Olympic Auditorium in LA. It was scary for Gary Floyd. It was scary for me.

Teresa Taylor: The Butthole Surfers got pulled over *all the time* when we had our Winnebago. And we'd say, "Well, we're in a band." And the cops would ask, "What's your band called?" Oh no.

So I don't know how MDC handled that situation . . .

Back in Texas, Houston's Dirty Rotten Imbeciles, a.k.a. DRI, were pushing ninety-mile-a-minute hardcore to its limits. Tim Kerr remembers seeing the band set up to play and then unfurl a six-foot scroll of paper, which spilled off the edge of the stage. It was their set list. Around the same time, the school of all-ages hardcore reached its logical conclusion with the youngest Austin punk band ever: Crotch Rot.

These pioneers of hardcore didn't last long in Texas, but they flourished elsewhere. In 1983, DRI followed MDC and moved out to San Francisco. Both bands developed international reputations and are still touring today. Crotch Rot drummer Felix Griffin played with DRI for a time, while singer Rob Buford dropped out of the punk scene, went into recovery, and is today a practicing attorney in Austin.

7 | FREETHINKERS

For some Texas bands, punk simply didn't go far enough. While others thought of punk as a sort of wild freedom, these bands stretched that freedom into perversity, playing slow songs instead of fast ones, florid warbles instead of expressionistic yelps, or long horrible drones instead of short, sharp shocks. By 1982, punk had compressed itself into a rubber band ball of rules and norms, although not all of us noticed it at first. In England, the freethinking bands who broke through and pressed ahead were called postpunk. In Austin and Dallas, they just seemed . . . contrary.

Radio Free Europe were the ur-Raul's band in one sense: They were mostly RTF students, with compelling side gigs and conflicting interests. They used synthesizers, tape effects, and guitars to create shrieking noise and the occasional song. Cofounder Brian Hansen was also a promising young director whose student film *Speed of Light* had attracted the attention of cult filmmaker (and future Academy Award winner) Jonathan Demme. Keyboardist Dan Puckett was a member of the Huns, while bassist Neil Ruttenberg wore more hats than any of them: He also played with F-Systems, worked at the scene hangout Inner Sanctum, and, as the Reverend Neil X, was a DJ for student radio station KUT, inspiring and fostering the first wave of Austin punk. Seen from the outside, Radio Free Europe might have seemed like an underground supergroup. But the band ended in tragedy.

Dan Puckett (Huns, Radio Free Europe): Radio Free Europe was formed in late 1978 by Brian Hanson, RIP, and Stephen Miller, after they taped a Huns show. To buy synthesizer kits, they borrowed money from a roommate, Dennis Parker, who worked on an oil rig in the Gulf. They began by taping songs on a four-track tape recorder in an old fire station on Blanco. They were strongly influenced by Chrome and Throbbing Gristle. "Borrow More Money" came from those sessions. Since I shared their enthusiasm for Chrome and TG, they recruited me in early 1979. Among other things, we recorded a cover of [the Monkees'] "(I'm Not Your) Stepping Stone."

Lynn Keller: Brian Hansen was like a scientist, and then an artist and a filmmaker, but he was from *Fargo*. He was a really interesting character. His film *Speed of Light* kind of questioned the JFK assassination. He ended up meeting Jonathan Demme, because Demme liked Brian's film.

Neil Ruttenberg: Brian and Steve just wanted to play noise. Dan and I were more into structure. I mean, I liked Throbbing Gristle, but I wanted something more like [British postpunk group] Magazine or Siouxsie and the Banshees. I was in the group for about six months.

Dan Puckett: Neil's song "Alien Day" was the closest we got to pop.

Neil Ruttenberg: "Alien Day" was recorded in someone's living room. RFE was mostly influenced by German electronic bands like Neu!, Can, with a little King Crimson. One day, we were supposed to rehearse for the taping of our single. When I walked in, Brian said to me, "We just dropped acid. Do you want some?"

Louis Black: Radio Free Europe once said they would play a forty-minute version of [Iron Butterfly's song] "In-A-Gadda-Da-Vida" at Raul's. But after ten minutes, they didn't know what to do anymore, and they walked off. It was hilarious.

Neil Ruttenberg: [The "In-A-Gadda-Da-Vida" cover] was all about a performance. It ended up getting us banned from Raul's. I guess Joseph didn't like it. *The whole idea* was to walk away from the stage after ten minutes. Brian had this ancient drum machine—it sounded like a game of *Pong*. Nobody really stayed. Nobody got it.

We were way, way ahead of our time.

Jeff Tartakov (manager, Daniel Johnston): Radio Free Europe got banned from Raul's, and I thought that was great. It wasn't because of any lyrics—it was just because of their *music*.

Neil Ruttenberg: And then I left because I wanted something else.

Lynn Keller: Brian Hansen moved up to New York. When David Byrne went on his honeymoon, Brian was staying at his house. Then Brian contracted meningitis. And basically, he just died on the floor of Byrne's house. It was horrible.

At the first rehearsal, in 1982, a beginner guitar player invited himself into the group. Then the singer started refusing to sing. To hear them tell it, Scratch Acid didn't know what they were doing, but that's another way of saying they were working intuitively. They may not have known what they were, but they were certain they were *not* a hardcore band.

David Yow, the group's eventual singer, was a great screamer: lunatic, surprising, and strange. His good friend David William Sims was quiet, imposing, and a brutish bass player. On guitar, Brett Bradford added a serrated, lysergic edge. Drummer Rey Washam was some sort of percussive savant. Scratch Acid songs were slower and weirder, but at first, it was hard to articulate why their shows were so unhinged and delirious. In fact, they were breaking with punk rock tradition—and good old Texas anti-intellectualism—by daring to think of their music as an artistic project.

One of the underlying tenets of our scene was that one could never admit to aspirations of greatness—that would be putting on airs. Texans may be loud, but they know they're *supposed* to be humble. Like the Butthole Surfers, Scratch Acid didn't talk about their ambitions, but they were driven by them. They crafted their sound out of influences from far away (namely Australia's Birthday Party) and beyond the pale (especially the prehistoric beast known as Led Zeppelin). They crafted their records too: Those cellos on their debut EP were a shock! Yet much of their inspiration remained obscure. Were Yow's gruesome and gynophobic lyrics a nod to serial killers like Henry Lee Lucas or Tobe Hooper's film *The Texas Chain Saw Massacre*? Where on earth did the harrowing, Gothic quality of their songs come from? Who knows?

What's more certain is that the band flamed on as live performers in 1983, released a startling, original debut record in 1984, and were blowing minds across the United States by 1986. *Spin* magazine devoted several features to them—one of which included the first photograph I'd ever sold to a national magazine. Out in Seattle, an astonishing photographer named Charles Peterson, future Sub Pop Records cofounder Bruce Pavitt, and the young Kurt Cobain were all devoted Scratch Acid fans. SA were actually well-mannered fellows, but perhaps the band resonated with people on the left and right coasts because their violent sound and lyrics seemed of a piece with Texas killers like Lucas or UT tower sniper Charles Whitman. Like many other Austin punks, Scratch Acid were keenly aware that much of the world thinks of Texans as occasionally literate, trigger-happy mutants, so they played with that perception. Butthole singer Gibby Haynes was still doing the same in 2020 when he poetically remarked to a reporter for Phawker.com that Whitman was "the wrong guy with the right rifle."

David Yow: Did I ever think to myself, "I've gone too far?" I don't recall that *ever* happening. But there was a time when I was living with my parents again, and I had written some lyrics for Toxic Shock, and one of them was "I wish that my father would hurry up and die so I can get his money!"

I came home one day, and everything that I'd ever given to my mom was on my bed. She had found those Toxic Shock lyrics. She said, "David, I have seen *The Exorcist*, but I didn't think anything that evil existed on earth."

And I loved my mom so much. [*his voice cracks*] I couldn't stand that I had hurt her that much. I said, "Mom, it's just a joke! I don't want Pa to die!" And I really, *really* had to work to win my mom back.

Rey Washam (Scratch Acid, Big Boys): Scratch Acid was a sissy, dress-up band.

David Yow: David Sims and I just had a lot in common. It's hard to put my finger on it exactly. But we had a cat named David too.

[When I was in Toxic Shock,] David Sims told me all his friends were in bands, but he wasn't. He was depressed about it. So when I invited Steve Anderson, Rey Washam and Brett Bradford over to first see if we could play together, David just set up his amp and guitar in the room and started playing along with us. Nobody told him to leave, so . . . he was in the group.

Rey Washam: I thought we sucked. We didn't know how we sounded, but we thought we sucked.

David Yow: After a while, Steve Anderson didn't want to sing at practice because he said that would blow out his voice before the show! We unceremoniously played a show without him, and he was really hurt. We were besties, but then he was really mad at me. But the same thing had happened with Toxic Shock. I think we only played one show with Steve singing. That's a big part of Steve's résumé: "Joined a band with David Yow and got kicked out of it after one show."

Maria Cotera: I met Steve right after [he left Scratch Acid], when he was starting the Cry Babies. We started dating—well, if you can call going to the Circle K for twin chili cheese dogs "dating." So just like he did with every single one of his girlfriends, he would complain about Scratch Acid. "Those *pussies*—they couldn't handle me!" [*laughs*] He would complain about how they couldn't recognize his *genius*. All of that was performance because he was still very good friends with them, and with David Yow in particular.

Rey Washam: I think David Yow is tone-deaf. He can't sing notes. Brett just plays very simply, but he really pours his heart and soul into it. David Sims is the heart of the band—he keeps everything on track. Without David Sims, Brett and I would both go off, lose a wheel, and end up in the ditch.

David Yow: David Sims was part of the Chris Gates school of songwriting. Chris told us one time, "Just take a riff from one of your favorite band's songs and change one note." One time, David had a new song for the Jesus Lizard, and it was a riff from the Bad Brains. He knew exactly what he was doing. I said to the rest of the band, "You guys can play the song, but it's gonna be an instrumental because I'm not gonna sing it." I don't think we ended up using that song.

Maria Cotera: There were so many psychedelics rolling around the scene, and in some cases, the bands themselves were distributing them. It was a really big part of that scene.

Tarbox Kiersted: The rumor was that Scratch Acid would be giving away a hit of LSD to the first hundred people through the door.

Brett Bradford (Scratch Acid): It was our first show and the first time I'd made a Scratch Acid poster for a factual show. Prior to this, there was a year's worth of posters we made for fictitious shows, like ZZ Top and Scratch Acid at the Frank Erwin Center.

As far as the LSD is concerned, there were twenty-five squares of blotter, and I halved them into triangles. The twofold intent being that it would go a lot farther, but much more importantly to me . . . I didn't want anyone

Brett Bradford and David Yow of Scratch Acid play a garage party, Austin, spring 1985. *In the crowd:* Caroline Tinkle, Sally King, Tim Kerr, Kelly Lynn, Frank Kozik, Adriane "Ash" Shown, Bill Anderson, and Mike Carroll.

to get *too* weird or freak the fuck out. I gave them out with a smile, free of charge, to the first fifty people who said, "Yes, I would like one." Not everybody did, but there were no leftovers. Didn't you get one?

David Yow: I really loved the Birthday Party. I was so taken with the way Nick Cave sang that I think that I—unintentionally—copied [him] too much. But I think that that's normal and healthy if you are inspired by someone's art.

[When the Birthday Party played in Dallas,] David and I flew up there to see the show. We actually walked to the airport in Austin and almost missed the plane. Then, at the show, David and I decided to act like we were magazine journalists, so we could meet the band. I was the "writer" and David was the "photographer." And David was standing behind Nick Cave when he popped the flash on the camera. Nick Cave turned all the way around without a word and stared at David because he knew David hadn't taken a photo and didn't know what he was doing.

But just before we were going to interview them, they started kicking everyone out of the club. So Nick Cave and the other guys said, "We're going to eat tacos—why don't you come with us?" But we couldn't because then we would have missed our ride home.

Adriane "Ash" Shown: There was a lot of finesse in Scratch Acid, a lot more sophistication than 90 percent of the bands that were in Austin or coming through Austin. Then, of course, there was the theatricality and the possibility of mayhem, that element of danger. Because Yow was playing with that.

Teresa Taylor: I remember one night I was sitting on the loading dock outside of Voltaire's Basement, when a bunch of us decided to climb the construction crane across the street. I had a calking gun, and I was snapping it at everyone. We all climbed up this makeshift ladder to the top. All of a sudden, David Yow starts walking backward out onto the arm of the crane. This thing was, like, fifteen stories high. We were all fucked up. But I had a moment of clarity, and I thought, "This is exactly how *really bad shit* happens! When people are tiptoeing backward on a fucking crane in the sky." I was scared to death. And Yow didn't seem to care. He was testing which way it would go. "This is gonna go either one way or the other." And it seemed like he wasn't that concerned about which way it went.

We thought, "Whoa, dude, you're punk rock." He was a bird on a wire.

Life was cheaper then.

Sally King: Scratch Acid had gotten better and better in an almost scary way. They were good when they got together, but after they had played for a year or two, they were scary good. I think part of it had to do with the songwriting and the lyrics. Their songwriting was beautiful and . . . stupid. [*laughs*] I remember a really incredible Scratch Acid show at the Colony. They just melted your face off, they were so good. David Yow was writhing around in 100-degree heat on the asphalt, with no shirt on.

Karen Ruth Getchell: David Yow is made out of gristle. He's a really physical performer. But I've never seen a dark side to him. He loves life.

Rey Washam: When we recorded that first record, and we listened to the playback of the first song, we said, "*That's* what we sound like?!" We listened to the tapes a lot. We didn't know what it was, but it didn't suck. Then people started saying they liked it, and *Spin* magazine said they wanted to write about it. But I thought that was probably because they wanted to laugh at us.

Laura Croteau: Both Stacy [Cloud] and I were very proud of how Scratch Acid were received. I was not involved in the production of their first EP—that was Stacy's baby. I became involved in the promotion and distribution phase. They got interviewed in *Spin* magazine—it was a few pages, with big color photos, and that felt like success.

Rey Washam: Tim Kerr came up to me one night and said, "Hey, do you want to be in the Big Boys?" I was in shock. And he just said, "Well, let me know tomorrow!"

I went home and just cried. I knew I couldn't turn down this chance. But I knew that once I joined the Big Boys, I'd never get to see them play again, at least not from the audience. And the guys in Scratch Acid were my best friends. I knew they would be really fucking bummed when I told them. And when I told them, they were really fucking bummed.

After the Big Boys broke up, Scratch Acid welcomed me back into the band with open arms. I don't really know why.

But after my time in the Big Boys, I brought professionalism to Scratch Acid. I wanted to take it to the next level. I was practicing all the time. And Brett wasn't into that. He'd say, "I can't practice because I'm going *fishing*." Or he'd make a mistake onstage, and he'd say, "That's okay—it's *punk rock*."

I think David and David and I were leaving Brett behind.

I started to understand Scratch Acid better by photographing them. At one show, Bradford was wearing tie-dye and a puka-shell necklace; it was the first time I noticed how trippy their music could be. So I gave the camera a woozy tilt as I made a picture of him. Then, in 1986, I met the band in central Austin to take a group photo of them. I shot a few rolls of film, but nothing seemed to work until we clambered down into a little limestone creek. Down there, posed under scraggly cedar trees next to primordial pools of stagnant green water, Scratch Acid stood around in their disheveled clothes and wild uncombed hair, and they fit right in. They looked so native to that landscape that I think vines and moss would have started creeping over them if I'd turned my back for a moment. The band finally made sense to me—as part of a long history of verdant, drippy, Texas psychedelic music stretching back to the 13th Floor Elevators and beyond.

They broke up a year later.

Glass Eye were a nerdy anomaly in Austin underground music. Instead of torn T-shirts, they wore shirts with actual collars. They were less post-punk than pre-alternative, their sound a wash of inflatable bass, wispy synthesizer, and hard rock beats. Singer-guitarist Kathy McCarty was in a first-wave Raul's band and then in the beloved but primitive Buffalo Gals. Before he moved to Texas, bassist Brian Beattie was a founding member of the Berkeley punk band Fang. And even though they loved the Butthole Surfers, Glass Eye were themselves way more politely provocative. They blended dissonance with melody, art rock with folk, and then added a dash of AC/DC. They played like kids who wanted to use every one of the sixty-four colors in the crayon box.

Kathy McCarty: [In the late 1970s,] the music on the radio was pretty shitty, and I thought I could do better. Songs like [Paul Anka's] "(You're) Having My Baby" and [Starland Vocal Band's] "Afternoon Delight." It seemed poorly crafted, and I thought I could do something with more lasting value.

Stella Wier (Glass Eye): I was part of an artier crowd—I ran around with David Yarritu and Josh Jordan. I didn't go to hardcore shows. I guess I liked the movie *Cabaret*. And then almost everything sprang from my love for the Cure's album *Pornography*. But frankly, I got tired of trying to keep up with that level of pretentiousness—it was exhausting.

[Note: Yarritu later moved to New York and became a member of the English new wave group ABC; Jordan followed and became a photographer who worked with popular dance group Deee-Lite.]

Kathy McCarty: My first band, Sinequan, [was named after] one of the very first prescription antidepressive drugs. That band was like Glass Eye, but more hypnotic and more new wave. It wasn't poppy. We did get to play at Raul's. But then our guitar player told me, "Your songs are terrible, and you need to stop writing songs."

Stella Wier: I can't remember how I met Kathy. Maybe while we were working at Pecan Street Café. I remember thinking she was a little weird. She was still in the Buffalo Gals when I met her, but I only saw them play once. And I did live in the Buffalo Gals warehouse briefly. Kathy came into my little room with a sledgehammer and knocked a hole in the wall, so I would have a window. I taped some plexiglass up over it.

Kathy McCarty: My mom thought it was dangerous hanging around with these scary-looking punks. I said, "Oh no, Mom, they're getting all their aggression out with their music. They're all teddy bears and sweethearts. The *music* is the scariest thing they do." Austin always had the most polite mosh pit. Nobody would ever hit a girl in the breast or gang up on girls to try to get them out of the pit. It was just good, clean fun.

Stella Wier: One day, Kathy said, "Well, we've been thinking about adding a keyboard player. Stella plays piano—let's put Stella in the band."

Chris Gates: I loved Glass Eye. So weird and sparse and *musical* . . .

Stella Wier: In Glass Eye, we were always surprised when we would win Best Avant-Garde Band in *The Austin Chronicle* Music Poll because we just thought we were writing rock music. We weren't trying to be weird when we wrote a song like "Lake of the Moon"—we were making fun of R.E.M. We were just writing what came out of us.

> Glass Eye consists of four true "new music" iconoclasts whose minimalist sound and parsimonious lyrics make their six-song debut effort *Marlo* . . . one of the most gripping independent releases from Texas in recent memory.
>
> JODY DENBERG, *TEXAS MONTHLY*, MAY 1985

Stella Wier: When Glass Eye toured in 1986, we played a little gay bar in New York. Josh Jordan—from my old arty clique—actually came to our show. We played my song where I sing, "I forgive you for not being my boyfriend." And Josh came up to me afterward and said, "Oh, I love that line—'I forgive you for not feeding my orchids.'"

While we were there, David Yarritu got me and Brian into [hip night-club of the moment] Arena, and it was really chichi. David was wearing a diaper and jumping on a trampoline. I saw Matt Dillon being really

Glass Eye, Austin, September 1985. *From left:* Scott Marcus, Kathy McCarty, Stella Wier, Brian Beattie.

mean and yelling at his girlfriend. I don't think I would have liked living in New York.

On the axis of outrage, Stick Men with Ray Guns went further than almost anyone else. They took their name from a white supremacist comic book created by singer Bobby Soxx. Soxx was born Bobby Glenn Calverley and became the notorious front man for early Dallas punk band the Teenage Queers in 1979. Guitarist Clarke Blacker had played with the Nervebreakers and Bag of Wire before forming Stick Men with Soxx in 1981. In a dizzying race to offend everyone on the planet, Stick Men with Ray Guns toyed with homophobia and matricide before launching their most disgusting broadside ever, the blasphemous dirge "Christian Rat Attack." It sounded like Hieronymus Bosch with feedback.

But as with the paintings of Bosch or the films of David Lynch, the horror was laced with humor. For Blacker and others in the Dallas scene who knew him, the Soxx was a joker *and* a troublemaker. Punk rock rewards anyone who can balance between outrage and oblivion, and for a time, the band—who were as musically rigorous as the Soxx was unleashed—stayed on this side of the void. They recorded when they could, but did not tour, partly because Bobby Soxx was, well, hygienically challenged. Somehow, sometime in the late eighties, horror won.

Mike Haskins (Nervebreakers): I met Clarke Blacker in 1976, when we worked for Dallas radio station KCHU. We bonded over our love of sixties garage rock. In 1977, the Nervebreakers needed a bass player, and Clarke stepped up. He also took over our management. He scored us our opening slot for the Ramones that year.

Barry "Kooda" Huebner (Nervebreakers): I didn't care much for Clarke, and we were often at odds, but he had a tenacity and fearlessness in business, a talent that we were lacking. When we heard that the Sex Pistols were coming on tour, he called Stone City Attractions in New York and got us the opening slot for their Dallas show. *Pretty damn ballsy.*

Mike Haskins: After the Pistols date, Clarke bowed out of performing with us onstage. He formed Stick Men with Ray Guns in 1981 with Bobby Soxx. By that time, the Nervebreakers were not active, so we didn't play any shows together. I attended their first show, though, and I was very impressed with their wall of noise and Soxx's command of the stage.

Clarke Blacker (Stick Men with Ray Guns): We played a show in Austin at the Ritz, where the power kept going out. While we were waiting for them to fix the problems, I was leaning against a wall with my guitar, and I noticed the audience was laughing. I look over at Bobby, and he had found this mannequin head. He stuck it on a drumstick, then stuck the drumstick up his butt and started dancing around the stage with the mannequin head bobbing around out of his ass. It was hilarious!

Jeffrey "King" Coffey: Stick Men with Ray Guns hold a special place in my heart. I'm from Fort Worth, and Studio D was where my local punk teen crew would congregate. Stick Men were our band. We'd be in the very front for every show. I realize now how incredibly lucky we were to have Stick Men as the band we saw the most, our de facto house band. "Christian Rat Attack"!

Paul Leary: Butthole Surfers played with Stick Men with Ray Guns at Studio 29 in 1982. Bobby Soxx kicked me in the balls and peed in the monitor speaker. What a great band.

Clarke Blacker: Our bass player was good friends with Gibby—they'd known each other for a few years. The Surfers were years younger than us, and the first time we played in Austin, they got us the job. At the time, there was this local band there called the Stains, but they later morphed into MDC. When we were setting up for the show, the Stains came up to us and said, "Can we use your equipment to play three songs?" And we said, "Fuck no. But if the Surfers want to let you, you can play in between our sets." So they agreed to play three songs. In the middle of their *fourth* song, the Soxx went up and took a leak on the singer's foot. It ended up with the Butthole Surfers having to link arms and hold the people off of us when we played our set because the audience was coming after us. So that's the kind of chaos that could develop around the band.

Paul Leary: I sure do miss Stick Men with Ray Guns. Truly some of the best songs to ever come out of Texas.

Clarke Blacker: I wanted to terrify the audience. I wanted to overwhelm them with this experience, the way I'd been overwhelmed by some music before. [But] there were lots of times where Bobby Beeman and I were just laughing onstage. Who could have taken songs like "Christian Rat Attack" seriously? It was so over the top. It was so *funny*.

John Spath: None of those stories about Bobby Soxx are incorrect. At some point, one of the old punks—it may have been Neal Caldwell from NCM—said to me, "Bobby Soxx is the only punk rocker in Dallas."

I found Bobby to be the nicest guy. I would periodically run around with him, staying up late in the night snorting speed, but not really getting into trouble. He was a wild one. It was nice having a psychopath on your side. He got into some sort of tiff with [first-wave UK punk band] the Stranglers when they played at the Hot Klub. Supposedly he slashed all the tires of their van.

Clarke Blacker: I had to go to the people at the Hot Klub and assure them that Bobby would behave himself. They were terrified of him because he'd smashed a bottle on the head of one of the Stranglers. Bobby was not afraid of being hurt. That makes someone very dangerous.

> Stick Men with Ray Guns . . . play a kind of music that is largely ignored by Dallas radio stations. Music described as invigorating, raw, frenetic, angry, evil, blasphemous social commentary.
>
> TV NEWS REPORTER KAY VINSON, WFAA NEWS 8, DALLAS, CIRCA 1984

Clarke Blacker: Everybody has a hot button, one thing that really freaks them out. We were trying to find everyone's hot button. I mean, I wasn't a very nice guy at some points in this band. I don't know why I was an asshole. The price I paid? Our drummer won't talk to me anymore. He was more important to creating our sound than he knows, but now he just wants to believe the band never happened. I'm very ashamed of that.

Joe Nick Patoski: Bobby Soxx was the real deal, an honest punk, going back to the early times at DJs.

John Spath: I think Bobby got into a tiff with the Anti-Nowhere League as well. He was usually just poetically saying the funniest things in the world. There's a picture that Vern Evans took where I'm in a Black Flag T-shirt and Bobby's got the microphone, holding it in his mouth. If you look close, Bobby's wearing a Ku Klux Klan shirt. He was an East Texas boy, but I never saw a racist bone in his body. And I'm pretty sure that was a lot like wearing a swastika in England, yet another sort of "Fuck you–ism."

Clarke Blacker: Bobby once played me a record he had that someone in his family had given him. It was a record made by and for the KKK. It was horrifying. Racism was baked into Bobby. That meant that he could just call it up and spew it out.

Jeffrey Liles: Were Stick Men and Bobby Soxx an influence on the Butthole Surfers? *Yeah*. Gibby was much smarter.

Clarke Blacker: When Stick Men with Ray Guns took a break in 1987, we were just going to go and do other things. In the time that we took off from the band, Bobby became an alcoholic. He was a different person—the guy that I'd known was gone. He wasn't there anymore. We [the band] saw things that made us all sick, and we talked about it. We said, "I don't know if we can do this anymore" to each other.

John Spath: I remember Bobby for three weeks in a row wearing these leather pants with the whole back end ripped out. He was just walking around like that in public. Next week, you'd see him in a tuxedo. After I moved to Austin, he went to jail. Mikey Vomit [Soxx's roommate and singer for the Vomit Pigs] died. And then Bobby got into a fistfight and a knife fight and a gunfight. In that realm, I think he just disintegrated.

Clarke Blacker: Before he died, I went back to Dallas and tried to find Bobby. I went to a 7-Eleven he supposedly went to a lot. I couldn't find him. But a photographer that had made friends with him got in touch. I saw some of his pictures of Bobby: He had a beard down to his belly. He was on crutches because his legs didn't work anymore. He looked like a typical homeless guy.

> Last week, Bobby died of liver failure. At 2 a.m. on October 23 . . . he drank himself to sleep, as usual, only this time he would not wake up. Those who knew him best never expected him to live to see 46 or, for that matter, 36. Some thought [Soxx] had died a long time ago; they heard rumors, whispers that he'd been shot to death, stabbed, or that he had died in prison. Others thought he would never die; he wore the scars of the indestructible.
>
> ROBERT WILONSKY, *DALLAS OBSERVER*, NOVEMBER 2, 2000

Clarke Blacker: That was always in the cards for Bobby. It's very painful to think about. I miss him all the time. I love him a lot.

8 | CINDERELLA STORY

Roger "El Borracho" Manriquez: You couldn't get any freakier than the Butthole Surfers. I thought, "What happened—did Pink Floyd go punk or what?"

Gibby Haynes (Butthole Surfers): Can I think of a time when things got out of hand onstage? Well, *yeah*.

The year is 1984 AD, and a strange ripple is moving across Manhattan. Bleary-eyed New Yorkers who turn on their TVs and see a cable-access program called *The Scott and Gary Show* witness something weirder than anything they've ever encountered on the Bowery. Two slack-jawed, barefoot drummers are wailing a caveman beat in unison—their syncopation and their short, efficient haircuts mark them as obvious members of a cult. The bass player is twitchy, and the show credits identify him only as "Teheran." The half-naked singer smears lipstick on his cheeks, then grabs a roll of toilet paper and sings through it, "Take me, Mexican caravan! / Teach this white boy to be Mexican!" But for NYC viewers, the most repellent and fascinating creature is playing guitar. His haircut is a bizarre purple accident, and he alternates power chords with scribbles and scratches he makes across the lower frets. He lurches center stage, and the camera zooms in to his lolling tongue, his crossed eyes.

"Ah," the New Yorkers think, "*hillbillies.*"

The show host introduces them as the Butthole Surfers "from way down in Texas." And for many people, that explained everything. These were *Texans*, the folks who shot JFK, marry their sisters, and can't forget the Alamo. But if anything, the truth was stranger. The Buttholes were artists—well familiar with Andy Warhol's ideas about reproduction and representation—and knew exactly how to play the role of yokels, even when they were tripping their brains out, as they were on *The Scott and Gary Show*. Just months before, in a sweltering recording studio in San Antonio, I had watched them meticulously record and rerecord the songs that would become *Rembrandt Pussyhorse*, their most surreal and spooky album to date. The Butthole Surfers—their name, high jinks, and toilet paper stagecraft aside—were a rigorous, conceptual band.

Back in 1981, San Antonio native Paul Leary Walthall and Dallas boy Gibson "Gibby" Haynes were wide-eyed fans of the Big Boys and the Dicks. Their first project together was a fanzine called *Strange VD*. They began the Buttholes by choosing a name they thought would be unspeakable for TV news anchors and radio DJs, and they did not start compromising after that. In short order, they diagnosed and defanged a central drive of punk rock: authenticity. Instead, the Buttholes embraced artifice. For them, nothing was really real. From that perch, they were free to explore and replicate a black universe of sound, emitting everything from nightmarish psychedelia to warped country, Asian folk music, and horror film soundtrack vibes.

For the next decade, they practiced and recorded exhaustively. They toured like animals with a U-Haul. In performance, by accident or design, they refracted all the horrible, juicy reality of Texas: its wealth of music, its white-knuckle violence and murderous bigotry, its self-awareness, worldliness, and oblivion. Understandably, audiences couldn't believe what they were seeing. By 1986, I was certain they were the best band on the planet.

Gibby Haynes: I want one of those jackets like the country and western stars wear. With embroidery on the back of a big pot leaf, a yellow brick road leading to your high school, skulls, needles. . . . Those jackets can tell your whole life story.

Paul Leary: I've known Gibby since 1977, I guess. We met at Trinity University in San Antonio. Gibby was an accounting student, and I went on to fall a semester short of getting a master's degree in finance.

I once saw him cut a fart into his cupped hand and then put it up to his nose for a big whiff. Then he looked at me, and he said, "I like my own."

Did I think, "This is someone I want to hang out with?" Sadly enough, I did.

Scott Stevens: I was the first bass player of the Butthole Surfers. I met Paul [Leary] Walthall in 1978 in a life drawing class at Trinity University. "Life drawing" equaled "nude models"—hooray! Paul introduced me to Gibby, the accounting student in the black leather jacket. They were such a contrast to the vast majority of the students at Trinity. Those were people who grew up afraid of anything or anyone different from them. The majority of the other students were going to graduate, live in a gated community, and spray-starch their genitalia every day before going to work.

Gibby Haynes: I lived with Paul for a while in an apartment there in 1979. I remember one Sunday afternoon, he and his girlfriend and I were sitting by the pool. We'd been drinking beer a lot, and I was in my bathing suit, sitting in one of those slatted chairs. There was a big crowd of kids and singles around the pool. I just sat there and peed in my pants, just drained myself. It felt so good to sit there in the sun with a beer in my hand, talking to everyone while I did it. And there was this big puddle below the chair that was slowly traveling toward the pool.

It wasn't openly addressed in our conversation. But later on, the people from the apartment office called Paul and asked if I was on heavy drugs.

Paul Leary: We got out of college, and it was either go to work or be in a punk rock band. It was just something to do for the fuck of it, like everybody does. I thought I was gonna be a stockbroker. That would have put me six feet underground . . . [but] hell, I think being in a punk rock band got pretty close to doing that to me too.

> You know, growing up to shit like classic rock sucked and all of a sudden this shit is going on with bands like The Cramps doing traditional music but fucking it up! It was real noisy and it seemed as though it took a lot more imagination than talent to do and that is what we had—we had imagination. . . . We started making noise because it was idea based and not

musical talent based. . . . Idea music came along [and] we jumped on the bandwagon!

GIBBY HAYNES INTERVIEW, *CAUGHT IN THE CROSSFIRE.COM*, SEPTEMBER 17, 2004

Paul Leary: We were gonna change the name of the band every week. We had a bunch of names lined up for the future. We'd already used the Vodka Family Winstons.

Gibby Haynes: I still like Nine-Foot Worm Makes Own Food. Ed Asner Is Gay. The Philippi Meeple Peeps. Black Astronaut was another good name. There was the Againsters and the Againsters. The Againsters were against everything, and the Againsters were into doing everything over and over again.

Jeff Smith: The first time I met Gibby and Paul was when I was sixteen. I was hanging out in this bar called Eddie's—it was sort of a frat bar. And Gibby had heard that I was booking bands at this barbecue joint that I worked at. So Gibby came and took me out of Eddie's and over to the apartment he shared with Paul. They played me this blown-out demo tape that they'd made with one of those desktop cassette players. The song was called "Peggy from Mannix." It was the most god-awful thing I'd ever heard.

Adriane "Ash" Shown: The Butthole Surfers played their first shows at my dad's art gallery, the Shown-Davenport Gallery. I wasn't in Texas yet. But when I turned seventeen, I found one of their props at the gallery—it was a paper cockroach. My father told me it was from this band Butthole Surfers. He loved Gibby and thought he was artistic and funny.

Chris Gates: I have all these cassettes from back in the day, and one of them is a rehearsal tape of the Butthole Surfers that Gibby gave me [before they] opened for the Big Boys the first time. It's a phenomenal recording, made with one of those early eighties jamboxes with the great microphones. It's amazing. They're changing instruments on almost every song.

Bill Daniel: The first time I saw the Buttholes was on the Riverwalk in San Antonio. It was theatrically goofy. It was arty.

Chris Gates: Gibby played saxophone as literally a guy who doesn't know how to play saxophone. Then, when I listened to [New York "no wave"

The Butthole Surfers, San Antonio, July 1984. *From left:* Jeffrey "King" Coffey, Paul Leary, Gibby Haynes, Terence Smart, and Teresa "Nervosa" Taylor. On a break from recording what would become their second full-length album, *Rembrandt Pussyhorse*.

punks] James White and the Blacks, I thought, "Oh! James White is doing that *on purpose*. He can play the same part next time." But Gibby wasn't trying to pretend he was a good sax player. He was just making an interesting noise with an instrument that happened to be at hand. That's kind of how they approached all of their instruments in the early days.

Bill Daniel: Even before they moved to San Francisco, they had developed into what they were, with tight musicianship, a powerful sense of arrangement [*laughs*], and a fucking all-out, emotional performance, you know? After I saw them on the Riverwalk, they understood that the whole show was the piece.

Paul Leary: In 1982, we decided to go to California. We sold everything we owned, got a van and loaded it up, went to California. We had one show lined up, with the Minutemen or something like that, in Hollywood. So we played our one show and got our fifty dollars, and there we were . . . in California.

We would show up at punk rock gigs and start unloading equipment. Someone says, "Who are you?" "We're the Butthole Surfers." "Well, you guys aren't playing here tonight." And then we'd start crying about having no gas or food. And they'd say, "Okay, you can play *three songs*!"

It was one of those shows—at the Tool and Die in San Francisco—where the Dead Kennedys showed up. And Jello Biafra took a liking to us and let us open for them at the Whisky a Go Go, and the next thing you know we're on his label Alternate Tentacles and playing more live shows with the Dead Kennedys.

From inception, the Buttholes split the difference between shock and schlock, Black Flag and Black Sabbath, Grand Guignol and Grand Funk Railroad. As Haynes and Leary scuttled back and forth between San Antonio and Austin, they also studied the local legends. They noted Big Boys' disregard for the line between band and audience, but they had no interest in feel-good funk. They loved the spectacle of the Dicks' Gary Floyd—and later even named a song after him—but they had no use for politics. And they admired the way that Stick Men with Ray Guns bludgeoned their own crowds, but the Buttholes were after a more extradimensional sound.

Most important, while other bands in Texas and all over the United States were xeroxing Circle Jerks and Minor Threat, the Buttholes understood hardcore punk not as a set of loud and fast rules, but as an *aesthetic*. For them, *hardcore* was a synonym for *extreme*, and they decided to be the most extreme of all.

They began their Alternative Tentacles debut with "The Shah Sleeps in Lee Harvey's Grave," a squealing, atonal freak-out that is either the craziest hardcore punk song ever or a hilarious parody of one. It is probably both. Elsewhere on the record were perfect, almost winsome melodies ("Hey") and guitar solos that sounded like someone losing consciousness. The band were already distinguishing themselves by wedging huge, chunky-salsa riffs underneath the scabrous noise of the EP. Halfway through its recording, the Buttholes introduced a new drummer who preferred to play standing up: King Coffey, formerly of Fort Worth punk heroes the Hugh Beaumont Experience. They would soon add a second stand-up drummer, Teresa

"Nervosa" Taylor; together, Coffey and Taylor gave the group a sinister, ritualistic groove.

Paul Leary: After we went to California, we came back to San Antonio and recorded our first couple of records. Gibby and I started [the first record] by ourselves, and we got King part of the way through it. He's on "Bar-B-Q Pope" and some other songs.

Jeffrey "King" Coffey: The first show I saw in Austin was the Buttholes, and they were playing Bloodrock's "D.O.A." and it was *so* great! When I was invited to join the band, I felt like I'd won the punk rock lottery. I was living my dream.

The Buttholes were known as a great live band, but Paul and Gibby worked so hard on that first record. They grew out of the US hardcore scene—I use the word *they* here, since I joined the band *after* I was already a huge fan. I think the performance aspects of what the Big Boys and Dicks were doing in their shows set the template for what Gibby wanted to do. But the Butts approached a live show and a record as completely different, unrelated things. We tried to experiment in the studio and challenge ourselves.

Sally King: Musically, some of the stuff that the Butthole Surfers were doing was so different, even though the 13th Floor Elevators had already kind of plumbed those depths.

Jeffrey "King" Coffey: The Buttholes were seen as a moronic, drooling, knuckle-dragging band, but Gibby and Paul were essentially art students who were unafraid of everything. We were all attracted to punk, but it got so codified, so we said, "Screw that!"

Was there an intellectual aspect of the band? [*hesitates*] Well, it was all *instinctual*. An *intellectual* quality was something you didn't want to admit to. Paul made no apologies for lifting riffs from classic rock and blues.

Paul Leary: I have this bad habit of crossing my eyes when I play, so I can't focus on anything. You end up with drool running out of your mouth. You see this big puddle under your lip. Then you realize you've split your pants, and you forgot to wear your underwear.

Clarke Blacker: When we met the Buttholes, they were younger than us [Stick Men with Ray Guns], and they were much more rhythmic. They hadn't gotten so abstract yet. But after playing with us for a few shows, that changed. I think if I sat down with Paul, one on one, he'd tell me we influenced them. I don't think they influenced us so much. We were going down our own road.

Sally King: Buttholes shows at the Ritz were a full visual-oral spectrum of performance art and music. They played while projecting driver's education films with mangled corpses behind them. They were fucking *great*.

Rey Washam: Our relationship with the Butthole Surfers was a friendly competition. Gibby was really funny, and the band were just undeniable. I liked their *songs*. But Scratch Acid were the first ones to play with films projected behind us. [Future *Slacker* and *Dazed and Confused* cinematographer] Lee Daniel once came up to us and said, "Do you want to play with a screen behind you?" We said, "Sure!"

The next time I saw the Buttholes, they were doing it too.

Maria Cotera: My parents hosted a dinner for some Austin City Council members once, and the Butthole Surfers came. And then Gibby came over one Christmas—he gave my mother a Christmas tree ornament that was basically a tiny Budweiser beer can.

Paul Leary: Before we got King and Teresa in the band, we were pulling drummers off the street. Guys that couldn't play their entire drum kits. We got a guy named Kevin Layman from San Antonio, who had a wife and a child, to play drums. Before our first show together, he went on and on about how scared he was. He was not a punk rock sort of guy; he was just a drummer. We told him, "Oh man, nothing's gonna happen. Don't worry!"

We were playing at Studio 29, and Mike Milligan threw a bottle at Gibby from the back of the club and missed Gibby and hit Kevin in the nose. Stopped the show. His nose was bleeding profusely—it was probably broken. He went home and never showed his face again.

Rob Buford: Gibby pulled down his shorts, then Mike Milligan grabbed them and pulled them down some more. Gibby kicked Mike in the face.

Mike was holding a bottle of beer, and he got so mad that he threw it at Gibby as hard as he could.

He missed Gibby, but the bottle hit the drummer right in the nose. Blood everywhere, show over. All the kids who were flying on acid fled the scene.

A few weeks later, Mike was walking up the Drag, and Gibby was approaching from the other direction. Mike could not avoid him. He was terrified—Gibby is, like, six foot four—so Mike got down on his knees and said, "I'm sorry, Gibby!" Gibby put his hand on Mike's shoulder and said, "It's all right, Mike."

Michael Corcoran (journalist): Butthole Surfers, Glass Eye, and mydolls played at Uncle Sue-Sue's in May 1984. They pulled the plug on the Surfers after ten minutes because it was closing time, so the band did a free show at Laurie Greenwell's house the next night. There was a big frat party happening across the street, so there were a couple of fights. I remember a dumpster was set on fire, and Gibby did all his vocals through a megaphone.

Laurie Greenwell: They played on our front porch. There were people everywhere, all over the place and in the front yard. Our place was right in the middle of all these frat houses. The police came and told the band to stop playing. And they did. After the police left, though, the Buttholes played "The Shah Sleeps in Lee Harvey's Grave." *Then* they packed up and left.

Diana Garcia: I really loved the Butthole Surfers. I was at their show at Liberty Lunch, and Gibby was starting fires. I thought I was at a pagan ritual. I don't know if I hallucinated this, but I think someone took a dog to the show. And they had the dog in the mosh pit, and then they were crowd-surfing the dog. I got really scared because I thought they were going to sacrifice the dog.

Teresa Taylor: And, of course, there was that famous show that we played at Voltaire's Basement as the Jack Officers. Me and King had to play an air conditioning duct that was hanging from the ceiling, and we were breaking sticks every two minutes.

Sally King: There was something a little bit dangerous at those Butthole shows. But Voltaire's Basement itself was extremely dangerous—you know, an old bookstore basement *with one exit*.

Teresa Taylor: At the peak of the show, David Yow ran up and smashed a bottle over Gibby's head. Then El Borracho, I mean Roger Manriquez, jumped onstage and said—very sentimentally—"Don't do that to Gibby!" and he punched David in the face. They all took David to the ground and were beating the shit out of him. They thought they were defending Gibby, so that was touching.

Adriane "Ash" Shown: I was at that Jack Officers show. I was front and center, as I always was, and it was a mess.

Teresa Taylor: It was all a setup. Gibby had gone to a theatrical prop store and gotten a Jack Daniel's bottle made out of hard sugar. Then, before the show, he gave it to David and said, "Make sure everyone sees you guzzling this Jack Daniels, and act super drunk." I was in on it, but not everyone realized this was gonna happen. It was hard to explain to people that it had been planned. People got mad.

David Yow: Gibby told me to start bad-mouthing him early, to do it all day, and I did. He gave me two bottles to use. He had a cue—he was supposed to say, "We weren't gonna play, but David Yow's mom gave us all blow jobs, so . . ."

But I didn't trust Gibby. I thought he was gonna do something I didn't know about, so I hid the second bottle.

Rey Washam: Just before it happened, David Yow was running around, asking, "Where's that bottle, where's that bottle?" I saw him head for the stage, but I didn't see him hit Gibby. I was in the back, trying to pick up some girl.

Sally King: I was *surprised*—I thought everyone would know that this was part of the performance. Because the band kept playing, you know? Also, I mean, David had already done a [Scratch Acid] show *dressed like Hitler*. So it wasn't like this *wasn't* a direction that they had fully embraced. [*laughs*]

David Yow: After I hit Gibby with the first bottle, the guy going out with my ex-girlfriend, Kevin Scollan, jumped onstage and started beating the shit out of me within seconds. I was covered with hematomas. They pulled him off me just as he was about to kick me in the face with his steel-toed boot—his boot *just* grazed my nose—but if he had connected, he would have broken my jaw.

Gibby said, "Where's the other bottle?" Then he took it and smashed it over his head to show everyone that it was a joke.

Adriane "Ash" Shown: I wasn't angry that I'd been tricked because *I was there* for the theatricality. But I ended up in that little backstage dirt room, and I was talking with them, saying, "Oh my God, I thought it was real." It fooled me for a second.

David Yow: Kevin and I were hanging out backstage after the show. We became great friends that night. He's a good fighter. I am *not*.

Sally King: But once people realized, "Oh, that was a *shtick*; that was a *thing*"—it changed everything. I think everyone—all the other bands—stepped up their game after that show. People took performing a lot more seriously.

D Angus Macdonald (fan): You fucking guys and your art bands.

By 1984, the Big Boys had broken up, Gary Floyd had moved the Dicks to San Francisco, and everyone in Austin was talking (or arguing) about the Butthole Surfers. In addition to manufacturing bloodshed at their shows, the group had begun encouraging (or crafting) rumors about themselves, especially anything that made them seem more inbred or craven. But the Buttholes didn't even live in Texas anymore: They had begun a punishing international touring schedule that would last almost seven years. Beginning in a tricked-out 1976 Chevy Nova and ending in a series of sputtering used vans, the Buttholes made friends and enemies in faraway places like CBGB in New York, O'Cayz Corral in Madison, and the Effenaar in Eindhoven, the Netherlands. They finally settled on an unflappable bass player, Jeff Pinkus, and added a naked dancer, but somewhere in that decade, they lost Teresa Taylor. Their wild, psychedelic shows became a notorious rite of passage for punks and innocent civilians across the nation—Kurt Cobain and Courtney Love allegedly met at a Buttholes show in Seattle in 1991. No other Lone Star punk band had been so ambitious or relentless.

Like ambassadors or novelists, the Butthole Surfers explained Texas to the world, but they had to become stateless to do that.

Jeffrey "King" Coffey: So much of the eighties was just *brutal* for us: We had no money, no home, no girlfriends, no boyfriends, no possessions. No relief. But playing the shows was the payoff.

Michael Laird (skateboarder and fan): The Butthole Surfers would play a show, then get off stage and start rehearsing again. They were professionals. They always had the best equipment. I don't think they wanted to become famous. I think Gibby knew that wasn't gonna happen. If he'd wanted to make money, he could have been an accountant. I don't think it was about getting famous. They just wanted to get *better*. To be a better band.

> Like Vladimir Horowitz, The Butthole Surfers are virtuosos. Unlike Horowitz, they specialize in the domain of cheap special effects, free-associating over lots of drone and throb punctuated by strange noises. It used to be that you could understand a lot of what lyricist Gibby Haynes was free-associating, and that was the band's main appeal, because the most amazing stuff falls out of that boy's mouth. . . . The drum section, King and his sister Teresa (no last name), consists of floor toms and cymbals and is guaranteed to induce undulations in your orgones.
>
> CHARLES M. YOUNG, *PLAYBOY*, AUGUST 1985

Paul Leary: Our first bass player was Scott Stevens. He gave me this souvenir plaque from Apollo 1. Then there was Andrew Mullen, then there was Quinn, then there was Bill. We took Bill on some tours, and he kinda fried. And went home to be a computer programmer.

Gibby Haynes: Terence Smart. Terence had a Bozo [the Clown] haircut.

Paul Leary: Then there was Juan—he liked to wear dresses. And then there was Trevor. Trevor was the guy who brought a sousaphone with him. He was from Windsor, Canada. So when we played in Windsor, they ran a promo photo of the band in the Windsor paper. The high school band director recognized that stolen sousaphone, and he came to the show and took it back.

Brad Perkins: I actually played on a few songs on the first Buttholes record. And they asked me if I wanted to join the band and go on tour with them. But they were going to go on tour in a *car*, not a van or anything. They sawed out a hole in the back of this car. And I thought, "That will be fun for a couple of weeks, and then . . ." It just didn't seem like a good idea.

Paul Leary: It wasn't that people in Austin hated us. We were just homeless. Every time we'd show up in town—I mean, a lot of people were real nice and gracious. A lot of people put up with us for a long period of time. It's just that after a while, you can only expect so much from people. I didn't want to put people out.

Michael Laird: The Buttholes toured so hard. They toured for years. I saw them in Houston one year, at Numbers, and talked to them backstage before the show. Teresa and King were so white, so pale, from living that life: getting up at five in the afternoon, then staying up for 100 percent of the night, then just a few hours of daylight and then sleeping, for years. They were so white. They were so beautiful.

Paul Leary: Gibby's parents have bailed us out on a few occasions. We might be coming through at the end of some god-awful tour, with no money, and the van breaks down right as we're getting to Dallas. So where do we end up for two weeks over Christmas? Let's ruin the Hayneses' Christmas! That's what people suffer from us.

It took us three and a half years to save up enough money to buy sleeping bags. We were always sick. You'd get the flu, and six months later you'd still have the flu.

[My dog] Mark Farner protected our tour van for years. She's a pit bull blend, and when she's in protect mode, you'd be very startled to hear her. She makes a noise that sounds like flapping sides of beef.

Teresa Taylor: Once when we were living in Winterville, Georgia, our friend Cammy came to visit us. We told her we weren't getting anywhere as a band, so we were going to change our name to Stargazer. She started crying. King said, "No, Cammy, Stargazer is a name that could really take us somewhere."

Jeffrey "King" Coffey: We also told people that Teresa and I were brother and sister. There are times—when I'm looking at some of your photos,

Pat—that I'm not sure if I am looking at Teresa or myself. She might as well be my sister—certainly the closest thing to a sister I've ever had.

Teresa Taylor: I was the one who finally, finally, finally told everyone that King and I were *not* brother and sister. Then the next thing that I heard was that [San Francisco band] Frightwig—who I love—started crying when they heard this. Someone told me that [Frightwig bassist] Deanna [Ashley] said, "I know that King and Teresa are brother and sister because they are good friends of mine, and they would *not* lie to me." And I wondered, "How many people out there did I just *lie* to?" Instead of looking like we had a cool idea, we hurt a lot of our friends.

> As their sound developed, so did their ability to judge between right and wrong.
>
> BUTTHOLE SURFERS PROMOTIONAL BIO, CIRCA 1983

Paul Leary: We met [Butthole dancer] Kathleen [Lynch, a.k.a. Ta-Da the Shit Lady] through the Celebrity Club in Atlanta, Georgia. The Celebrity Club had nude lesbian grit wrestling, where they'd spike the grits with a turd. Six-foot-four drag queens dancing on the bar in lingerie with tampon strings coming out of their bottom ends. Whenever we played that place, there'd always be some guy in the pit with a machete, waving it around in the air.

We'd play there, and after the show, we'd take turns standing out by the truck with a two-by-four, guarding it from the guy with the machete. He was a regular at the club. One afternoon, we saw him passed out on the sidewalk. And then he came to the show that night. And he came toward the van with his machete. We were trying to show him we meant business with the two-by-four, so Gibby says, "Man, I remember you! You were passed out on the sidewalk."

And the guy goes, "Yeah, but it was only for *a second*."

Teresa Taylor: I shaved my head too. When the Buttholes were in New York City, I had people in the street trying to give me money because I obviously had some kind of cancer. Because my head was partly shaved—Paul had shaved around these three dreadlocks that I had. People started asking me, "Oh, how long have you had leukemia?" Ha ha! "No, I actually did this to myself."

Paul Leary: There was one night when Gibby got stabbed by some crazed woman up in Canada. Emilio Estevez was at that show. Gibby did some lyric about a "crippled midget lesbian boy," and somebody took offense. It was kind of hard to tell what happened because of the strobe lights and smoke machines. It all looked pretty weird.

Gibby Haynes: I got stabbed in the arm [*chuckles*] but we played it up a bit later. People thought I had been stabbed in the intestines and would have to pee in a bag for the rest of my life. Stabbings are always good.

> The coolest record ever made, this unbridled, surreal burst of imagination is enough to erase years of indoctrination by schools and television viewing. It's finally okay to do whatever the fuck you want. We can only go up from here.
>
> BRUCE PAVITT, REVIEW OF THE SURFERS ALBUM *REMBRANDT PUSSYHORSE*, *THE ROCKET*, JULY 1986

Steve Marsh: I was living in New York City in 1985, and I saw the Butthole Surfers eight or nine times there. They were at the height of their powers—nobody in New York would have disputed how great they were. And after one of these shows, everyone was leaving at the same time out of this one entrance, and just as I got to the door, I found myself face-to-face with Gibby. I'd never met him, but he was still in that after-show mode. And he said, "You're Steve Marsh, right? What are you doing here?"

I said, "Well, I live here now."

And Gibby said, "Dude, I was at a Terminal Mind rehearsal once, high on acid, and that was the thing that made me want to start a band!"

And I said, "Well, that's funny, because what you're doing now makes me want to keep doing a band."

Paul Leary: We played a show in Los Angeles in 1986, and then [*long sigh*] we drove from LA to New York to play two shows. Friday and Saturday night at the Danceteria. We had four days to get there, but we had to stop at Bryce Canyon [in Utah].

We get to New York, and they'd canceled one of our shows without telling us. We were really pissed off, so we were rambunctious. We had this drummer named Cabbage who was filling up this plastic Fred Flintstone bat with her own urine and waving it at the audience, and the little hole at the end of it was emitting this stream. And the hole was about an eighth of an inch across, and she and our dancer Kathleen were taking turns trying to pee into that little hole.

We'd lit a lot of the stage on fire. And the strobe lights and the flames and Gibby humping down on Kathleen . . . I've seen the video. It's shocking. I doubt there was penetration, but it looks good! There's legs in the air and butts.

Steve Marsh: A few weeks after that, Gibby called me. He told me they were going on a European tour, and he asked if I would like to go with them as their bass player. We talked about a few other details of the tour, and then I asked about money. He said, "Well, we put the money we make back into the band for recording and equipment. I mean, you'll get enough to eat and everything you need, but . . ."

I said, "It's one thing if you're asking me to join the band. But if you're just asking me to go on this tour with you, I gotta come back with *something*, some kind of money."

He didn't say much more after that, then he hung up, and I never heard from him again. I believe that was the point where they asked the bass player from Shockabilly [Mark Kramer] to go on the tour with them.

Teresa Taylor: King and I were the nice ambassadors. We would get embarrassed when Gibby would be rude. Especially in other countries. We were used to it. When we went to England for the first time, Gibby started yelling at everyone and calling them teabaggers. Gibby was the absolute provocateur. He would always say what no one else had the nerve to say. But then me and King would be, like, "Hey, do y'all like Hawkwind?"

Paul Leary: Gibby urinated at the customs checkpoint going into Switzerland once. We pulled in, and we were waiting for the equipment truck, and Gibby got out and right in front of all the guards, he just urinated. When they started yelling at him, he yelled back.

He wasn't high. We've been kicked out of Europe a couple of times. When you're in Europe, after you've been there for a while, you get to the point where you just want to go home. So it's like, "Let's see . . . let's kidnap the tour bus and make the driver go to Belgium instead of Norway" or "Let's urinate in front of the border guards." What are they gonna do? They're just gonna send you *home*.

Teresa Taylor: After I quit the band, I had a guilt trip because maybe the Butthole Surfers had led a lot of people astray. One of our first fans jumped off a building, and another one shot herself. We were getting older, and our fan base was getting younger. People would say, "I'm tripping my ass off, and I can't wait to see you play." We were showing heavy, strobe-lit shows and movies, and Kathleen was dancing. I think some of those kids left those shows *changed*. And not always for the better.

I just had to drop out. If I had stayed in the band, I was gonna die.

Even as they toured the USA relentlessly, melting faces everywhere, all of the Butthole Surfers knew they needed sanctuary. Some place of their own, a home and hearth where they could gather their wits for a few days or weeks between shows. They tried living in Athens, Georgia, where they allegedly stalked R.E.M. singer Michael Stipe and pranked former President Jimmy Carter. But by 1986, they returned to Texas and settled into a rambling estate just off of US Route 183 in Austin. They called it the Compound.

I was summoned to the Compound to take photographs of the band in the winter of 1987. Teresa had rejoined the band and was wearing pigtails and a Catholic schoolgirl's uniform. As King snuggled with their beloved pit bull Mark Farner, Paul showed me around. The den was draped with parachute silk, and another room featured a wind-powered turntable. It was, in its own Butthole way, a cozy place.

Not long afterward, the band moved to a communal ranch in the hill country outside of Austin. They were still the hardest-working band in Texas punk, so naturally they had been recording at the Compound and continued to do so at their new home in Driftwood. One of the results was *Hairway to Steven*, which might be my favorite Butthole album. When I saw them perform some of it a year later, I was astonished to hear some truly shocking sounds: a rooster crowing, bubbles bursting underwater, and even a folksy acoustic guitar. While they had been holed up, licking their wounds from the road, the band had produced their weirdest music yet, plugging directly into an inheritance of central Texas rock and psychedelia that stretches back through cosmic country, the 13th Floor Elevators, and ZZ Top, among many others.

Paul Leary: The idea of getting our ranch out in Driftwood was to get some place where there was peace and quiet. After years on the road, the idea of

Gibby Haynes with stuffed animal and strobe, Liberty Lunch, Austin, March 1986. The Butthole Surfers used minimal stagecraft to inflict maximum audiovisual trauma and hilarity.

waking up to chirping birds and deer and turkey in our front yard was real nice. It was real pleasant. We were there a couple of years.

Gibby Haynes: It was fairly secluded. It was nice. [*sighs*] It was a little far out, like twenty-eight miles outside of town. It was kind of dangerous driving that much. Jeff got in four wrecks. He hit three deer. Then, one time, he lost control of a van on a slick street. Flipped it—destroyed it.

I remember driving out there, going ninety miles per hour down those roads, barely holding the corners, my foot just *stomped* [on the gas pedal], with a twelve pack of beer—drink one, finish one. [*makes gesture of throwing something out a car window*]

Do I like driving fast? I'm more into acceleration than sustained high velocity. I'm not into that road-racing thing. I'm mainly into going straight quick. Zero to sixty in five seconds.

A few years later, the Butthole Surfers were the most famous Texas band on earth. One night in 1996, they were in Paris, appearing on the legendary French talk show *Nulle part ailleurs*. The were performing their hit single, "Pepper," from their Top 40 album, *Electriclarryland*. Haynes talk-smirked through the verses of the song, as if it were a Vanilla Ice cover. Leary solemnly began a guitar solo at exactly the moment where any other guitarist would begin it. There was no naked dancer, and nothing was on fire. "King" Coffey was playing the drums *while sitting down*. What in the Sam Hell had happened to them?

The Buttholes began the nineties by accomplishing the unlikely, then the unthinkable. First, they joined the first edition of Lollapalooza, the most high-profile US touring festival of the decade. Then they signed with Capitol Records, former home of the Beatles (and Grand Funk). The Buttholes' first Capitol record was produced by Led Zeppelin bassist John Paul Jones. *Electriclarryland* was their second, and a surprise breakthrough. "Pepper" was shocking in another way because it was the first Buttholes song that sounded like someone else (especially the alternative songwriter and "loser" Beck). The only trace of Texas in "Pepper" was the lyrics, which extolled various doomed characters from Gibby's adolescence in Dallas, including Stick Men with Ray Guns' Bobby Soxx.

Paul Leary (interviewed in 1991): Sometimes I still think of us as a Touch and Go band. We were real spoiled by that label because I can't imagine another label that's as nice to the bands or totally honest when it comes to royalties. They would send a royalty statement that was half a page long, paid on time—or earlier.

Except that [Touch and Go cofounder] Corey Rusk isn't into the major label distribution scene. And that's just something we wanted.

Teresa Taylor: Gibby and Paul are magic together. They're like Rock Hudson and Jerry Lewis. Someone asked me once, "Are you an equal in the band?" Well, of course, I was an equal human being. But I was a *drummer*. In how many bands do you want to know what the drummer is thinking? Paul and Gibby were the managerial team. They drove the van. King and I were younger. Gibby and Paul seemed so grown up. I just trusted them.

Paul Leary: One thing I like about the big shows, like Lollapalooza, was having big old barricades so those guys in the audience can't even spit far enough to get it on you. Sometimes I miss the interaction [with a small-show audience]. But Lollapalooza was fun as hell. Really, the most fun tour ever. It was a breeze. We played early in the afternoon. Made a bunch of money. Worked for forty-five minutes a day.

Gibby Haynes: [English punk and Lollapalooza performer] Siouxsie [Sioux] told me, "You're *so* good."

And my response? I just kept on lickin' her. "Gibby, you're *so* good."

Paul Leary: Led Zeppelin's John Paul Jones told my wife that I was the best guitar player he'd ever worked with. So you can take that with a grain of salt.

Gibby Haynes: What kind of girls want to hang out with me? Girls with dicks. Girls who dropped out of college, made pretty good grades, *but just couldn't get along*. Nah, no girls ever want to fuck the Butthole Surfers. I guess they're scared. Or we're too ugly.

Paul Leary: Usually, I assume they're just after a free beer. "Okay, here's your beer, here's one for your buddy, here's a backstage pass. Nine Inch Nails is down the hall." That's the kind [of fans] we get.

I was walking on the street here in Austin, and this teenage kid chased me down. He asked me if it was true that John Paul Jones was gonna produce our record. I said yes. Then he asked who John Paul Jones was. I told him, "He was the bass player for Led Zeppelin." And the kid says, "Oh I thought he was the pope."

That would have been the one person we would have turned John Paul Jones down for. I bet they got some badass studios in the Vatican.

> [Our audiences have] such a heavy grunge factor in them. . . . It's amazing, you light one guy on fire and he'll follow you all around the country wearing his scorched jacket—try and get backstage and everything.
>
> BH BASSIST JEFF PINKUS, QUOTED BY GINA ARNOLD IN *ROUTE 666: ON THE ROAD TO NIRVANA* (ST. MARTIN'S PRESS, 1993)

Paul Leary: *Locust Abortion Technician* is still my favorite record, probably. That was just a totally different recording procedure. We had this big, old, ancient, dinosaur, one-inch, eight-track tape machine and microphone out in the middle of Georgia. Recording in weird ways. We'd say, "Let's hit this one drum over and over and add this, that, and the other" or "Let's record something off the radio—that sounds good!"

With *Independent Worm Saloon*, we just made a rock record. It was something we just wanted to do. When you spend a quarter of a million dollars on a studio project, you kinda wanna know what you're gonna do. *Everybody* wants to know what you're gonna do.

Gibby Haynes: We wasted so much fucking money. That album cost as much as Billy Idol's record.

Paul Leary: After recording *Independent Worm Saloon*, we're in debt for a third of a million. We gotta go gold to break even. Otherwise, we're gonna be fucking bums on the street again.

> "[The Butthole Surfers are] no longer cool, totally uncool. It's hard living with this level of uncoolness. . . . People have been grumbling about us for our entire existence. I wouldn't even call it a career."
>
> GIBBY HAYNES, QUOTED BY JIM SULLIVAN IN THE *BOSTON GLOBE*, JULY 19, 1996

> Texas Sky [Festival Park] was the location of one of the more infamous stories involving the Corpus Christi concert scene. During a Butthole Surfers concert appearance on July 6, 1996, lead singer Gibby Haynes was hit in the hand by a wristwatch hurled onstage from the audience. . . . Haynes was furious, instructing the crowd to inflict punishment on anyone they saw throwing objects. He then called Corpus Christi a city of "white trash," saying he didn't care if people refused to buy the band's newest album. "We've got your money already," Haynes yelled into the microphone.
>
> ALLISON EHRLICH, "#TBT: CORPUS CHRISTI'S TEXAS SKY FESTIVAL PARK ATTRACTED POPULAR CONCERTS IN LATE '90S," *CORPUS CHRISTI CALLER-TIMES*, OCTOBER 4, 2018

The Butthole Surfers became a mainstream success story because they released a series of brilliant, compelling albums and crafted a reputation as the most insane live band in the United States. But they also understood marketing in a way that few bands do because their product was themselves: their bodies, their drawls, and, more than anything, their backstory. They were inspired by the terrible beauty of Texas and performed what King called "Texas drag" more believably than anyone since Willie Nelson. At Lollapalooza, the drummer refused to wear anything but cowboy boots, and Gibby punctuated his onstage patter with blasts from a shotgun.

But after *Electriclarryland*, Butthole Surfers' fifteen minutes were up. Their major label deal fell apart. Gibby descended into a nearly fatal spiral of drugs and public outrage, while Paul and King retreated to Austin. They had been the exception that proved the rule, the Texas punk band that left the scene yet epitomized it. They began as a group who didn't sound like anyone else and finished with an album that didn't sound like anything at all. In 2015, a reporter from *Texas Monthly* was speaking to Haynes and mentioned accusations that the Butthole Surfers had sold out. His reaction was characteristic and instructive: "Yeah, but who cares?"

Paul Leary: MTV used to have this jingle with their network logo and that little melody. They went through a few versions of that, and then they wanted us to do a version. They sent down this saxophone player who had played the solo on "We Are All Prostitutes" by [English first-wave punk band] the Pop Group. They came to our toilet studio in Driftwood, Texas. They were saying, "No, this way." "No, this way." And we were like, "Okay, whatever you want." And they used it. They used it on the hour, every hour, for at least a year and a half. We were on TV more than fucking Van Halen.

Gibby Haynes: I'm getting ready to build a house here. Just a little bit outside of Austin. It'll be a big, prefabricated metal building that looks like a garage, with a big fence around it and barbed wire and a gravel parking lot big enough for twenty cars. Make it look like a total business. Put a sign up that says something really weird.

Does that sound really ugly? It is what it is. What do you do when you get a house—look at the *outside* of it? I'm into going *inside* the house and looking *out*!

> I wrote this article in the *Austin Chronicle* headlined "Tell It Like It Is: Celebrity Sightings and Scandals of 1993" and three of the ten items were about Gibby. This was when Ministry was thinking about moving to Austin and Gibby was working with [Ministry singer] Al Jourgensen and they did "Jesus Built My Hot-Rod." It was around this time that Gibby got into heroin, and when he left the Ministry enclave in Chicago, he slipped into smoking crack and doing heroin all the time. He'd walk into the Black Cat bar [in Austin] and his eyes were going in two different directions. He smelled bad. He had that translucent look, like he didn't know what was going on. He was in rehab within four months.
>
> MARGARET MOSER IN "FEEDING THE FISH: AN ORAL HISTORY OF THE BUTTHOLE SURFERS," *SPIN*, NOVEMBER 1996

Scott Stevens: I am neither surprised nor baffled by the Butthole Surfers' success. Paul and Gibby worked very hard for what they have. Have they changed? Hell yes! Gibby wasn't a fucking junkie when I knew him back then! I think Paul is very well-grounded and has a wife who loves him for who he is, rather than [seeing him] as an ATM or a step up the social ladder. In some ways, Paul has mellowed. Gibby still needs to be the center of attention, no matter what. When the Surfers did a book signing at Waterloo

Records in Austin in March 2019, there was definitely an air of relief that Gibby was not there.

> The lyrics are everything. The lyrics are 100 percent of the song. All the music is something some Black dude did forty years ago, man. And then we're just putting new lyrics on top of it. Believe me, rock and roll is just what a bunch of Black dudes did in East Texas, and no one's giving them credit. That's what rock and roll is. I mean, the Beatles—they were just ripping off Buddy Holly, and Buddy Holly was rippin' off some Black slave that was down the street from him. It all boils down to Texas and Black and blues and rock and roll, damn it!
>
> GIBBY HAYNES ON *POLITICALLY INCORRECT*, ABC, MAY 26, 1997

Louis Black: The Butthole Surfers never lost sight of their humanism. That band went to some dark places, some places that are almost unimaginable, but it wasn't about evoking devils. They were saying that humans are complicated people, but you can be dark and still be a human being. We are just seriously complicated motherfuckers. It's the same with Rick Linklater's films.

Paul Leary: Ahh, we're just grateful that anyone wants to listen to these terrible records that we make. I know that I wouldn't buy our records if they were made by someone else. It's like Jiffy Pop—it's a lot more fun to make than it is to eat.

9 | "OUT ON THE STREETS"

Rob Buford: A lot of people claim they were trying to make some kind of social or political statement with punk rock. I think that's revisionist crap. There may have been a very small number of people who actually thought that way, but I never met any of them. Everyone I knew was there because they felt rejected or excluded in some way, and they were looking for a place where they would fit in. Poison 13 had a song called "Out on the Streets," and it captured this sentiment well. Word for word, that song describes how I was.

A lot of punk rock happens offstage: in record stores, student housing, secondhand boutiques, aftershow parties, and, of course, at the mirrors in teenage bedrooms all over the world. That's where people reconstruct and reinvent themselves.

In the 1980s, several adjacent cultural and commercial phenomena flourished simultaneously with American punk music. Independent record stores and carefully curated vintage clothing boutiques were a fixture of every college town. Head shops welcomed a new and spikier generation of pot smokers and psychic adventurers. The buzzing center of punk culture in Austin was Bluebonnet Plaza, which was home to nodes of all of these subcultures, plus a fake French café and a wonderful cosmic burger joint called Mad Dog and Beans.

Easy Rollers was the skateboarder shop in Bluebonnet Plaza, and both Biscuit and Tim Kerr from the Big Boys worked there at various times. This is not the only reason the Big Boys soon became US ambassadors of skate punk. Not all punks were skateboarders, and not all skateboarders were punks, but pretty much anyone skating in the United States grew accustomed to hearing rednecks and frat boys yell, "Hey, Devo!" at them whenever they rolled down the street.

Michael Laird: Texas has long periods of drought and periods of extreme rainfall. So they have these long concrete ditches—storm drains—that you don't see anywhere else. They're great for skating. And you don't have those in Minnesota.

In the late 1970s, there was this guy in Dallas named Jeff Newton, and he bought a blue half-pipe from a skate park that was closing. Then he started hauling that half-pipe around Texas and setting it up at all these backyard parties. Texas pioneered the backyard skate contest.

And Newton would play music at these things. Skaters don't care about whether music is punk or new wave or whatever. They just want to hear something *other* and aggressive. Fast and aggressive. Oingo Boingo—they're not a punk band, but a lot of skaters like Oingo Boingo.

All these skaters were hearing five or six or eight hours of this other music at every contest. And guess what? There were lots of nonskaters at those contests. Hundreds of them. All of them listening to hours and hours of this *other* music.

Rob Buford: The Austin scene was more about drugs, music, and parties than skateboarding. You can't get good at a dangerous and difficult sport while you are blasted out of your mind all the time on acid and quaaludes. The guys in the bigger cities like Houston and Dallas prioritized skateboarding and were way better. They had better ramps, better parks, et cetera. We had shitty ramps, like the one on Speedway, and an abandoned skate park that was later demolished, and the Bastrop Pool that was later demolished, and the Pflugerville ditch—which was later demolished.

We did like to skate parking garages on acid after shows. Skateboarding parking garages on acid is about the most fun you can have. Tim Kerr was the best skater in the Big Boys. He made these great slide moves at Pflugerville that I still can't do.

Michael Laird: I was a sponsored amateur for Sims and Vision for a while because I was, well, I was really good at skating those half-pipes. I wasn't a pro, and I didn't ever want to be. But I'd get a box of new boards and clothes sent to me every month. And that was really cool.

Inner Sanctum Records was the fount of secret music wisdom in Austin in the late seventies and early eighties. The store had all the newest, coolest, weirdest records, and perhaps more important, the staff there knew everything about everything they had in stock. The people at the cash register almost always passed judgment on whatever you were buying, and it was often not cool enough. They also hosted in-stores and concerts in their parking lot. For all these reasons, Inner Sanctum had a huge influence on underground music in Austin.

Polar Bear: I recall finding a great, antireligious pamphlet at Inner Sanctum that spoke of "the spermon on the mount"! It was more than just records—they had [Austin fanzines] *Sluggo!* and *Contempo Culture* too.

Chris Gates: I started going there in junior high, probably not long after it opened. Bought a ton of used records there. For a long time, it was the *only* place to find any punk or underground music in Austin. I believe it was also ground zero for the cosmic cowboy movement earlier in the seventies.

Justin McCoy (Buzzcrusher): Inner Rectum was my "go-between" on days that I had a little scratch. A black bean tostada and a cold beer at Les Amis, then into Inner Sanctum to search through the stacks of vinyl. Then over to Pipes Plus for papers and/or incense, then over to Mad Dog and Beans for a small but glorious mint chocolate chip milkshake.

Scott Conn (fan and filmmaker): Who was the girl working there who sometimes had the Adam Ant stripe across her face? She insisted that I buy *Meat Puppets II*. She said that it was God. And it was good.

Judy K. Frels (fan): The Ant Girl was Dina. She worked the door at Club Foot too. She had a tip jar for donations to send her to "Ant Camp."

Sammy Jacobo: None of us can be faulted for having a crush on Ant Girl. She was kind of gorgeous. Tall, long dark hair, dressed in black, always. Alabaster skin. The prettiest eyes. The perfect stripes, always. She could take a punch: "You know Adam Ant sucks, don't you?" The perfect eye roll and sigh. Very mysterious. We'd invite her to hang, but she never did. She was a wonderful, amazing woman.

David McCreath (Hugh Beaumont Experience): I think it was one of the first places we went when my band moved from Fort Worth to Austin. Like, unpack the car, go to Inner Sanctum, *then* go buy toilet paper.

To the west of Inner Sanctum, the UT campus area was a warren of antebellum sorority houses, crappy apartment complexes, and student collectives called co-ops. The neighborhood had once been a kind of hippie paradise. But by the time I got there, punks were invading, and some of these places started to feel like the fraternity house from the 1978 comedy *Animal House*, except with more Dead Kennedys posters. I lived in a co-op

Criminal Crew and bystanders behind the Drag, Austin, November 1984.

with the hopeful name of Halcyon; three doors down was the Ark, a collective that was well-known for its great pool parties and a Coke machine stocked with fifty-cent bottles of Lone Star beer.

A couple of clever punks engineered the takeover of the Campus Colony III apartment complex, and it quickly became a bacchanalian hive of late-night parties as well as the Fort Apache of the great Punks Versus Frats War. Hardcore haircutter "Texas" Terri Laird played the John Belushi role at the Colony, much to the delight of a cast of Dicks, Hickoids, teen runaways, and skate rats. It was all good, clean fun—until it wasn't.

David Roach: Texas Terri lived at the Colony. One night in January, there was a party, and Terri starts throwing her furniture off the second floor for a bonfire. The cops come and tell her to put it out. Terri throws a bucket of water on one of the cops.

"Texas" Terri Laird: Once at the Colony, Pat Roach told me that all these young boys that he hung out with, they just liked to take acid and come to the Colony to watch Terri Laird. That was their idea of a good time.

Rob Buford: Terri Laird's apartment was upstairs. I absolutely loved it when she would show everyone her tits. She would do this all the time.

"Texas" Terri Laird: Another night, I was walking by David MacDonald's room, and I heard him ask some of these little punk rock kids, "How do you know when Terri Laird is on the rag? Because she's only wearing one sock."

So I turned right around and told him, "Well David, I'm wearing two socks, but"—then I reached down and pulled my tampon out—"I'm on the rag." Then I threw my tampon into the middle of all of these boys, and you've never seen a room full of tough, hardcore boys move so fast, trying to get away from that thing.

To his credit, Pat Roach went over and picked it up and started swinging it at every boy and scaring them. Then he took the tampon down to this tree in the parking lot, and he hung it up in the tree like it was a Christmas tree ornament.

I moved to LA, but when I came back, some of these boys had gotten tattoos that were recreations of my tattoos. Tommy Pipes got a tattoo like the one of teeth marks on my shoulder. His had exactly the same colors as mine. I was really moved.

Rob Buford: I spent *a lot* of time at the Colony. It was right next to the Contessa, this big UT dorm. Jeffro (a.k.a. Jeff Cowell) figured out how to purchase noise permits from the City of Austin and would buy them for Sundays. The Offenders would set up drums and amps on the roof, and pretty much anyone could get up there and play all day long. I'm sure it was terrible for the sorority bowheads trying to study next door. It was also directly across the street from a frat house, so there was always trouble with them brewing.

> "There is this one guy who's always out there with a bass guitar and he plays the same song over and over and over," [Contessa resident and business major Mary Young] said. "They even had a little sign up last week that said, 'Go ahead! Complain! We're legal!'"
>
> More than 100 Contessa residents have signed a petition asking the City to intercede on their behalf . . .
>
> "It's a social problem," said [drummer and Colony resident Jeff] Cowell, shaking his shoulder-length hair. "They resent that we are low income when they are right next door paying big money."
>
> *AUSTIN AMERICAN-STATESMAN*, DATE UNKNOWN

Cindy Melbie: I lived at the Colony. I was there when they hung John Slate. That was ugly. There was this noose in one of the trees outside. It had a Barbie doll attached to it. And one night, Rat went over to it and put it around his neck, like, "Look at me!" As a joke.

But then Santiago and some other guys—three or four people—grabbed the rope and started pulling Rat up with it. Hoisting him up. And he was struggling. Then he was turning purple.

I was at the door of my apartment, and I yelled, "That's enough! Stop it, stop it! He's struggling, stop it!"

For years and years after that, John wouldn't speak to me. He thought I was part of it. He didn't know I'd saved his life.

Sociologists can dispute the boundaries of public and private space, but generally speaking, in those years, the West Campus area was a staging area for adulthood. Most of us living and hanging out there were no longer children, but we were still unsure about what kind of grown-ups we wanted to be. Punk records assured us that we could obey the laws we wanted to and forget the rest. (See the Slits' wonderful "Shoplifting.") Petty crimes aside, even those of us who had to work wage-slave jobs still had plenty of time on our hands. This time allowed for misadventures, popsicles, and lots of boredom. We had no idea how lucky we were.

Karen Ruth Getchell: We were the last feral generation. There weren't any parents helicoptering behind us. And that was a gift—we were able to be wild and free. But it's a razor's edge, too, and some of us were neglected. My parents weren't interested in what I was doing.

Diana Garcia: I worked at a restaurant with Muffy. She let me stay at her house for a week once. She turned me on to Brian Eno and his song [sings] "Baby's on Fire." We'd go buy orange popsicles, sit by the side of the road, and just watch cars go by and talk.

David Roach: One night, me and Chico and Ralph and some others were on the roof of the Ritz Theater, just hanging out. And Ralph fucking disappeared. She fell off the roof and—amazingly—landed on a bed. She was not injured.

Lisa "Ralph" Armstrong: Martha and Anna both had pretty decent racks. So we'd go to convenience stores, and they would unbutton the top button of their shirts, grab a six-pack of Heineken, dump a pocketful of change on the counter, and then lean over as they counted it out. The one guy in the store, his eyes were not on people walking around the store, he was looking straight down the cleavage. I'd be stuffing my backpack full of beer, and that's how I got away with it so many times: my decoys.

Maria Cotera: Atomic City was one of those places where we'd just hang out. The reason I can remember it so well is that I went there *during the day*! Spend hours on the front porch, smoking clove cigarettes—ugh, we were disgusting! I got my first pair of Doc Martens there, and it was one of the only places in Austin where you could get them.

It was a home away from home—a place where you could go to see other people. We spent a lot of time just loitering out front. Frank Kozik was working there, and he was a very gruff person—that was his whole pose. He'd come out of the store and say, "Y'all get off the porch—you're discouraging customers!"

Bethany Johnson and Lynda Stuart at Lynda's house, Austin, November 1984.

We'd say, "You idiot—we're the only customers here!" "Fuck yourself, Frank!"

He was such a *loser*! We would always make fun of him. But obviously, he was an incredible artist, even then. The first time I saw a poster by Frank, I realized he was very talented. But quite insecure. Like we all were.

Some of the party houses in Austin became informal hostels for touring punk bands, as well as laboratories for some dubious notions of personal hygiene. I spent my last months in Austin sleeping on the cruddy couch at the House of a Thousand Beers on West Thirtieth Street—that was the place with the seven-foot pink papier-mâché penis hanging from the trees.

After the punks were evicted from the Colony, some of them simply padded up the street and moved into a Victorian hovel at Twenty-Eighth and San Pedro. The place was quickly dubbed the OAF House. Early incarnations of the Red Hot Chili Peppers and Jane's Addiction stayed overnight at the OAF, and the photographs of one of their Sunday afternoon barbecue parties show several motorcycles parked in the front yard, about a dozen punks on the roof of the garage, and lots of underage boys and girls. Some of these kids used the OAF House as a safe space, others as a place to buy mushrooms, and some used it as both.

Adriane "Ash" Shown: I lived at Chris and Mike's house behind the funeral home—I wasn't just hanging out. I was getting ready to move back to DC, and Chris asked me to live with him. There were a lot of aftershow parties, like when Glenn Danzig came over after some show. He and Mike were just geeking out and talking about Japanese toys with Tim Kerr. Then they were lip-synching to "Danke Schoën" by Wayne Newton. It was a very sweet moment. Danzig's just a little guy. I thought, "He's a kid geeking out."

When Fang came to Austin in 1984, I had to go retrieve [singer] Sammy and bring him to the house. He's got a six-pack under his arm already. And he goes, "Oh my God, what time is it?" He had to watch his favorite soap opera. He sat there, drank his six-pack, and watched his soap opera. No talking during the show.

Rob Buford: The OAF House was punk headquarters after the Colony. Some people actually lived there, but anyone could just stop by and hang out. [Hickoids guitarist John Thomas Jackson, a.k.a.] Jukebox might be on the porch doing a painting, or this other guy K-9 might be just getting up. He was the one who lived in the trashed, yellow Toyota Celica that was always parked out front.

We frequently used the first-floor bathroom to fix up before we headed out to a show. I think that guy Speed Baby (RIP) lived there for a while. I remember that when they couldn't find any speed, they would go steal a bunch of Vicks inhalers and melt them down in a spoon to shoot up. Supposedly, it gave you this *insane* menthol rush. I never had the balls to try that.

Dotty Farrell: The OAF House was a huge old mansion with six or seven bedrooms, probably built in the 1870s or some shit. With the twenty-foot ceilings and the woodwork and the backstairs to the kitchen. A totally bad-ass old house. But it was full of punks, and it was right in the middle of all the fraternity houses. They used to call the cops on us all the time. We were sitting outside on the front porch one time, and someone had some poppers—amyl nitrate. They said, "Have you ever tried this?" And then right as I did it, this cop comes walking up. There had been a noise complaint about a party, but the party was at the frat house—it was really loud. The cops just immediately thought it was us.

Bill Anderson: There wasn't anyone in charge at the OAF House—there weren't any adults living there. I stayed there one weekend when I was between places to live. It wasn't dangerous—I never felt unsafe in Austin—it was just fun.

If you walked out of the OAF House and turned left, you'd be in that student housing complex with a pool and a hot tub. In the summer months, it was empty, and you could just walk right in there. So that summer, there were all these punks in the swimming pool and in the hot tub. Do you remember when Richard Mather had that three-foot-high Mohawk? Well, he got that thing to stick up straight like that with *soap*. He went over to that hot tub with us once, and his Mohawk just dissolved. The hot tub had three feet of pure bubbles in it for the rest of the summer.

Rob Buford: One night, right before my eighteenth birthday, we were at a keg party at Sound Exchange, then we dropped some hits of Black Cat [blotter LSD] and went skateboarding. We were rolling down Twenty-Ninth Street when the left half of my body just collapsed. I'm pretty sure it was a stroke. I fried some circuits, for sure. I basically went into shock. But somehow, we made it to the OAF House. I sat on the front steps there, staring down at the sidewalk for about four hours. Then I finally regrouped and made it home. That was kind of a turning point for me.

I started phasing out of the scene not long after that. My childhood friends were all graduating from high school, and I was a street criminal with a ninth-grade education. My punk friends were also moving away from the fun punk scene and toward more serious crimes, like burglary, guns, stealing cars, and large-scale drug dealing. Some of them were becoming genuinely dangerous people. Some were getting into white supremacy. Heroin started to become popular. It was more than I signed up for. I cut ties and ended up in military school, which saved my life. From there, I began the long and difficult process of picking up the pieces.

10 | RADICAL PRIMITIVES

Brecht Andersch: Austin was very receptive. I wasn't fully formed, and people there were very accepting of me as I was. There was a kind of humanism, a humanistic element to the scene. People were interested in everything. But they were also interested in *people*.

In the summer of 1985, MTV dispatched a film crew to Austin to report on a burgeoning scene of postpunk and "New Sincerity" bands. They found something else: a strange young man who could barely play or sing, who invited himself into the program and stole the show. Daniel Johnston soon became an international cult figure; six years later, Kurt Cobain, the most famous rock star in the world, was wearing a Daniel Johnston T-shirt.

Johnston wasn't even a Texan, so it seemed a bit random that Austin claimed him. But Texas has a long history of embracing radical primitives—musicians and artists with negligible skills and loads of angst. One can draw a straight line from Johnston back to Raul's bands like Reversible Cords, who played oddball instruments and had a penchant for run-ins with the law, or to the Houston group Culturcide, who gleefully blurred the line between creation and copyright infringement. Long before Texas punk began, another Houston group called Red Krayola were more commune than band: they launched their career in 1966 by sharing their stage with a fifty-person nonmusical group called the Familiar Ugly. All these groups took DIY principles to new conceptual and expressive heights—rarely have musicians with so little yearned to express so much.

Why do these birds alight in Texas? The essayist Charles Pierce has written about the American crank, suggesting that we embrace crackpots because their reveries push a conversation forward. And in *Mystery Train*, Greil Marcus illuminated the Texas crank who became a US president, Lyndon Johnson. Explaining LBJ's penchant for obscenity, Marcus writes, "The American, Johnson might have been telling us, is alive only as long as he is uncivilized." The false (and racist) dichotomy between civilization and savagery notwithstanding, these myths still hold Texans and other Americans in thrall. Is there a line between performance and provocation? Between genius and madness? Is there a difference between music and noise? For radical primitives, it was all on the table.

Lynn Keller: Our band, Reversible Cords, lasted about a year. From '78 till the beginning of '80. We were broken up before we did our album.

Tom Huckabee: How were the Re*Cords different from the Huns? They were a better band. They were fun to be around. I was intellectually compatible with them. And politically compatible. Three of the Huns voted for . . . Reagan. That broke my heart.

Lynn Keller: Ty Gavin was the one I went up and talked to [at Raul's]. He said, "Oh, you want to be in a band?" And I was like, "Okay." It was totally random. And then a week later, after I met Bert and Doug, we had our first show. Halloween 1978. I mean, you didn't have to know anything. You didn't even have to be a good singer. It was just like, "Okay, I'll do it. Let's go." It was nuts.

Tom Huckabee: [Reversible Cords guitarist] Doug [McAninch] and [keyboardist] Bert [Crews] were always letting people know that they were the culprits, just scofflaw, delinquent criminals, with complete and utter disrespect for authority. We were even banned from Raul's. Bert was an incorrigible person. If he found out somebody liked him, he'd do something to aggravate them. He was kind of an equal opportunity insult machine. Anyway, he was a beautiful friend to me during this whole time.

Steve Chaney (fan): The thing about Bert was that he was a total academic—erudite, skinny guy, patches on his elbows, the whole bit. But bad . . . very bad.

Lynn Keller: I trashed my voice in the punk scene because the music was so loud. And I didn't know how to sing. I had to scream over the music. There were no monitors, nothing. I was just trying to appeal to myself and interpret what these guys had written or whatever I had written.

Jeff Tartakov: When I first went to Raul's, I liked the Skunks and Standing Waves. But the Re*Cords and Radio Free Europe were leaders, not followers, at Raul's. I thought the Re*Cords were politically radical—they would perform acoustically on the Drag, in front of the UT Co-Op. Nick West would be there, handing out copies of *Sluggo!* I saw Doug from the Re*Cords vomit onstage once, and Lynn Keller just kept performing—she was dancing in the vomit.

Neil Ruttenberg: I liked the Reversible Cords. Lynn was a great singer, although they were pretty challenging.

Lynn Keller: We weren't copying anybody. And most people were. They were listening to English punk or West Coast stuff or Iggy Pop, whatever. But other Texas punk bands were derivative.

Ty Gavin: The Re*Cords were a very politically charged band. Anything Bert Crews was involved in had to have some militant element. He was one of the most militant people in the Raul's scene.

Lynn Keller: I don't think we were communists or even anarchists—we were just aware that we were being taken over by the man. We had a lot of songs about corporate capitalism and corruption. There was a feeling at the time of *foreboding*. Bert wrote "Guyana Holiday" [about the Jim Jones cult and mass suicides]—and that was just a *horror*. I wrote a song called "Video Cassette Machine"—we were heading down this road of technology. I didn't want people to live with a false sense of security, and I felt that was a threat in Texas. People were in their own dust bowls in their minds. We were pretty serious, actually. I know that no one wanted to admit that, but that's why we didn't stay together.

Tom Huckabee: [After our run-in with the Feds (see chapter 5),] Bert called all the local TV stations, and we did a protest show at the State Capitol rotunda. It was one of our favorite places to drop acid and drink beer and hang out, you know?

Lynn Keller: We showed up at the Capitol at noon, so everybody would be going on their lunch hour. We came in singing "Guyana Holiday," and I sang with a bullhorn. I wanted people to be a little scared. I felt like it was my job. In those days, people weren't really paying attention. Maybe they thought, "This doesn't affect us. This isn't in our country." But meanwhile, there was all this crazy manipulation, these horrors that were happening to people, and it was happening in the US too.

Tom Huckabee: One of the TV crews filmed us playing. We got twenty or thirty of our friends to join us. The state legislature was in session, and they were annoyed by the noise. Supposedly, after that, they passed a law to ban future musical performances in the Capitol rotunda.

Lynn Keller: We called ourselves a guerilla band. We played in the parking lot of the Austin Opry House at an Elvis Costello concert. We also forced ourselves onto a bill with [Big Star guitarist and producer] Alex Chilton. He was playing at the Rome Inn. We went in and said to him, "We want to play *now*."

And Alex Chilton said, "Well, can you come audition in the back?"

We were kind of pissed. We were like, "*No*." But [then] we said, "All right."

We went to the back and just started singing to him. He said, "All right, you guys can go onstage." Then we played a set.

Tom Huckabee: When our record came out, it became one of my favorite albums. [Texas music producer and executive] Bill Bentley loved it. [Velvet Underground guitarist] Sterling Morrison loved it. Brian Hansen from Radio Free Europe. Everybody that mattered to me loved it. Gary Floyd just recently told me it was his favorite record from that time.

Lynn Keller: But we got kicked out of Raul's. Because Bert and Doug had pulled out the bathroom sink or some ridiculous thing.

Tom Huckabee: Oddly enough, they loved us at that Dallas club DJs—the Nervebreakers and all the Dallas bands would come out to see us. That's where the B-52s and the Talking Heads saw us. David Byrne invited us to open for them at the Armadillo three days later.

We knew that we were persona non grata at the Armadillo, along with all of the other Austin punk bands. But we showed up at sound check at the

Armadillo that day anyway. David Byrne came out really sheepishly, and he said, "I can't believe it, but they're not gonna let you all play. They've booked a mime to open the show."

But he said we could hang out with them backstage and drink their beer and eat their food. Except that then the Armadillo staff closed the backstage to us. Doug started mouthing off to them. The bouncers picked him up, threw him out through the back door, and sailed him as high as they possibly could into the air. He landed on his face, lost ten teeth, and broke his jaw.

Lynn Keller: We found out later that the Talking Heads were being filmed that night for the news show *60 Minutes*.

Tom Huckabee: A friend of ours was a telephone operator, and she had been privy to a long-distance call made by Roky [Erickson] to his manager in San Francisco. And she had written down the number. Bert got the number and made the first call to Roky. And the phone call went more or less like this:

> ROKY: Hi! Who's this?
> BERT: This is Bert Crews, Roky, and I'm a local musician with a hot band called the Reversible Cords. We play regular gigs at this punk rock club called Raul's . . .
> ROKY: Oh, I've heard of Raul's! What can I do for you?
> BERT: Well, why don't we play a show? Because we've got all these fans that don't know your music, and you've got a million fans that don't know our music. So why don't we do a show together?
> ROKY: Well . . . all right! I don't have a car, you know. You'll have to come get me.

We were just dumbfounded. Roky was a big, big influence on all of us.

So we started rehearsing with him, and Roky was completely prepared. He had just written all those songs on [Erickson's legendary solo album] *The Evil One*—we may have been the first people to hear songs like "Creature with the Atom Brain" and "Don't Shake Me Lucifer," and they were just fucking awesome. But he sussed us out really quickly. At the first practice, at one point, he stopped in the middle of a song, and he says, "Look, you guys, you've got to get *the beat . . . and the notes . . . and the chords too!*"

We played this fantastic show at Raul's. The punks and the hippies were officially enemies at this time. There was practically a red line drawn down the middle of the club: hippies on one side, punks on the other side. The hippies were irritated that this band that they've never heard of had gotten hold of Roky. They were very suspicious—and also concerned for their physical safety. Meanwhile, the punks were giving the hippies the stink eye. But then we started playing, and I think we won them over.

> There was no better time for Roky Erickson's debut at Raul's than Mayday last Tuesday. In honor of Russia's national holiday, Erickson, backed by the Reversible Cords, opened an eight-song set with his anthem "Two Headed Dog." . . . When the chemistry was right . . . it was like the Thirteenth Floor Elevators jamming with Devo. Raul's regulars . . . honored Erickson as a returning hero. They yelled, "We love you, Roky" so much it could have been the summer of love all over again."
>
> JOE NICK PATOSKI, *AUSTIN AMERICAN-STATESMAN*, MAY 5, 1979

Buffalo Gals were less confrontational than Re*Cords, but their central proposition was no less radical: They thought women should be able to live and create in their own way. They shared a downtown Austin warehouse, worked shitty jobs, and practiced their songs. Their hilarious gig posters stuck it to punk patriarchy. Within months of forming, they became a favorite opening band for the very popular cowpunk outfit Rank and File, but the Gals always stood up for themselves: After one show with the Butthole Surfers, singer-guitarist Kathy McCarty got into a tussle over money with Surfer Paul Leary and punched him in the nose!

In 1983, Buffalo Gals contributed their lilting and sweet "I Love Dancing with Joshua" to the *Mighty Feeble* compilation for a label run by legendary California punks Mike Watt and D. Boon of the Minutemen. They'd become one of a small handful of Texas bands who were platformed by much better-known California punks. Still, some Austin hipsters continued to grumble about the Gals. Why was it so hard to take a female punk band seriously?

Kathy McCarty: The first song I wrote was about how the cosmic cowboys and the punks were all into the same things, but they hated each other for no reason. When the Buffalo Gals played with the Big Boys and Dicks, we couldn't believe they were letting us open for them.

The thing about Texas was that it was cheap to live here. The Buffalo Gals paid $180 per month to live in the front of a warehouse. It was downtown, on West Fifth Street, right where the Waldorf is today. My room had no windows and no heat, so I took a sledgehammer and knocked a hole in my wall for a fan. I slept on an army cot and drove my motorcycle right into the warehouse. My cousin wrote me a letter, and she just wrote on the envelope, "Kathy McCarty, she lives in a warehouse in Austin." And I got the letter.

Pat Doyle: [Buffalo Gals bassist] Liz Gall was from Killeen! She wore the Renaissance Records "Remember, Disco Sucks!" T-shirt to school three times a week, and then Lou Reed and Cramps T-shirts on the other days. She was a total freak among all the Killeen potheads and heshers. Liz was way ahead of her time.

Kathy McCarty: We all had these wage-slave jobs. I was a busboy at Pecan Street Café. And we spent the rest of our time rehearsing, playing, and trying to get shows. Both the Buffalo Gals and Meat Joy rehearsed at our warehouse. When Meat Joy was practicing, I was at work, and when the Buffalo Gals practiced, Meat Joy were at work. The Butthole Surfers may have rehearsed there too while I was at work. I think they played there for a party. So did Hüsker Dü.

Chip Kinman (Dils, Rank and File): I was impressed with some of the Texas bands, although that didn't mean that I liked them. Joe "King" Carrasco—he was something. The Judy's, *wow*, they were something. We liked the Buffalo Gals because they were very passionate and straightforward. We didn't care that some people said they couldn't play their instruments. As a matter of fact, their drummer, Jamie Spidle, played in our most recent band, Cowboy Nation. She's great.

Kathy McCarty: We *tried* to be good. We really tried. It's scary to say, but I was the most technically proficient musician in the Buffalo Gals. And you know me—I'm not *that* good. We were remarkable for our incredible bravery and pretty okay songwriting.

Gretchen Phillips: I had been in bands in Houston since I was twelve but hadn't really started playing yet in Austin. Then I saw the Buffalo Gals at the

Ritz in 1982. I seem to remember that stage being *so* high! As I was looking up at them, something snapped inside of me, and I vowed to myself, "I am going to be up there on that stage too." I loved the Buffalo Gals and everything that was so fucking weird about them musically and visually. Plus, they made amazing posters.

Kathy McCarty: The Buffalo Gals weren't together all that long, but we got very popular. Probably because we had three young, relatively attractive girls in our band. We didn't try to be sexy or trade on our sexuality. We were not flamboyant. Our songs spoke to people and their time of life, of being a young girl.

Culturcide lumbered out of the petrochemical wastelands of Houston like a swamp thing toting a primordial drum machine. The band, led by visual artist Mark Flood, who was then calling himself Perry Webb, were enthusiastically transgressive: They didn't care about guitars, and they preferred shrieking noise over melody. They didn't like punk songs. They didn't like songs.

Working with partner Jim Craine, Flood launched Culturcide as a Lone Star response to the industrial, synthetic sounds of Throbbing Gristle and Cabaret Voltaire. By the mid-1980s, Culturcide began splattering overdubs of their own vocals and music across Top 40 hits like [USA for Africa's] "We Are the World" and [Grand Funk Railroad's] "We're an American Band." One of these pasteups, "Houston Lawman," brutally indicts racist police violence, even as it evokes the southern Gothic conditions that produced such violence. When Culturcide released their 1986 masterpiece *Tacky Souvenirs of Pre-Revolutionary America*, American major label record companies were not impressed with the bands' use of their intellectual property. After things got hot, Flood arranged for a few friends to impersonate Culturcide, in order to distract lawyers who were trying to sue the band on behalf of various copyright owners.

Mark Flood, a.k.a. John Peters, a.k.a. Perry Webb (Culturcide): One thing that's hard to pin down is how singular it all was. At first, nobody had ever heard of punk rock, except me and a couple of people I knew. Then, when people started showing up at the club, it was like we were a secret cult group. And everything that happened was something that had never happened before.

Most of my friends went down the road I called Talking Heads. And I moved into a completely different world of all the people who'd been caught up by the punk rock thing. It evolved so rapidly. I started buying punk singles and going to the club. I lost interest in my life as a college student and flunked out.

At first, the local [Houston] response to punk rock was not stereotypical hardcore. For about five years, it was all kinds of experimental weirdness, and I was into *that* version. Throbbing Gristle was the actual inspiration for Culturcide—I met the other guy, Jim Craine, because of our interest in Throbbing Gristle. He worked in the edgy record store, and he told me that if I could get the money, he knew how to make a record, which was mind-blowing to me. So I got the money, and we made the first record.

> Formed in 1980, experimental noise rock band Culturcide recorded their debut single . . . *"Consider Museums as Concentration Camps"* at MRS Studio in Houston . . . [and dedicated it to] Museum of Fine Art Houston.
>
> WILD DOG FANZINE, HOUSTON, DATE UNKNOWN, REPRINTED IN WILD DOG ARCHIVES (FLICKR), OCTOBER 30, 2014

Mark Flood: Eventually, we decided to start playing gigs. Despite my lack of musical skills and my mediocre vocals, I was in a band. It was something I had vaguely wanted but never really imagined could happen.

> The stomach-turning sonic manipulation on "Feeling I Was Gonna Die" is disorienting and abrasive in all the right ways. This song in particular makes even the crudest Coil and Throbbing Gristle records seem accessible by comparison. Hell, even Suicide sounds downright melodic next to the pummeling electronics of "Laughtrack," the industrial quasi-boogie of "Another Miracle," the screaming guitar gauze draping the existential nightmare of "The Tapes" and the back-to-back cacophony of "(C'Mon) Let's Talk About It" and "Penis-Vagina." . . . An important document of Culturcide's legacy as creators of some of the most utterly unforgiving and brutal music to come out of the early and mid-'80s.
>
> CHRIS HENDERSON, REVIEW OF CULTURCIDE ALBUM *GIGS FOR AN IMAGINARY AUDIENCE*, *HOUSTON PRESS*, MAY 14, 2008

Mark Flood: [Our first album] *Year One* was made from cassettes we had used to record our rehearsals and live gigs. I had met a recording engineer who showed me how you could transfer cassette recordings to reel-to-reel tapes without too much hiss. Hiss was a problem in the analog age. I assembled *Year One*, but I couldn't afford [to press it up on] vinyl. So at first, I just put it out as a cassette release. I would put each cassette inside a blank LP cover, with one of our flyers pasted it onto it.

> This LP . . . is pleasingly aggro all the way through. Hearing Perry Webb mumble "Hey cocksucker, I wanna beat the shit out of you" to a nonplussed audience in Houston, TX circa 1981 over the cheapest drum machine sound known to man is a moment that is nothing short of magical.
>
> HOME BLITZ, REVIEW OF CULTURCIDE'S *YEAR ONE* ALBUM, *DUSTED MAGAZINE*, N.D.

Mark Flood: In the early eighties, I tried to apply the ideas of punk rock to my painting. It was certainly a source of energy. I would paint little stick figures and text onto paintings that I bought at thrift stores. Only a couple of the paintings actually had an obvious punk rock dimension. There's one painting that has clippings about Sid Vicious's trial [for the murder of his girlfriend Nancy Spungen].

Trish Herrera: Mark Flood—or John Peters—and I were so close back then. He started incorporating corporate logos into his artwork. He'd go to secondhand resale shops and buy, like, a Mexican [black] velvet painting, then draw an Exxon sign in the middle of it or a McDonald's logo. So it had this meaning of, like, "Oh my God, these things are creeping up on our beautiful, natural world!" When he started nabbing songs and singing over them for that one album, he had a lot of trouble because he didn't ask [the copyright holders for permission to] do that. My very favorite one is "They Aren't the World." So funny.

Mark Flood: *Tacky Souvenirs of Pre-Revolutionary America* came out six years later. We had been playing some of those songs since about 1983. We were just playing one or two per set. I'd gotten used to being in a band and playing live, and I had discovered all the unwritten rules of those kinds of concerts: How the audience wanted you to succeed, and what it was like to have their attention. How all the familiar rock and roll clichés were great for the concert and for the audience.

Instead of accepting these concepts, I started trying to mess with them. I had the idea of starting a gig like a regular rock band playing rock and roll stuff, with a lot of noise. Then we would get weirder and weirder and destroy the comfort of it all. And nothing was more uncomfortable than when we had a record player on stage, and the band would almost stop playing, and I would put [Paul McCartney and Stevie Wonder's] "Ebony and Ivory" on the record player and then sing new lyrics over it while the band made noise or played along.

> The situation is addressed by the American group Culturcide, who, on "Tacky Souvenirs of Pre-Revolutionary America," record a vicious polemic over pirated tracks by leading rights owners like Michael Jackson and Paul McCartney. "Plagiarism is necessary. Progress implies it," they state, occupying the opposite pole to an industry attempting, as ever, to catch the lightning and control the impact of technological change.
>
> SIMON FRITH AND JON SAVAGE, "SAMPLING THE SOUNDS," *THE OBSERVER*, OCTOBER 18, 1987

Mark Flood: After we broke the concert down to nothing, then we would start up again. Play some actual music. It wasn't popular, but audiences were tolerant back then. I decided to put all that material on one LP because it was very problematic, in many ways.

> Home-taping is killing the record industry . . . so keep doing it.
>
> LINER NOTES, CULTURCIDE, *TACKY SOUVENIRS OF PRE-REVOLUTIONARY AMERICA*, 1986

> The first of Houston's underground bands to play in Europe, Culturcide received a warm welcome from Dutch and Belgium audiences. They landed in Den Hague and went on to play a government-sponsored rock festival in Amsterdam at the Paradiso theater, with such acts as Bad Brains, Nick Cave, SPK, and many other bands. . . . Another week of dates in Germany unfortunately fell through, but Culturcide made lots of new contacts and friends in the cities where they played. . . . While

> in Antwerp, they caught an art-video installation about violence in America which featured Ed Gein and replicas of some of his gruesome "leather" crafts.
>
> *SICKO*, NO. 2, 1987

Mark Flood: To me, Culturcide don't seem that important as a punk band!

Like Marcel Duchamp, musicians such as Culturcide and Daniel Johnston are often misunderstood because they use the materials at hand, the cheap throwaways of our age. "Hey, anyone could talk over a record," people say. "Anyone could repurpose a urinal!" They hear the noise and miss the signal. Much of Johnston's music is poorly recorded and psychically raw, but underneath is a songwriter who spent years poring over the collected works of Lennon and McCartney.

Johnston grew up in a fundamentalist Christian family in West Virginia and began recording his music, making art, and fiending on comic books long before he made it to Texas. He traveled the USA with a carnival before landing in Austin in 1984, when he got a job at a McDonald's location across from the University of Texas campus. Johnston wasn't a punk, but he was electrified by the hardcore and postpunk scene he saw flourishing around him. I saw him walking the Drag and handing out duplicates of his self-recorded tapes after his shifts at McDonald's. One of these tapes found its way to a former Raul's regular named Jeff Tartakov, who began to represent and support Johnston.

After Johnston's appearance on MTV's *Cutting Edge* program in 1985, his cassettes started to spread via word of mouth throughout what would soon become known as the Alternative Nation. Meanwhile, Johnston himself was revolving in and out of mental institutions, where he was diagnosed with bipolar disorder. Occasionally, he attacked people. The noisy New York postpunk group Sonic Youth took an interest in him, and they invited Johnston east to perform and record in 1988. He stopped taking his medication and went to New York City, but after several area shows, he lashed out at Sonic Youth drummer Steve Shelley and ended up wandering the streets of Manhattan for days. In the midst of all of this, I saw one of his performances at a downtown venue called the Cat Club. Johnston was a frightening, quaking apparition, his eyes glued to the heavens as he sang. Afterward, he walked through the club, and I said hello. "You're in the darkness, Pat," Daniel said. "Come into the light." I stepped back and declined the invitation.

Sometimes the noise surrounding a challenging performer reveals more about their audience than it does about them. Shortly after Johnston's first appearance in the national music press in 1989, a debate began swirling around him: Was he a genuine talent, or an unstable victim being exploited by managers, journalists, and family members who were just out for a buck? I believe all these things were true, but Johnston was also more in control than he might have seemed. Two allies were more sincere than the others. In 2005, documentary film director Jeff Feuerzeig made a fine film about Daniel, and the movie then drew even more attention to the performer. But if Johnston had never met manager Jeff Tartakov, he probably wouldn't have survived the 1980s.

> It was really wild in West Virginia, because all we had was records. When I was 19, I wanted to be the Beatles. I was disappointed when I found out I couldn't sing.
>
> DANIEL JOHNSTON, INTERVIEW WITH LOUIS BLACK, *SPIN*, MARCH 1989

Jeff Tartakov: Austin in 1984 was the perfect landing spot for Daniel. For the first time in his life, he was able to see bands on a nightly basis, and he was exposing himself to a wide array of bands and singer-songwriters. He already had this amazing catalog of albums recorded in the family basement in West Virginia that nobody would know about for another couple of years, but he chose to reinvent himself in Austin by handing out [his self-released cassette album] *Hi, How Are You* as his calling card. I don't think he would have chosen this tape first anywhere else.

Kathy McCarty: Daniel was living in San Marcos, Texas, and having a mental breakdown. So he joined a carnival, traveled around the US, and he was coming back on his way to San Marcos. Then he injured himself, and the church helped him find a place to stay. He was in the right place at the right time because there was a big songwriter scene here. He became the talk of the town really quickly.

By this time, we had formed Glass Eye. Daniel gave me a copy of *Hi, How Are You*, and I told him I would listen to it. I didn't, and the next time he saw me, he asked if I had, and I felt guilty, and I lied and said I had and that it was great. He asked if he could open for us, and I said yes. And those

Daniel Johnston performing for (and directing) a music video for his song "The Stinker," Cactus Café, University of Texas, 1986. Note his McDonald's uniform. "He was totally innocent and totally manipulative."

slots opening for Glass Eye were gold, baby, because we were *popular*. I went home and finally listened to his tape, and I thought, "OMG, this is so good!" Then I played it for the band, and everyone loved it, super-duper loved it. We thought, "OMG, this guy is an insane genius!"

Jeff Tartakov: When I heard his piano-based music and tapes that he recorded before *Hi, How Are You*, that was when I knew he had created this body of work that would last in importance and last until long after he was gone. It's all of these songs of unrequited love that people can relate to. And until he left Austin in 1987, Kathy McCarty and I were the only people that had heard that material.

Brecht Andersch: The first time I heard Daniel Johnston was in a record store, in the first location of Waterloo Records. This girl behind the counter put on "I'll Do Anything but Breakdance for Ya, Baby." It had this haunted, isolated, and very expressive quality to it. The girl at the counter had this sly expression—like she was thinking, "I'm gonna subject them to this and see if they can take it."

Kathy McCarty: Daniel was so bad at playing live. The Austin bands loved Daniel, but the audiences were like, "What is this shit?" The audiences felt like he was being foisted upon them. He could never do more than three songs because he was so nervous.

> I wish I had never got manic depression. When I was in junior high I didn't know what was the matter with me. It was as if I'd died or something.
>
> DANIEL JOHNSTON, INTERVIEW WITH ROSANNA GREENSTREET, *THE GUARDIAN*, AUGUST 5, 2011

Teresa Taylor: [The Butthole Surfers played a show at] 505 East Fifth Street, which had once been the Buffalo Gals–Meat Joy warehouse. This was the same show where somebody thought it was a good idea to give Daniel Johnston LSD. I wish we really *could* roll back the hands of time. Like so many things in life, he had fun at first, but it led to a psychotic break. Acid is not for everyone.

Jeff Tartakov: Austin was in no way to blame for his troubles, although he was obviously not equipped to handle LSD. One could argue that becoming "famous" made things difficult for Daniel, but it was what he wanted.

Brecht Andersch: [When I was living with Rick Linklater,] I came home from work one day, and I was bounding up the stairs. I could see Rick at the top, talking to someone. This person was wearing some sort of green monster mask and was making all of these yelps and strange noises. I thought, "What the hell is going on here?"

When I got to the top of the stairs, the guy took off the mask, and Rick said, "Brecht, this is Daniel Johnston."

Kathy McCarty: Daniel made all of his dreams come true, but only after he appeared on *The Cutting Edge* show and then [had] a lot of sophisticated management by Jeff Tartakov.

Jeff Tartakov: At the time, his family believed that Daniel had no talent, and that I was misleading him. They were [members of the Church of Christ], and they were pretty close-minded. I had a falling out with Daniel's father. I have a soft spot for Daniel's mom, even though she yelled at him [as heard on some early DJ tapes]. She told me I was the first Jewish person she'd ever met. She thought I was this evil showbusiness Jew that would do anything to sell records. And [that] since I was Jewish, I controlled everything.

Louis Black: Daniel had two football teams in his head, and they were arguing all together at the same time. He was like *Sybil*, but instead of sixteen personalities, he had thirty. But even when he was acting crazy, I never thought he was *crazy*. He was totally innocent and totally manipulative. People talk about how he was being exploited, but he was exploiting the people who said that!

> You've probably noticed I'm no ghost. . . . It's just that I identify with Casper so much. It's simple. He always had a good attitude and he was always helping people. That's the way I feel I should be. Though I sometimes ruin things for people instead. I've been told that my music bugs some people. I say crazy things that upset them. . . . But I feel like I'm a good person who just wants to entertain.
>
> DANIEL JOHNSTON, INTERVIEW WITH *HOT PRESS*, 2006

Jeff Tartakov: There were times that Daniel was in the State Hospital, and I didn't know why, but we couldn't get him out. Then there were times when he was out of the institutions, and he *really* needed to go back, but we couldn't get him back in unless he committed a crime.

> I was stuck. I couldn't get out of the system; every time I'd come home, if I got upset and raised my voice a little bit or something, Mom and Dad would say, "back to the hospital." So the last time I got out I said, "Hey, this time I'm going to stay out." But I spent almost five years in mental hospitals and it was like a bird in a cage.
>
> DANIEL JOHNSTON, QUOTED IN LAURA BARTON, "'I KNOW THE DARKNESS,'" *THE GUARDIAN*, APRIL 21, 2006

Jeff Tartakov: You asked me about one or two of the most stressful moments in our history together, but they were all stressful: getting him out of Austin State Hospital for the first time, the trip to New York that led

Daniel Johnston sits onstage at a Butthole Surfers show, with Kathy McCarty of Glass Eye and Brett Bradford of Scratch Acid, 5th St. Theatre, Austin, September 1985.

to his falling out with Steve Shelley and Sonic Youth, the elderly woman who went out the window [to flee from Daniel], the plane crash with his father. It was all very stressful.

> Yeah, I got in a bunch of trouble. I beat up a bunch of cops and went to jail and then they put me in the mental hospital. Man, I knocked those guys around.
>
> DANIEL JOHNSTON, INTERVIEW WITH JASON COHEN, *OPTION*, NOVEMBER 1994

Jeff Tartakov: On the day that Bill Clinton was inaugurated, I got a phone call from a Washington, DC, hotel room, and it was Terry Tolkin asking about signing Daniel to Elektra. After that, Elektra flew me up to New York, and it became a bidding war. Unbeknownst to me, [Elektra Chairman and CEO] Bob Krasnow had a relative with mental illness. And during the one conversation I had with Krasnow, he asked me, "If we sign Daniel and the whole thing blows up, and he never makes a record, is this money still going to help him?" I could not have been more impressed by that.

[Contrary to what he said at the time,] Daniel didn't think Elektra was bad because Metallica was satanic. He liked Metallica. He just didn't want Metallica to think he was not as good as them.

Daniel wanted to get rid of me. With Elektra, it was like a package deal: for Daniel *and* me. He did try to get Elektra to sign him [without me], but Elektra said, "No Jeff, no deal."

> Most of the worst things said about me, I've said myself.
>
> DANIEL JOHNSTON, INTERVIEW WITH ROSANNA GREENSTREET, *THE GUARDIAN*, AUGUST 5, 2011

Jeff Tartakov: We still could have salvaged the deal. A little while later, I got the phone call from Tom Gimbel. He told me he was now Daniel's manager. That's when I knew it was over between Daniel and I. Daniel had found Gimbel by looking through the Austin phone book. Gimbel was a low-paid employee of Amazing Records, which was the first name under "Record Labels" in the Yellow Pages.

Everyone else in Austin knew that Daniel had fired me multiple times, and it never took. But Gimbel didn't know that. He was the first and only person who intervened. He's the only person I'm still bitter about. He had zero experience in signing a major label deal. And eventually he did get Daniel a contract with Atlantic Records—which was worth about one-third of what we were being offered from Elektra.

> It's a lot different being in the big time. It means I'm not making little records anymore. It's a big deal. It's great.
>
> DANIEL JOHNSTON, INTERVIEW WITH JASON COHEN, *OPTION*, NOVEMBER 1994

Jeff Tartakov: [After that call from Gimbel,] I went four years without talking to Daniel, until 1997. I was suicidal at the time. I was also thousands of dollars in debt because when the Elektra deal blew up, I still had to pay the lawyer.

Then, in 1997, Daniel was in town for South by Southwest, and I ran into him at the Electric Lounge. We talked, and he apologized to me. It was a really lengthy, sincere apology, where he said all the right things, everything I could have wanted him to say. So from that point on, we were friends again.

> The most important thing in music is absolute honesty. People like Daniel and [Roky] Erickson—'cos they're slightly damaged—have this great ability to touch your heart because they don't know where to stop. When a child hits a piano he makes untainted music, and that's there in Daniel. He goes between extremes of naivety and darkness.
>
> JASON PIERCE (SPIRITUALIZED), QUOTED IN LAURA BARTON, "'I KNOW THE DARKNESS,'" *THE GUARDIAN*, APRIL 21, 2006

Jeff Tartakov: I'm very proud of him. I feel like he's my little brother who did well. I can't imagine my life without Daniel. Our relationship gave my life meaning. I never married or had kids, so there's nothing more important to me than what I did for Daniel.

> Everything is really happening for me. I've just bought a new house. I've built it right next door to my parents because I couldn't do without them. My dad is my manager now. I've had some other managers but as soon as my dad took over, I was rich and travelling all over the world. Now, what I really, really want to do is get enough money to buy my dad a B-51. That's what he flew when he was with the Tigers during the war. I'd like to get him a restored model. He'll flip out when I do.
>
> DANIEL JOHNSTON, INTERVIEW WITH *HOT PRESS*, 2006

11 | THE REVISIONISTS

Clark Walker, a.k.a. Jean Dodge (fan and filmmaker): In Tulsa, in the winter of 1978, a month or so before the Sex Pistols played Cain's Ballroom there, my brother came home from Starship Records with the Ramones first album and *Give 'Em Enough Rope* by the Clash—and our entire trove of rock records was *shoved* to one side on our shelf so that the punk albums would be physically separate from the other LPs. We didn't want the two groups of vinyl touching one another. And yet, what Joe Strummer taught us—quickly—was that there were no borders, no categories, no separation. As Neil Young once told a heckler who said his stuff all sounded alike, "It's all one song." We loved Buddy Holly already, and yet, it took the Clash playing "I Fought the Law" [written by the Crickets' guitarist Sonny Curtis] for us to truly appreciate "Not Fade Away." The piles had to be separate before they came back together.

Punk had been a year zero, a blast center where everything old was destroyed and everything new was improved. It wasn't articulated as a rule, but everyone knew it was no longer cool to talk about Aerosmith. For many of us in Texas, this began to change around 1982, after the release of three key records on the Los Angeles–based Slash Records and its sublabels. On *The Days of Wine and Roses*, the Dream Syndicate channeled their love for the Velvet Underground and 1960s psychedelia into a seemingly fresh take on postpunk. With *Fire of Love*, the Gun Club married a dank memory of Mississippi blues to high-speed punk songs. And the Misfits, from Lodi, New Jersey, created their *meisterwerk*, *Walk Among Us*, by fusing their devotion to horror films and the Ramones with their love for a 1970s band so loathsome that many punks dared not utter their name.

In January 1983, the Misfits brought their monster makeup and bone-shaped guitars to the Ritz in Austin. I didn't go, but I regretted that immediately and spent the next week scrambling across the West Campus area, asking everyone, "How were the Misfits?" Almost all of them said the same thing: "They were terrible! They were just like Kiss!" But when I finally caught up with my best friend, Steve Collier, and asked about the Misfits, he said, "They were so great! They were just like Kiss!"

As a source of inspiration for Texas punks, country and western music *should* have been off-limits. It was our parents' music, the songs of our oppressors. For me, it was music for people who used the N-word. But even that changed when Rank and File came to town. Chip and Tony Kinman and Alejandro Escovedo were California punks who'd been in the Dils and the Nuns, and they played like the Everly Brothers with more adrenaline. Then they scored a record deal with Slash. Like the best revisionists, Rank and File seemed to have gone back to the future. Plus, they were very dashing in those pointy black cowboy boots.

Chip Kinman: I had this epiphany outside of the Lone Star Café in New York City. I didn't have the money to get in, but Merle Haggard was playing. I could hear this loud, thumping "boom-ba-ba-boom" sound. And I thought it sounded like the Sex Pistols. I'd been looking for something new, something *honest*. I was done with punk, but I couldn't have played jazz or reggae. And right then, I knew it had to be country. I knew I could *play* country. We'd grown up with it.

I wasn't interested in the myth of the cowboy or cowboy music. There's a big difference between "Home on the Range" and "Okie from Muskogee." But our parents were country. My mom's name is Dixie Lee. Our cousins—our family—were *country*. Before my dad went to Vietnam, we lived in North Carolina, near the Ohio River. I thought of country music as something that was about the Everyman.

Joe Nick Patoski: Rank and File were *ambitious*. I didn't think of them as a punk band. The punks were always saying they hated country music and the cosmic country scene. But Rank and File tricked them into liking it.

[Bassist] Tony [Kinman] wore that huge ten-gallon black cowboy hat, and it became comical. Like a shtick. And it worked.

Chip Kinman: We thought about moving to Nashville—but we thought that might be a tough nut to crack. We thought about Memphis—it was sort of country-adjacent. But the Dils had played in Austin. People knew us there. We had connections there. And we'd also seen lots of other places in Texas. The bayous in East Texas, little West Texas towns, El Paso. Texas was everything I thought it would be. Maybe we didn't know so many Texas punk bands. But we loved Bill Neely. Absolutely worshipped him.

Bill Bentley (producer and executive, Warner Bros. Records): Dave Alvin from the Blasters was the first person to tell me, "Hey, you gotta check out this band from Austin called Rank and File."

Chip Kinman: One day, we were practicing in a garage near Avenue D. And this Austin punk luminary walked in. I can't remember who it was—it wasn't Biscuit. But he heard we were playing country, and he told us point-blank, "You're not punks."

We went to Brad First at Club Foot and said, "We were in the Dils, and Alejandro was in the Nuns. Can we have a gig?" And he said, "Sure, you can open for Pylon." We played that show, and it seemed to go okay. But then we were told that we would never be playing there again. Because we were country.

You know how we did it? We started playing at the Short Horn, which was a down-and-out honky-tonk next to the Stallion, where everyone ate chicken-fried steak. They gave us a gig playing five sets every Sunday night, even though we only had about twenty-three minutes' worth of songs. Then we started playing acoustically at the Alamo Lounge and Emma Jo's. And UT students started coming. And then people like Lucinda [Williams] started coming. People started hearing about us.

Chris Gates: Rank and File made me laugh. I remember they showed up in Texas, in their dude outfits, thinking somehow they were radical. Discovering traditional country music was a radical thing for them because they're fucking Canadians. But don't come to Austin—where the Big Boys were having to fight with Willie Nelson's road crew on a regular basis—and talk to me about fucking country music. For me, Rank and File were also kind of edge-free. And the last thing I wanted was edge-free.

Chip Kinman: Our song "I Went Walking" was about something that happened to me on St. Mark's Place in NYC. Alejandro and I were walking down the street, and this punk was walking toward us. This guy had everything: the Mohawk, the black leather jacket, the spikes. And I just said, "What a loser! Doesn't he know all that is over?"

Then he passed us, and I looked back, and the back of his jacket said "The Dils." I just thought, "I'm the loser." So that song's really about me.

Joe Nick Patoski: Nobody else was doing what Rank and File did. They were really like the next generation of the Flying Burrito Brothers. But their timing was not good. Country radio wasn't going to play them, and KOKE-FM, the progressive country station in Austin, had just gone out of business. They would have been perfect for college radio, but that wasn't yet what it would become a few years later. [The other problem was that] Slash was a DIY label, and they were breaking groups like Los Lobos out of Los Angeles, but they didn't have the wherewithal to break their own records on radio.

Chip Kinman: I really wanted to learn to play better. I was actually taking guitar lessons. Alejandro just wasn't headed in that direction. Rank and File was really becoming the Chip and Tony show. That wasn't what he wanted. After he left, something was missing. But we didn't know what it was. The only regret I have after all these years is that we couldn't keep that version of Rank and File together.

If Rank and File presented themselves as cowpunk heartthrobs, Hickoids were more like goat ropers who'd spent too much time under the stars and out of their minds. Singer and San Antonio native Jeff Smith formed the band in Austin with guitarist and inevitably hallucinating tepee-dweller John Thomas Jackson, a.k.a. Jukebox, in 1984. Hickoids threw everything and the meth lab sink into their version of cowpunk: howling, LSD, screaming, psilocybin mushrooms, Eagles covers, and drag queens too. A key moment of the band's classic *Waltz-a-Cross-Dress Texas* album arrives when Smith describes waking up to see their drummer wearing a dress and being beaten by a cop. Smith merely hollers, "That ain't no way to treat a lady!" Hickoids never made the mistake of taking themselves too seriously, which is ironic because they have survived as a working band longer than any other Texas punk group mentioned in this book.

Jeff Smith: Why have the Hickoids lasted so long? Well . . . some people just never learn.

Karen Ruth Getchell: When I got to Austin, in 1984, I met Jeff Smith at the [UT Student] Union bar. He said, "Do you want to come see my band?" I thought, "He's probably the bass player or something." Then I get to the Beach, and I see this completely different person, singing for the Hickoids. He wasn't the same quiet guy. He was wearing pants made out of duct tape and throwing corn at the audience. I thought, "Who is this person?"

He came over to our house once, and he saw my Tears for Fears record. He said, "Oh, you like Beers for Queers."

Jeff Smith: When I was a kid, hard country was what I heard from the back seat of our car when my dad was driving and smoking a cigar. In the Hickoids, we were interested in that sort of country—George Jones, Tammy Wynette, Merle Haggard.

Jukebox came from Lamesa, out by Lubbock. His father sounded like a real asshole, and his mother sounded pretty mean too. Jukebox didn't talk about it too much; that was just my impression. He wasn't the most trusting individual. On that first album, he was obsessed with being able to hear every nuance of his guitar—his sound took up a lot of space.

I'd been hanging out with Jukebox for about six months in Austin before I knew he could play guitar. He kept saying, "Look, I want to start a band with you." But I was pretty hesitant. When I finally heard him, I thought, "Okay, this guy can really play." And he had a very unique style.

Jukebox wanted to call us the Wang Dang Doodlers from Tijuana, and I just said, "No way." Then one day, we went over to Davy Jones's apartment—this was before Davy was in the Hickoids. And while we were talking, Davy was looking out the window. There was this rumpled old guy wearing a cowboy hat and digging through a dumpster. And Davy said, "Look at this old hickoid."

And we said, "That's it—that's our name." It was meant to [suggest] a hick in the big city urban context. Jukebox said he wanted us to be a cross between Gary Stewart and Black Flag.

Our first album doesn't sound like any other thing you've ever heard. It was a flawed experiment. We probably could have used an outside perspective, a producer [who] would have had some ideas for us. But we did it in two days—that's all the time we had.

Davy Jones's dad saw us play in Athens, Georgia, in the mid-1980s, and there were only two people in the audience: Peter Buck from R.E.M. and Davy's dad. Afterward, Davy's dad famously said, "Well, I heard the punk, but I didn't hear the cow." The Hickoids weren't country enough for the country people, and they weren't punk enough for the punks.

Around 1988, when Jukebox was no longer in the band, we were playing out at the Austin rugby fields. We were all high and drunk and were doing our traditional "sunrise" set, but because of a series of delays, it was already 10:00 or 11:00 a.m. It was hotter than hell and really muggy. After the previous thirty hours of drinking and doing whatever other drugs we could get our hands on, we could barely make it through a song. So Jukebox is at the front of the stage, drinking this cheap tequila out of a gallon jug, and heckling us real hard. That didn't bother me—I started the band with him, and he quit, but he was welcome to say his piece. Anyhow, my girlfriend was one of our "corn dancers"—I can't remember whether we had them in chicken wire go-go cages that day or not—but Jukebox starts addressing her and saying something like, "I can't believe you're dancing with these guys; they're a bunch of sexists!" or "Quit demeaning yourself!" So homegirl asks for a drink of the tequila, and Jukebox offers it up. She takes a slug, then hits him with the bottle. That put an end to his play-by-play commentary. And the band finished off his tequila during the set.

Even before New York punks like Patti Smith Group guitarist Lenny Kaye were pledging their love for long-gone 1960s garage bands like the 13th Floor Elevators, rock and roll could be understood as a kind of corpse love, a barely disguised necrophilia. The Rolling Stones worshiped the doomed and possibly demonic Mississippi bluesman Robert Johnson as much as Jim Morrison did moldy old Friedrich Nietzsche. The deepest and most sophisticated performers cover it up with a kind of magic—they make their devotion to older artists disappear in a rush of new sounds and electricity. Punk was no different. When I first heard the Sex Pistols, I thought they were a disgraceful mess. But after a few more listens to *Never Mind the Bollocks*, I was surprised at how much glam rock I could hear in their songs.

Many Austin punks scorned Texas blues and its devotees, at least partly because those sounds belonged to an older generation and their nightlife. Antone's was *the* central Texas mecca for blues performers and fans, but for a while, a younger crowd crammed into the Rome Inn to see upstarts like Stevie Ray Vaughan and the Fabulous Thunderbirds. After it closed in

1980, the Rome Inn became—tellingly—a punk rock and hardcore space called Studio 29.

The Dicks underscored their songs with blues chords, but onlookers sometimes missed that when they saw Gary Floyd in a nurse's uniform. When Big Boys guitarist Tim Kerr and bassist Chris Gates started Poison 13 in 1984 as a side project, they became the first US punks to truly *assimilate* the blues. Unlike the Gun Club, who simply made a sandwich out of blues changes and punk velocity, Poison 13 used that old trick to make the blues (and punk rock itself) disappear inside a sick storm of feedback and fuzz. Singer Mike Carroll squealed like the spawn of Robert Johnson and Darby Crash, but the band's songs were so thick with distortion that it was nearly impossible to hear the Mississippi and Texas blues inside of them.

Poison 13 was heavier and slower than every other Austin punk group, which is part of why they would later be cited as a key influence on Seattle grunge bands like Mudhoney. At first, I had no idea that one of their songs was actually a cover of a tune by folk singer Buffy Sainte-Marie—she was literally my parents' music. We were just beginning to understand that punk was part of history. Poison 13 used their weapons-grade roar to cut right to what makes old country tales of death and betrayal so compelling. It was a kind of tribute, even if blues purists would have called it heresy. Like so many other Texas punks, the group was grappling with a difficult question: How do you honor the past while setting yourself apart from it?

Bill Anderson: Poison 13 were definitely in-betweenies. We were too punk for blues clubs and too bluesy for punks. I think we just wanted to play loud rock songs about drinking, fucking, and killing.

Chris Gates: Poison 13 had a couple of great things going for it. The first was that we were *not* the Big Boys. We weren't responsible for the scene. The Big Boys had this "We have to take care of everyone" mindset. But that's a burden—being the peacekeepers and the big brothers to the scene. There's a lot of weight to that, and I didn't want that anymore. Poison 13 got to just be a band. And two—Poison 13 was a band full of people my own age. Tim is seven years older than me, and Biscuit was nearly thirteen years older. It makes for a different dynamic.

Bill Anderson: I had always listened to blues. But the old stuff. Like, I knew more about Robert Johnson recording in a hotel room in San Antonio than

Poison 13 shooting a music video for "One Step Closer" in their rehearsal space behind Weed Corley Funeral Home, Austin, fall 1984. *From left:* Tim Kerr (*turned away*), Jim Kanan (*partially obscured*), Mike Carroll (RIP), Chris Gates, and Bill Anderson.

I did about the Vulcan Gas Company. Chris came to me and said, "Do you want to be in this psychobilly band?" And that sounded pretty cool.

But then he told me Mike was gonna be the singer. And I said, "You mean, Mike *Carroll*?!" Mike, who has said, maybe, *ten* words to me, *ever*?

But it was Mike's band. It was his music, his sense of style, his aesthetic. Tim and Chris wanted to be in a band with Mike. It was one guy with a quiff, and four other guys with almost no hair.

Chris Gates: Mike [Carroll] was always around, right? He looked cool as shit from the word go. He and I moved in together in '83 and lived together until I left Austin. We were best friends, even though he probably only said, you know, one hundred words to me in our entire friendship.

I liked the garage stuff. I *loved* the blues stuff. Mike and Bill were listening to Tex and the Horseheads and the Nomads and the Lime Spiders. The Gun Club's first record was mind-blowing. And a lot of these bands were actually putting out records at the same time we were making our first record.

Bill cut his teeth playing [Elvis Presley guitarist] Scotty Moore–type riffs. And Jim Kanan, the drummer, was like the punk rock Charlie Watts—he did not speed up or slow down unless it was on purpose, but there's a little *giddyup* in there, you know? I loved the polar opposites of what Tim and Bill were doing because without Bill, Tim's parts are just bushy. Fuzzy. And without Tim, it would have been a little bit more traditional and not as exciting. But the two of them together was an awesome thing.

Sally King: I liked Poison 13 because I love the blues, and anyone covering Bukka White is okay by me. I get my love of blues from my older brothers. I remember hearing them playing Freddie King, Johnny Winter, John Lee Hooker, and Bugs Henderson albums throughout my childhood. Austin was a music town long before Raul's.

Jeff Smith: Poison 13 was one of my favorite bands. But they got a lot from the Ideals. And Austin punks weren't impressed with either of them.

Bill Anderson: Poison 13 never really toured. We just went to LA a few times. We seemed to go over well there. It was almost like being from Texas was exotic for California audiences.

The story of Doctors' Mob also began with the Big Boys: Singer-songwriter Steve Collier had been their first drummer. After discovering the Jam, Collier left to form a mod group called the Capris. But his musical ambitions were more diverse than loud and fast reinventions of early Who and Stax soul songs—Collier loved everything from the Misfits to the Replacements, a young Minneapolis garage band who were making waves. The Capris morphed into Doctors' Mob, with Collier leading an entirely different group who adopted a new slogan: Show Up Late, Show Up Drunk, or Don't Show Up at All.

Full disclosure: At one point, Collier asked me to be the group's manager, which was an unfortunate development for everyone. This was not why he later wrote a song called "Pat Blashill," but that song is also notable because it begins with a parody of Golden Earring's "Radar Love" before becoming Doctors' Mob's parody of hardcore punk. It was a very meta moment. Among other things, Texas punk could now be a revision of a revision—a hall of mirrors reflecting rock music history.

Steve Collier: I was fixated on melodic *heavy* music, like the Jam and the Who. At first, I think we were self-conscious about how melodic our songs were. We thought, "We're gonna be the loudest band in town, and we're gonna play really fast." We thought that would *trick* people, so they would think, "This is not *really* pop music."

But dressing like mods was ridiculous in Texas. People would ask, "Why are you wearing a parka when it's 100 degrees outside?"

"SHUT UP!"

Chris Gates: I loved the Capris when Steve first started doing that band. And then, when it shifted into Doctor's Mob, I loved that because it felt like Steve was getting serious about songwriting.

Jeffrey "King" Coffey: I loved [Austin's Byrds-influenced band] the Reivers—they wrote beautiful *songs*. They played in Minneapolis one night when we were there, too, so we went to see them. It was, like, 20 degrees outside. There were ten people in the crowd, and half of them were Butthole Surfers.

Chris Gates: One of the underlying premises of punk rock was that it was all about inspiration. Like, we just have these ideas creatively, and we blurt them out, and we move on. Much later in my life, I was hanging out with Steve Earle, and he explained to me that songwriting has two elements: inspiration and craft. Inspiration is uniquely yours. It should be protected. That's yours! But craft is something you can get better at. And it requires a thoughtfulness around song arranging, like, "How fast should this song be? Does this song need a bridge?" And that sort of thoughtfulness was frowned upon in punk rock.

[The Replacements'] Paul Westerberg drove Steve Earle nuts. [Earle] said, "[Westerberg] has some of the most brilliant, creative inspirations I've ever heard. But he never finishes the fucking song." Earle thought "Unsatisfied" by the Replacements was a brilliant *idea*, but there's no song. It's two verses and a chorus, and then it wanders around for a minute and stops. He thought Westerberg could have done so much more with it. But he didn't because punk rock doesn't teach you that.

Beth Kerr: We were living up on Avenue H, and Tim had the car. I was at work on campus, and I saw a poster that said, "Doctors' Mob—Last Show—Continental Club." So I went through all this hoopla—go to the ATM, get money, get a cab down to the Continental Club. And I see Steve, so I ask him, "Hey, why is this your last show?" And he says, "Oh, it's not—we just put that on the poster."

Kathy McCarty: I loved Doctors' Mob, and I think Steve Collier should have been nationally famous. It's too bad the 1980s aren't known for all the bands that were really good—like Doctors' Mob, Hüsker Dü, and X. Instead, the 1980s are known for Bon Jovi.

Marcy Buffington: Doctors' Mob was what you'd get if R.E.M. and the Replacements had a baby, and Pete Townshend was the godfather. We were all growing up—rents were still cheap, but once you graduate, most people have to foot their own bills. And if you were still in school but spent more time on bands than books, Mom and Dad might have shortened your leash. At some point, everybody realized they needed to get paid for their music. Suddenly, there was some ambition and competitiveness, an effort to get better bookings, better time slots, a bigger part of the door. There was an awareness that bands could actually get record deals, and "success" started to look like a goal. It wasn't just fun anymore—on some level, "music" started to look like a career choice, and that complicated things.

Steve Collier: We took it for granted [that] we would do this three-week tour up the East Coast to New York, and then we would be famous. We'd start making some money. It would all happen. They just needed to *see* us!

And then you realize, it's nothing like that. No one [in those towns] has your record, no one can get the record . . . usually we played to hardly anyone. We played the Jetty in Bloomfield, New Jersey, and we had heard it was the greatest new wave club in the state. It looked like a Long John Silver's. We set up next to the salad bar. Hardly anyone showed up. And after the show, we didn't have a hotel. It was cold and rainy, and everyone in the van was saying, "C'mon, Steve, you gotta do it! We got nowhere else to stay!" So we parked at a convenience store, and I went to the pay phone, and I called Glenn Danzig.

At the time, Danzig was *fairly* nice. He wasn't the Arnold Schwarzenegger Danzig yet. We had played with Samhain in Austin, and Glenn had

Steve Collier, Doctors' Mob, Liberty Lunch, Austin, January 1986. By this time, Texas punk could be a revision of a revision.

talked about producing Doctors' Mob that night. Tim Kerr had given me Glenn's number. He said, "When you're in New Jersey, just go to Lodi and call Glenn. He'll put you up."

So I call the number, and it rings.

"Hello?"

"Hey, Glenn, this is Steve Collier from Doctors' Mob. You know, Tim Kerr's friend from the Big Boys? And anyhow, he gave us your number, and he said you could probably put us up. We're here in town, and we were wondering if we could, like, stay with you tonight?"

And there was the longest silence ever.

Then he just says, "Uh, I don't like people much."

[*takes long pause*]

"Okay, well, bye!"

But it was my dream Danzig reply. And I think he was being honest.

EPILOGUE

Aftermath and Aftershocks

Mike Alvarez (Max and the Makeups guitarist, Woodshock promoter): After the Woodshock shows at the Hurlbut Ranch, the first thing I always did when I woke up the next day was to go to the swimming hole to see if there were any bodies floating in the water.

If you want to understand the essence and legacy of Texas punk, I humbly submit that you take a look at two institutions. The first was real in the 1980s, but now seems ephemeral, like a wild crescendo of all the noise and fire in our scenes. The second was a crazy scheme in 1987, puffed up by former Austin punk rockers, but is today all too real—in fact, it is a cornerstone of the Texas economy.

Almost as soon as punk shows were happening in Austin and Dallas, ambitious promoters were putting together punk festivals and Battle of the Bands shows. Woodshock was just another one of these: It was promoted with a cartoon by David Yow that replaced the dove-and-guitar logo for Woodstock with a dead bird and a toe tag. But Woodshock became an annual—and transcendent—affair after it was moved *way* out into the hill country, to a site that had also hosted Willie Nelson's first Fourth of July Picnic. The Hurlbut Ranch was a gorgeous spot, with several unbelievable swimming holes. The only problem was getting there.

Mike Alvarez: Blaine Hurlbut and I met in 1982 in a hot check–writing class. I had written a twenty-dollar check to an H-E-B grocery store, and

I was facing a prison sentence for it. Blaine knew I was a punk rock musician, and he said we should have a party at his mom's ranch. He persisted until I finally agreed to visit the ranch. The dirt road that led to the site was like a blown-up minefield—it was nuts. When we finally cleared the road, I saw the ranch. It was one of the most beautiful places I'd ever seen. There were tons of Native inhabitants' arrowheads and tools all over the place and under the dirt.

Jeff Smith: Chris Wing [of Raul's band Sharon Tate's Baby] put together the first Woodshock festival in 1981. The first one [my first band] Bang Gang played was in 1983, out at the Hurlbut Ranch. That's when Mike Alvarez and I became friends. The Woodshocks in 1985 and 1986 were where I did the most as a promoter. Mushrooms were free-flowing and cheaply available . . .

Mike Alvarez: Before the festivals in 1983 and '84, Blaine took Charles Gunning, a.k.a. Doug the Slug, and [me] around the property. I told him, "These punks are gonna get into everything and jump off everywhere." We had to go through all the possibilities. Gunning did a perfect dive off the eighty-foot cliff at Dead Man's Hole—he was showing off for Lisa Gamache, the singer of our band Max and the Makeups, who was with us too. I jumped off the fifty-foot cliff. We just wanted to be sure there was enough water to make the dives safely.

Jeff Smith: Mike had a team—he had Doug the Slug and another guy. Then Blaine Hurlbut was there with a couple of other people from the area—they were the local, "country" part of the team, and we were the "city" part of the team. And we had some off-duty county sheriffs out there.

Mike Alvarez: Gunning, Blaine Hurlbut, and I headed up matters. I was thirty years old in 1985, and Gunning was older. We were adults in age only. Gunning was a professional bouncer, and I was the peacemaker when necessary. But we never had to defend anybody from anything.

Some of our conflicts came from the locals out in Dripping Springs. On the night before the 1985 Woodshock, while we were setting up the stage, Blaine's brother was passed out underneath a tree. A scorpion was crawling on his face. A couple of cowboy [neighbors] came up on horses, with rifles. Blaine was fuming, and he said something to the effect of, "Get off my property, or I'll shoot your ass." They left.

Johnny Medina ran the sound system, and he kept the tape recorder loaded. Gunning was Minister of Defense—he was in charge of security and backstage management. Blaine was Minister of Land, and I was the Prime Minister of Woodshock. Jeff Smith brought in the San Antonio element and recruited a few out-of-town bands—like the U-Men [from Seattle]. And he was the key to later getting the *Woodshock '85* double LP released. Buzzy Bills was our keg runner, but [after the 1985 festival,] he told us that he had passed out on the roof of his pickup truck and remembered nothing of the show.

Sally King: Woodshock 1985 is a good example of an earlier phase, when the drugs were not so dangerous and not so self-destructive. We were hanging out with the Hickoids. We'd all go camping every year at Mustang Island and then take over a biker bar. We were on mushrooms for, like, three days straight. And then we went to Tacoland in San Antonio, where Tex and the Horseheads played, and we barbecued. Then we went straight to Woodshock. That was all in the same week, with lots and lots of mushrooms.

Chris Gates: The day before Woodshock '85, twenty-five people from around the country showed up at my house unannounced. This big pink, Indian school bus with about half of the U-Men. David and Lisa Nobody. Tex and the Horseheads show up. We all started drinking at four in the afternoon. By 8:30 or 9:00, when other people started showing up for the party, we were all already unconscious. Mike Martt from Tex and the Horseheads walked out to the U-Men's bus, and he was wearing shorts and cowboy boots. He dropped his cigarettes, bent down to pick them up, and kicked them inside of my dog's doghouse. So he crawled into the doghouse and passed out. His legs were just sticking out of the doghouse. I have a picture of that.

Bill Anderson: Woodshock was so peaceful. There were no fights, no trouble. And no adults either. I jumped off the forty-foot cliff about twenty times. For the sixty- and eighty-foot cliff jumps, you really had to keep your legs straight and your toes pointed, or you could be hurt. It's amazing that no one got seriously injured.

Poison 13 played a set, too, but that's pretty blurry.

Jeff Smith: Until then, punk rock had mostly been a failure. Normally, we'd be pushed into the darkest corner of the darkest clubs. But that was a high-water mark for anything that had happened in Texas punk. It was pretty surreal. We played at sunup. I think we were the last band to play.

We had 1,200–1,500 people out there. It really blew up. We mounted the best production we could—with no money. And it was all fueled by local bands.

Maria Cotera: Woodshock 1985 was, ugh, *beautiful*. The U-Men were staying on our living room floor. So we went out to the ranch with them in their school bus and, of course, took some mushrooms on the way.

It was a difficult time because Steve [Anderson] and I were breaking up, and his band the Cry Babies were playing. Steve always had to vomit before he sang—every time, ever. He would spontaneously vomit or force himself to vomit before going onstage. And I was *pretty high*.

I walked up to Steve right as he was going through this vomiting ritual. I thought, "Ugh, I really gotta move on to something better." It was horrible! [*laughs*]

Kim Longacre (Zeitgeist / the Reivers): I don't remember how much fun it was because I had so much fun.

Chris Gates: We get out there, and somebody gives me a bunch of acid for the band. So I give everybody a piece of acid, and I take a hit. But it turns out the sheet of acid he had given us had been doubled over, so I had actually given everybody *two* hits apiece. By the time we hit the stage, I'm fully hallucinating. I look at my bass, and it's undulating in my head. I remember looking at the frets at one point and thinking, "I never played that note."

The funny part is that when you listen back to the live album that was recorded out there that day, we sound just the same as we always did. Which I guess shows that we had developed our *craft*.

Steve Collier: Woodshock was right before [the MTV show] *The Cutting Edge* would be taping in Austin. There was a lot of insider talk at the festival about which bands would be chosen for the episode. None of which was true.

Bill Anderson: Chris and I had all these fireworks, like bottle rockets and M-80s. So when the U-Men or the Hickoids or someone else were playing, we went down to the swimming hole. There was no moon that night, so it was really dark. And, you know, M-80s are waterproof. The first one we

Woodshock pastoral, Hurlbut Ranch, Dripping Springs, June 1985.

lit and threw down in the hole, it went off in the water—like, "Glub, glub, glub . . ." We were all on mushrooms and speed and whatever else, but we felt great. I lit the second M-80 and held it for a second, then threw it really high up in the air. It exploded when it was way over the water. It was *so* loud, like this sonic whiteout. It nearly blinded us.

So we had to do that a few more times.

Brad Featherstone (fan): Capt. Trip [guitarist Steve Hunt] from [Sacramento band] Tales of Terror was a constant source of amusement that day. I remember Rat's Ass [singer Pat Stratford] running with a can of beer, jumping off the cliff, cracking open the beer and chugging it down as he fell, and then watching the can float up to the surface when he went into the water. What a day that was . . .

Steve Collier: I wanted to get back to Austin that night to see Robyn Hitchcock play at the Continental Club, but I pretty much destroyed the undercarriage of my car getting out of Woodshock.

Chris Gates: I remember thinking, "I don't know if this could happen anywhere else." I think this is a uniquely awesome thing, partly because of the "outside" element of it. There was a certain element to Austin punk because of the heat, and because none of our houses had air conditioning. The style here wasn't really a style. It was more of a response—to the heat. Punk was an indoor sport in most other places. But here, there was an engagement with the physical world that might not have happened in other places.

It got cold that night at the ranch, and we were all in shorts and drying off from being wet after swimming. People were starting fires to stay warm. And I'm on acid. I remember looking around and thinking, "Punk rockers in the woods starting fires? *That* seems like a good idea."

As an American outdoor music festival, Woodshock built on the legacy of both Woodstock and Altamont, but Alvarez, Smith, and Hurlbut were working with a solid understanding of the local scene. They were confident their festival would be peaceful, not a violent, drug-orgy disaster. Woodshock *was* hedonistic, but it wasn't cynical. The location was idyllic and lush. The mood was euphoric, not aggressive. It was good, clean fun, with hallucinogenics and water sports. That day in 1985 was the ultimate refutation of the punk aesthetic. Or its reinvention.

We had kidnapped the tropes of Texas—barbecue, cutoff shorts, and fun in the sun—then transformed and reanimated them as our own incarnation of subcultural hoorah. We had turned the honky-tonk inside out.

As usual, I had my camera with me, but I was different too. I had learned how to be a photographer at punk rock shows in Texas. Punk quickly became much more than a kind of music; it became a way to see the world and all its fabulous disasters. I learned how to stake out an artistic position and how to sometimes fail beautifully. I tried to document everything that was happening around me, then realized that was impossible—maybe even counterrevolutionary—because the ephemeral nature of this universe is possibly *the* most beautiful thing.

Austin today, like many American cities, is a fractured landscape, a disjointed mash-up of junkspace, ugly new houses, and the occasional spot of beauty and wonder. If you know where to look, you can revel in the traces of previous glories and the scars of good times past. Just don't do it in July, like I did, under the heat dome of 2023.

Out on the streets, on front porches, in record stores and Austin-themed restaurants, I found the ruins and ancient burial sites of the Texas punk rock which formed me. I cased the burned-out wreck of Texas French Bread, which had once been the transitional hardcore punk paradise called Studio 29 and, before that, the crucial little Rome Inn. I went to see Hickoids at Hotel Vegas, a club deep in the heart of the previously segregated Black and Latino districts of the town. When the band took the stage, singer Jeff Smith was wearing the same grin—a mix of mischief and dazed oblivion—which he wore in 1986. He still can't keep his pants up.

As I loitered on the sidewalk of a downtown noise music festival, a woozy younger man quizzed me about Led Zeppelin before showing me his Butthole Surfers tattoo. While he chattered, I gazed up at the glittering battalion of new skyscrapers above Fourth Street.

Austin began aggressively branding itself as the "Live Music Capital of the World" in the mid-1990s. I don't know about all that, but the city lights are brighter now because of its brain-melting cultural history *and* the boosterism of the massively successful music and media festival South by Southwest.

The annual event was cofounded by Roland Swenson, former manager of Raul's band Standing Waves, and Louis Black, an RTF student and punk fan who codirected a student film with Radio Free Europe bassist Neil Ruttenberg. The third cofounder of SXSW was Nick Barbaro, one of several people arrested at the 1978 Huns riot at Raul's. Black and Barbaro first worked together to found *The Austin Chronicle* in 1981. They joined with Swenson and a fourth partner, Louis Meyers, to launch SXSW in 1987. The first year's festival had seven hundred registrants. South by Southwest has steadily grown into a behemoth festival, with guests like Barack Obama and Lady Gaga and an estimated economic impact of $356 million (in 2019).

Whether South by Southwest is a cornucopia of music and pop culture or a lurching, all-devouring demon out of H. P. Lovecraft—or both—is an open question. But these days, Black and his cofounders explain themselves with some of the same language I have used to grasp the punk innovation and shenanigans we all witnessed in places like Duke's Royal Coach Inn and the Hot Klub in the early 1980s. That is, they say they were in the right place at the right time.

Jeff Tartakov: More than anything else, South by Southwest is the reason Austin is what it is today. It comes with good and bad. I thought the festival was all good up until 1993 or 1994, when it started having growth problems.

Louis Black: With *The Austin Chronicle*, we really wanted to focus on local music, local bands. *The Chronicle* was very much influenced by *The Village Voice* and other alternative weeklies, but SXSW was more shaped by my experience in the punk scene. What we brought to the festival was the [punk] idea that the difference between the band and the audience is about one and a half feet.

Austin was full of great B-list bands. Not the Rolling Stones, but bands like the LeRoi Brothers, who could always fill a club in Sweden. [Internationally renowned tattooist and Austin resident Michael Malone, a.k.a.] Rollo Banks once told me, "I feel sorry for guitar players who move here because they're the best guitar player in their hometown. Or the best guitar player in two states. They move to Austin, walk into a bar, and immediately know that the barback is, like, five times better than they are."

But the thing musicians in Austin didn't have was *access*. You could be a great band or guitarist in Austin and not talk to a producer or label for ten years. With SXSW—after it got going—producers and label people and engineers and journalists were coming to Austin—you could meet anyone because you'd end up standing next to them in a club.

Did we bring the mountain to Mohammad? Yeah. People tend to think we created these geological formations. They say, "Oh, they took over that mountain, and they did it badly." No, we built these things *by hand*. We did all this stuff because this is the place [where] we *could* do it.

South by Southwest was not the only surprising aftershock of Texas punk, but it was the most conspicuous. Less surprising—given the precariousness of life as a musician or an artist—is that many of us didn't get out alive. After a tragic life and a miraculous recovery, Roky Erickson, perhaps the true godfather of Texas punk, died of unknown causes in May 2019. Just a few months later, Daniel Johnston, who had struggled with some of the same demons that beset Erickson, died of a suspected heart attack.

In 1997, the astonishing Dicks guitarist Glen Taylor died from liver and kidney failure. Eloquent and hilarious Huns drummer and filmmaker

Tom Huckabee died of cancer in January 2022. Steve Anderson, who was the original singer for both Toxic Shock and Scratch Acid, passed away in 2015. The fabulous front man for Poison 13, Mike Carroll, contracted bacterial meningitis and died in 2018. And in 2013, the founder of the Texas Blondes, journalist Margaret Moser, was diagnosed with colon cancer; she beat it back until she succumbed to the disease in August 2017.

Three of the four members of the ferocious Offenders have left this vale of tears. Tony Johnson, J. J. Jacobson, and Mikey Donaldson (who also jump-started the Austin hardcore band MDC) are all gone, leaving drummer Pat Doyle as the last Offender standing. "Losing all three of them was . . . well, it does suck," Doyle has said. "I'm only fifty-seven, and I've lost three of my siblings, and three of my original bandmates. I've got a lot of dead people in my life."

When the larger-than-life guitarist we all knew as Jukebox died in 2013, his partner in the Hickoids, singer Jeff Smith, posted a eulogy on Facebook. It was a heartbroken and mythopoetic chronicle of a life in Texas drag:

> He died of a pulmonary aneurysm on Saturday November 16th in Ouray, Colorado.
>
> Jukebox . . . bridged the countercultures of '60s and '70s hippie philosophy with the newer punk ethos. He made a living selling psilocybin mushrooms. . . . He had an outlandish sense of style . . . favoring bright colors and loud patterns, manly baubles . . . and in almost any weather, his trademark short-short cut-off jeans that would quite often reveal one testicle or the other. . . . What I can remember of the first couple of years of the band were the most fun I've ever had, a crazy dream where things just kept getting better, so much so that you never wanted to wake up. . . . [Later in life,] Jukebox would talk at great length about a desire to "go live with the Indians," and about how he thought the modern world was all fucked up. His spiritual longing was real but the West and the Indians he was looking for had all disappeared when *Little Big Man* wrapped production. Serenity and peace seemed to constantly evade him. . . . He was a small town hustler and would-be shaman with big dreams, a heart of gold and a silver tongue more suited to life at the end of

> the 19th century. Jukebox, I hope you find all the things that escaped you in this life on the other side. . . . I wish you peace my friend.

More recently, I was well into writing this book when Teresa "Nervosa" Taylor left the planet. We had done several interviews, and she began one of them with a sweet, crystal-clear memory of sitting with me outside a club forty years ago, laughing about stupid shit, without a care in the world. As she looked back, Teresa was as fiercely honest and funny as she had always been. I knew she was ill. Nevertheless, when I got word she was gone, I reeled for days, unable to grasp the fact that I would never laugh with her again.

The only two losses that may have been more devastating to the Texas punk diaspora were the deaths of Randy "Biscuit" Turner in 2005 and, shortly after I interviewed him for this book, Gary Floyd in 2024. They had been the heart and soul of our scene . . .

Gary Floyd: I ended up moving to San Francisco in 1982, but me and Biscuit stayed in touch. After the breakup of the Big Boys, he moved on. He had many different projects, great bands, and a house that he owned. He was beloved by most everyone. Whenever I returned to play in Austin, I usually stayed at his house. He was depressed, he told me. He held onto past unpleasant situations that wouldn't let him go. I loved him, and it was heartbreaking to feel the pain he carried. I could see a loving, multitalented brother suffering inside. His health was not great, either. He couldn't sleep.

Dotty Farrell: Randy was a deeply sensitive person. The greatest joy for him was to see other people happy and entertained. But if that was a lake—and you were on top of the lake, having fun—underneath the lake, there was a lot of sadness, a lot of heartache. He'd carry negativity, and I'm sure a lot of it had to do with growing up where he grew up and the messages that he received there. He always rose above it in public, but in his heart, his feelings would get hurt, and he could be profoundly sad. When the Big Boys broke up, it broke Randy's heart.

Laurie Greenwell: Gary was better friends with Biscuit than he was with the rest of the Big Boys. And Biscuit had so much vitriol in him before he died. I think it's part of what killed him.

Randy "Biscuit" Turner (RIP), onstage with the Big Boys during their last performance, Liberty Lunch, Austin, September 23, 1984.

Dotty Farrell: *Tragic* is the word for it. Both Gary and I told him, "Maybe you should get some counseling." Any time he met a person who didn't know the story of the Big Boys' breakup, it was like watching him crucify himself again. He really carried a grudge.

"Texas" Terri Laird: [When Biscuit got older,] he was just mad at that one person—probably Chris Gates. But he didn't let it into his love for everyone else. He died doing what he loved: making art. And even if he was bitter about that one person, he was all about the love.

Gary Floyd: I was thrilled to hear of his upcoming art show. He was needing some positive attention and public love. But that call came . . . that call. An unbelievable call that changed a fun and wacky scene to bleak darkness. The big art show went on without him. Heartbreaking and bleak. What could we do but think of this giant public entertainer who lived to make us feel good?

He gave us hope by telling us, "Start you own band." We have to celebrate him. He's living in this powerful voice, a funky, loud punk doctor healing whatever needs it! I miss him almost every day. He was a dear friend.

Now, move on!

Laurie Greenwell: I never felt like the Dicks got their due. Maybe it's because they broke up too early. Or maybe it was just because they were scarier. They weren't fun, like the Big Boys. They weren't going to make an album called *Fun, Fun, Fun . . .*

Gary Floyd: Oh, I still like [the Dicks' first recording,] "Saturday Night at the Bookstore." I didn't hear it for years, and then I was at a gay bar here in San Francisco that only plays rock and roll and punk. The DJ knew me, and he put "Bookstore" on, and it was really loud. It sounded great. And some old queen turned around and said to me, "What in the hell is that? '*I'm at the bookstore!*'" Then he sort of fluttered off into the crowd. And I was so *touched*.

In the Dicks, we wanted to feel the emotions our audience was feeling and then feel *our emotions*. And then do something about it. Which isn't just going out and raising hell. It's going out and helping people. Serving people. Whether you're serving food on a lunch line or you're helping a street person get up off the ground.

When you're young and finding yourself, you make a lot of mistakes. And I *drank so much*! But all of those things were leading me to this very day, when I'm sitting here, looking out the back door.

Those Dicks reunion shows were fun, but they were only stirring up a memory. Because I'm not mad like that anymore. I'm really disappointed that the world is in such weird shape, but I'm not *mad*. I'm too old for that. Do I like what's going on? No, I hate it. But I'm just trying to do my best, you know? If that means going to a big demonstration or sitting at home, looking at a bee buzzing around a flower, you gotta put those both in the right perspective. And I have.

Texas punk wasn't a craze, like the Twist or the Mashed Potato. No one became a superstar. It just isn't that kind of story. Instead, what happened in the 1980s in Austin, and Dallas, Houston, and San Antonio, is a story about transformation. Local music scenes, like other fantastic regional cultures, only become important and compelling when people reinvent music to suit their own purposes. When they rewire and translate culture in a unique and tasty way.

But the musicians and artists and hustlers and poets in Texas were themselves transformed as well, and not just because they took acid at a Butthole Surfers show. Creative communities are quietly powerful things—they can supercharge people. Folks get bold, and they learn that sometimes, the only thing to it is to do it.

Back in Austin in 1978, a provocateur named Nick Modern, a.k.a. Larry Dickson, put these words on the cover of a fanzine: "Someday All the Adults Will Die!" As a kind of Peter Pan hot take, it was mean, it was funny, and it was correct. Today, all our parents, and most of the adults like them, are gone. John Wayne and June Cleaver have left the building.

Some of us died, too. Some of us became parents before we were adults. And many of us suffer from a peculiar generational syndrome that has been much noted in the popular press: an inability to *think* of ourselves *as* adults.

Perhaps we don't entirely recognize ourselves. My generation does parenting differently: We're generally more permissive and less inclined to hit our kids. We may think about gender and gender roles in a more critical and expansive way. Those of us who are gay are able to marry each other, and those of us who aren't are more likely to be guests at the wedding. We're less likely to work for the same boss, in the same job, for thirty years. Unfortunately, we're not kids anymore, and we *know* that because actual young people roll their eyes when they talk to us. Those kids have their own word for what we are doing. They call it *adulting*.

I very much like what one punk rocker of my generation has said about who we are. Ian MacKaye is not a Texan, but he is a Big Boys fan. He led the amazing 1980s Washington, DC, hardcore band Minor Threat and then the equally terrific postpunk band Fugazi. In *Punk Is Dead, Punk Is Everything*, an excellent 2007 book about punk art, MacKaye told author Bryan Ray Turcotte, "Punk rock, really, if you ask me what it meant, it just means human. It's just human beings, just life, it's just about being alive."

From my own perspective, punk has been about being a new kind of human. Back in the way back, when we whirled through Raul's and Tacoland and the Island, we didn't know where we were driving, but this is where we ended up.

Dayna Blackwell: [After those punk rock years,] I applied to grad school and joined Mensa because it looks good on your application. I tested out at 152. Back then, very few people—including myself—knew that I was quite brilliant. Seriously! Idiot-savant-level, guess-the-number-of-jelly-beans-in-a-jar, human-calculator sort of thing. At UT, I majored in microbiology and genetics and minored in applied mathematics. I was almost ashamed of being bright—I didn't want it to single me out in any way. How weird is that?

Richard Mather: I have a lot of trouble sitting still, ha ha! I'm working on an animation right now for a kids show, making fine art, an animated music video, a horror video, rebuilding part of my deck, working on motorcycle engines, riding dirt bikes, and playing musical instruments. In the eighties, when I found punk rock, I was so very excited to be a part of it, and I felt like these people could accept me for who I am, and they could digest the weirdest stuff that I could come up with. That was really a new thing for me. It was super inspiring.

Caroline Estes: Raul's really defined who I am. I'm sixty-five now, and these days, I'm an agitator and a topless protester against the open carry gun guys. I follow around the gun guys while I'm topless, and they hate me because it steals their thunder and [scares away film crews] and keeps them off TV. *Rolling Stone* said I was the forty-eighth coolest thing at South by Southwest. So Raul's made me into the troublemaker and hell-raiser that I still am today.

Ty Gavin: I joke around. I tell people that I'm sixty-three, but I'm still on parole.

Stella Wier: After I quit Glass Eye, I moved to LA, but I only lasted six months. I thought, "I don't have the drive or the ambition for this, either." So I moved back home and house-sat for the Butthole Surfers.

I have a weird affection for UT. It's like the mothership. I always like to live within a mile or two of UT.

Carlos Lowry: I'm still friends with the Dicks that are still alive, and they're both still lefties. David Dictor and Ron from Millions of Dead Cops are still lefties. Ron may still live in Venezuela—he was a supporter of the [Hugo] Chávez regime. And Pat Doyle from the Offenders is still about as clearly left and intelligent as you can be. At first, it may have been a fad for some of them, but it remains who they are today.

Laurie Greenwell: Sometimes, when I'm driving, "Saturday Night at the Bookstore" will come on, and it still sounds really good, so I'll turn it up. But when I get to a stop sign, I'll turn it down again. I wouldn't want to offend the people in the car next to me.

Those Dicks songs are still not acceptable. There is still so much rage in them, so much *seething* under their skin. Those songs are still scary.

Holly Hock (fan): I remember seeing the B-52s on *Saturday Night Live* in 1980—I thought my head would explode. Now, they play the Sex Pistols at the H-E-B.

Trish Herrera: Texas had a unique position in the world and still does. Houston has always been a blue city; it's always been multicultural. I'm definitely proud of the city. But it has been hard to find feminist power in Texas. We found it by working with Girls Rock Camp, by working for Planned Parenthood as volunteers. We tried to keep a positive attitude that we weren't going to end up in a fascist regime, but it looks like it's happened. I mean, you can't get an abortion here anymore. I'm ashamed of the government that we have now. Texas has been taken over by racists and assholes.

Lynn Keller: Education in Texas has been abominable. At least it was in El Paso. When I was young, you had to seek out your own intelligence. Through hanging around with the right people, or whatever, you had to figure it out. And I mean, look at the result. If I look back at my friends, most of them voted for Donald Trump. He's the result of something, not the cause.

Laurie Greenwell: I wish that Amy Winehouse would have recorded the Dicks song "Shit Fool." The Dicks never made any money. They're all poor. I mean, I'm looking out into our backyard, and Buxf's got a wheelbarrow out there, and he's still doing this really heavy, blue-collar work. I mean . . . there's always a sense that the Dicks never quite got their due.

Dayna Blackwell: There's a group of us, about twenty, maybe thirty people. The Raul's family. Dottie Swenson? Can't stand her; she hates me. I fucked her boyfriend—who didn't? But if she calls me at three in the morning, I'm bailing her out of jail. We've got each other's back.

As for some of the rest of us, "Texas" Terri Laird left Austin for LA, where she continued cutting hair before becoming an internationally beloved punk rock singer and front person for the Stiff Ones and Texas Terri Bomb! She now splits her time between Berlin and Thailand.

After breaking up Scratch Acid, David Yow and David Sims formed the Jesus Lizard, a critically acclaimed band that achieved greater financial success than their previous groups and gained widespread recognition as godfathers of noise rock. In 2024, they released *Rack*, their first album in twenty-six years. Yow lives in Los Angeles these days, where he also nurtures a burgeoning acting career. Sims lives in New York City; when not touring or recording, he works as an accountant.

After the Big Boys and Poison 13, Chris Gates also moved to Los Angeles, where he formed Junkyard with fellow former Austin punk David Roach. After a wild ride, Gates is now back in the Austin area and still playing live music.

Diana Garcia finished college and became an award-winning elementary school teacher in Austin. She has made social justice, as well as a focus on Chicano and Black activists, a cornerstone of her lesson plans.

Carlos Lowry is a commercial artist in Austin.

Big Boys guitarist Tim Kerr has returned to painting, specializing in a series of portraits of jazz and civil rights heroes.

Maria Cotera continued her education at Stanford and has now returned to UT—as an assistant professor of Latin American studies.

Until 2023, Roger "El Borracho" Manriquez was still in Austin and working nights. He posted to an Austin punk Facebook group and peppered his comments with Spanish. After suffering some health problems, he is now again living with his family in Vidor, Texas.

Photographer Bill Daniel did indeed stop taking punk rock pictures after that Minutemen show, and he hit the road to document the DIY lives of artists, musicians, bike messengers, and filmmakers around the country. He has lived in his van and set up darkrooms in industrial parks in the petrochemical swamps outside of Houston. He's the most truly punk rock person I know. Maybe he'll settle down one day.

In 1987, I moved to New York City, where I continued taking pictures of punk, postpunk, and independent musicians. I worked as a music journalist for some of the slick magazines. After I met my wife, we moved to Vienna, Austria, in 2005. Since then, I have worked as a refugee educator and a high school teacher. I try to mention the Butthole Surfers to my students as often as possible, and sometimes hilarity ensues.

I remain hopelessly, embarrassingly enthralled by all sorts of rock and roll music. When I was five years old, I loved the Beatles. When I was thirteen, I thought Led Zeppelin were gods. But rock and roll only taught me how to be cool. Punk rock made a man out of me.

ACKNOWLEDGMENTS

I am indebted to all the friends, fellow travelers, inspirations, coconspirators, crushes, elders, and heroes whose voices animate this book. Thank you for trusting me, inviting me into your lives, and helping me to understand what happened back there, all those years ago.

To all of our brothers and sisters who have left this vale of tears, rest in power: Gary Floyd, Teresa Taylor, Randy "Biscuit" Turner, Tom Huckabee, Daniel Johnston, Brian Hansen, Roky Erickson, Tomas Levy, Tommy Pipes, Mark "Chico" McCullough, J. J. Jacobson, Mikey Donaldson, Tony Johnson, Jerry Patterson, Dixon Edge Coulbourn, Chris Wing, John Thomas "Jukebox" Jackson, Steve Anderson, Mike Carroll, Dee Montgomery, Glen Taylor, Davy Jones, Margaret Moser, Michael "Rollo Banks" Malone, and Mark Farner.

Thank you, Steve Collier, for a lifetime friendship and the invitation to my first punk rock show. Marc Griffin, you turned me on to Wire—best of health to you, sir! Chris Ball né Stewart, you were always too cool for school, and I loved sharing Conan's pepperoni-and-jalapeno, whole-wheat-crust pizzas with you! Bill Daniel, you were the pathfinder and my inspiration. And Luke Torn, thank you for the rides in your Camaro, hipping me to the *Psychotronic Encyclopedia of Film*, and tirelessly attempting to turn me into a Bob Dylan fan—you may yet succeed!

A special shout-out to Clair LaVaye—I esteem the invaluable work you have done to preserve the archive of Austin punk rock posters at flickr.com/photos/n1t3_bo1yz/albums.

Thank you, David Menconi, for making first contact. I am so grateful for the advice, support, and friendship of Michael Azerrad, one of my very favorite authors. My gratitude to you, Casey Kittrell and Jessica Hopper, for your guidance, ideas, and patience.

Adinah, Vivien, and Anette, I love you to the moon and back again.

CAST OF CHARACTERS

Mike Alvarez: Guitarist, Max and the Makeups; producer-promoter, Woodshock Music Festival.

Brecht Andersch: Fan.

Bill Anderson: Roadie, Big Boys; guitarist, Poison 13.

Steve Anderson: Fan and singer, Toxic Shock, Scratch Acid. Rest in peace (2018).

Tony "Autoharp" Arena: Artist, *J.D.s* fanzine.

Lisa "Ralph" Armstrong: Fan.

Bill Bentley: Journalist, producer, and executive, Warner Bros. Records.

Alice Berry: Fan and member, the Texas Blondes.

Louis Black: Editor and publisher, *The Austin Chronicle*; cofounder, South by Southwest.

Clarke Blacker: Guitarist, Nervebreakers, Stick Men with Ray Guns.

Dayna Blackwell: Fan and member, the Texas Blondes.

Brett Bradford: Guitarist, Scratch Acid.

Marcy Buffington: Fan.

Rob Buford: Singer, Crotch Rot.

Yuri Campbell: Fan.

Sherri Canon: Drummer, Technicolor Yawns.

Steve Chaney: Fan and proprietor, Big Mamou restaurant.

Jeffrey "King" Coffey: Drummer, Hugh Beaumont Experience, Butthole Surfers; founder, Trance Syndicate record label.

Steve Collier: Drummer, Big Boys; guitarist-singer, Doctors' Mob.

Scott Conn: Fan and director, *Dirt Road to Psychedelia: Austin, TX During the 1960s*

Michael Corcoran: Texas music journalist. Rest in peace (2024).

Maria Cotera: Fan.
Cathy Criss: Fan and singer, the Negros.
Laura Croteau: Cofounder, Rabid Cat Records. Widow of Anthony Johnson, guitarist for the Offenders. Rest in peace (2012).
Bill Daniel: Photographer and filmmaker.
Dave Dictor: Singer, MDC, a.k.a. Millions of Dead Cops, formerly the Stains.
Pat Doyle: Drummer, the Offenders.
Caroline Estes: Fan and activist.
Dotty Farrell: Fan and singer, Technicolor Yawns, Jaws of Life, Punkaroos, Jefferson Trout.
Brad Featherstone: Fan.
Jane Fletcher: Writer, editor, and seamstress, *The Western Roundup* fanzine.
Mark Flood, a.k.a. John Peters, a.k.a. Perry Webb: Guitarist-vocalist, Culturcide.
Gary Floyd: Singer, the Dicks, Sister Double Happiness, the Gary Floyd Band. Rest in peace (2024).
Judy K. Frels: Fan.
Diana Garcia: Fan.
Chris Gates: Bassist, Big Boys, Poison 13; guitarist, Junkyard.
Ty Gavin: Singer, the Next.
Karen Ruth Getchell: Fan.
Laurie Greenwell: Fan. Married to Dicks bassist Buxf Parrott.
Diane "Muffy" McGee Hardin: Fan.
Mike Haskins: Guitarist, Nervebreakers.
Gibby Haynes: Singer, Butthole Surfers.
Trish Herrera: Guitarist-singer, mydolls.
Holly Hock: Fan.
Ken Hoge: Photographer.
Tom Huckabee: Drummer, the Huns, Reversible Cords (a.k.a. Re*Cords). Rest in peace (2022).
Barry "Kooda" Huebner: Guitarist, Nervebreakers.
Garinè Isassi: Guitarist, Chlorine.
Sammy Jacobo: Fan.
Darryl Jenifer: Bassist, Bad Brains.
Brit Jones: Fan.
Lynn Keller: Singer-keyboardist, Reversible Cords.
Beth Kerr: Manager, the Big Boys. Married to Tim Kerr.

Tim Kerr: Guitarist, Big Boys, Poison 13.
Tarbox Kiersted: Journalist. Rest in peace (2014).
Sally King: Fan.
Chip Kinman: Singer-guitarist, the Dils, Rank and File.
Jim "Straightedge" Koppenhaver: Fan and roadie, the Big Boys.
Michael Laird: Skateboarder and fan.
"Texas" Terri Laird: Fan and singer, Texas Terri Bomb!
Clair LaVaye: Fan and member, Dykes with Dicks.
Paul Leary: Guitarist, Butthole Surfers.
Jeffrey Liles: Fan and promoter.
Kim Longacre: Singer-guitarist, Zeitgeist / the Reivers.
Carlos Lowry: Artist.
D Angus Macdonald: Fan; apartment manager, the Colony; bassist, the Jeffersons.
Jacob Mackey: Fan.
Roger "El Borracho" Manriquez: Fan.
Steve Marsh: Singer-bassist, Terminal Mind, Miracle Room.
Tim Mateer: Singer, percussion, and ring oscillator, Meat Joy.
Richard Mather: Cocreator, *Buttlikker Comix*; guitarist, Criminal Crew, the Rock Busters.
Kathy McCarty: Singer-guitarist, Buffalo Gals, Glass Eye.
Justin McCoy: Fan and singer, Buzzcrusher.
David McCreath: Guitarist, Hugh Beaumont Experience, Drain.
Cindy Melbie: Fan.
Gary Miller: Fan.
Mikey T. Milligan Jr.: Skater and drummer, Fudge Tunnels.
Joe Nick Patoski: Journalist; manager, Joe "King" Carrasco.
Brad Perkins: Drummer, Marching Plague, Fearless Iranians from Hell.
Gretchen Phillips: Singer-guitarist, Meat Joy, Two Nice Girls.
Polar Bear: Fan, poster artist, and anarchist.
Dan Puckett, a.k.a. Dan Transmission: Keyboardist, the Huns, Radio Free Europe. Rest in peace (2020).
Donna Rich: Fan.
David Roach: Singer, Pagans, Junkyard.
Neil Ruttenberg, a.k.a. the Reverend Neil X: College radio DJ, KUT-FM; salesclerk, Inner Sanctum Records; bassist, Radio Free Europe, F-Systems.
Larry Seaman: Singer-guitarist, Standing Waves.

Adriane "Ash" Shown: Fan.
David Wm. Sims: Bassist, Scratch Acid, the Jesus Lizard.
John Slate, a.k.a. Control Rat X: Editor, illustrator, and publisher, *Xiphoid Process* fanzine.
Jeff Smith: Singer and founder, Hickoids.
John Spath: Photographer; guitarist, the Mel Coolies.
E. A. Srere: Violinist-singer, Chickadiesels; gossip columnist, *Sluggo!* fanzine; member, the Texas Blondes.
Scott Stevens: Fan and early bassist for the Butthole Surfers.
Jeff Tartakov: Manager, Daniel Johnston.
Teresa Taylor: Drummer, Meat Joy, Butthole Surfers. Rest in peace (2023).
Roy Tompkins: Artist and author, *Trailer Trash* comic series.
Kathy Valentine: Guitarist, the Violators; bassist, the Go-Go's.
Clark Walker, a.k.a. Jean Dodge: Actor and filmmaker.
Rey Washam: Drummer, Scratch Acid, Big Boys, Rapeman, True Believers.
Bob Weber: Drummer, Really Red, Culturcide.
Stella Wier: Keyboardist, Glass Eye, Prohibition.
Paul Crow Willis: Singer, Agony Column.
David Yow: Bassist, Toxic Shock; singer, Scratch Acid, the Jesus Lizard.

INDEX

Page numbers in *italics* refer to photographs.